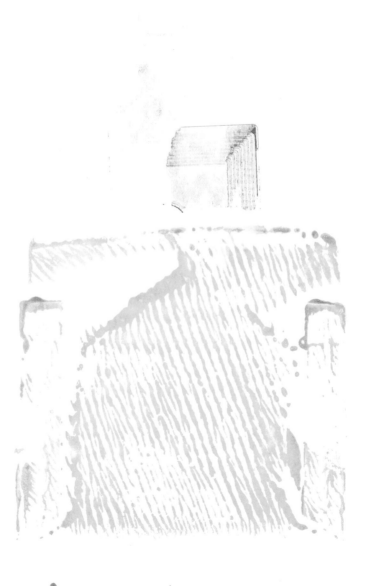

Russell Kirk

Russell Kirk

A Critical Biography of a
Conservative Mind

James E. Person Jr.

MADISON BOOKS
Lanham • New York • Oxford

Published by Madison Books
4720 Boston Way
Lanham, Maryland 20706

12 Hid's Copse Road
Cumnor Hill, Oxford OX2 9JJ, England

Distributed by National Book Network

Library of Congress Cataloging-in-Publication Data

Person, James E., 1955–
    Russell Kirk : a critical biography of a conservative mind / James
E. Person, Jr.
        p.   cm.
    Includes bibliographical references and index.
    ISBN 1-56833-131-2 (alk. paper)
    1. Kirk, Russell—Criticism and interpretation.   2. Conservatism and
literature—United States—History—20th century.   3. Conservatism—
United States—History—20th century.   4. Kirk, Russell—Knowledge and
learning.   I. Title.
PS3521 . I665Z8   1999
808´ .0092—dc21   99–39707
[B]   CIP

Excerpts from "Little Gidding" in FOUR QUARTETS, copyright 1942 by T. S. Eliot and renewed 1970 by Esme Valerie Eliot, reprinted by permission of Harcourt, Inc. Outside the
U.S., its territories and possessions, and the Philippine Republic, by permission of Faber
and Faber Ltd.

Excerpt from "East Coker" in FOUR QUARTETS, copyright 1940 by T. S. Eliot and renewed 1968 by Esme Valerie Eliot, reprinted by permission of Harcourt, Inc. Outside the
U.S., its territories and possessions, and the Philippine Republic, by permission of Faber
and Faber Ltd.

Excerpt from "The Dry Salvages" in FOUR QUARTETS, copyright 1941 by T. S. Eliot and
renewed 1969 by Esme Valerie Eliot, reprinted by permission of Harcourt, Inc. Outside the
U.S., its territories and possessions, and the Philippine Republic, by permission of Faber
and Faber Ltd.

Excerpt from "Choruses from 'The Rock'" in COLLECTED POEMS 1909–1962 by T. S.
Eliot, copyright 1936 by Harcourt, Inc., copyright © 1964, 1963 by T. S. Eliot, reprinted by
permission of the publisher. Outside the U.S., its territories and possessions, and the Philippine Republic, by permission of Faber and Faber Ltd.

♾ ™The paper used in this publication meets the minimum requirements of American
National Standard for Information Sciences—Permanence of Paper for Printed Library Ma-
terials, ANSI/NISO Z39.48-1992.
Manufactured in the United States of America.

To
Lista Joyce Haist Person

Contents

Preface

A little over ten years ago, when I lived in a small Michigan community near the birthplace of Russell Kirk, I fell into conversation one day with a younger friend, a teacher, about the state of education in the local schools. Midway through our talk, we turned to the subject of authors who have written on education. "You really ought to read this man's work," I said, referring to an essay I had recently read. "It articulates exactly what you're trying to say."

"What's the author's name?"

"Russell Kirk."

"Who's he?"

"Well, he grew up near here, in Plymouth, but he went on to become famous for helping found conservatism in America after World War II."

A conservative. Oh.

Images rose in my friend's mind of men with crewcuts, American-flag lapel pins, a dull, straight-arrow way of living, closed-mindedness, and voting Republican without fail.

Like all stereotypes, this description has a shadow of a basis in fact among some but not all who call themselves conservative. But it does not describe the man whose writings I had just commended to my friend. Kirk had written not only on education, he also wrote social criticism, literary criticism, ghost stories, novels, an economics textbook, and a host of other works, not to mention the work by which he is best known, a history of ideas called *The Conservative Mind*.

The questions my friend asked then are pertinent today: Who was Russell Kirk, what did he accomplish, and does his work live today? In the study that follows, I have endeavored to answer these questions, and in so doing illuminate the life and works of an extraordinary man.

As is already evident by the heft of this volume, I have not sought to write the final word on Kirk's accomplishments, nor a deeply detailed one. Rather, I have tried to craft a critical primer, an introduction to Kirk's thought that will serve the intelligent, interested reader, in a manner accessible to the nonspecialist, and at the same time provide a starting point or springboard for those scholars who will in time depart from this study to write more in-depth works on a man William F. Buckley Jr. has called "a neglected prince of conservative thought."[1]

The impetus for this study sprang from a steadily growing perception, which came about during the last years of Kirk's life and the years that immediately followed, that the word "conservatism" and certain terms used by Kirk himself, especially "the permanent things," were falling from the lips of men and women who had little understanding of the meaning behind these concepts, much less a defensible understanding of the terms' substance. The very words "conservative" and "conservatism" had come to mean nearly anything the speaker had in mind, whether it be former Russian communists who longed for the days of Josef Stalin or any wealthy, self-absorbed American who cared to adopt the motto "He who dies with the most toys wins." Words serve very little purpose if they have a meaning so malleable that they would not be recognized by those who coined them. Russell Kirk gave twentieth-century American conservatism its very name, and even he would find it hard to recognize as a distinct habit of mind among people who apply the term freely.

In a largely favorable review of Kirk's *Eliot and His Age*, sympathetic critic John Chamberlain lamented that he could not tell what Kirk meant by "such terms as Right Reason, the Higher Reason, the Permanent Things, and Demon Ideology. They demand what might become whole libraries of qualification, and so they become thought-stoppers instead of thought-liberators."[2] A valid concern—other reviewers, some of them hostile to Kirk, have made the same point. This book, then, intends to serve the purpose of making clear distinctions so that Kirk's terms become "thought-liberators."

Along the way, I seek to demonstrate a truth brought to my mind by way of imagination in the opening chapter of Owen Barfield's novel *Worlds Apart* (1963). There, the principal narrator, G. A. L. Burgeon, relates that something distressing had occurred to him while reading the many book reviews spanning several disciplines in *The Times Literary Supplement*: "What struck me so forcibly, and not for the first time, was that a new book on any subject—history, philosophy, science, religion, or what have you—is always dealt with by a specialist in that subject. This may be fairest from the author's point of view, but it conveys a disagreeable impression of watertight compartments." Burgeon explains:

> The trouble was this. Behind each review there lay a whole network of unspoken assumptions about the nature of life and the universe which were completely incompatible with the corresponding network behind the review on the next page. It was obvious for instance that for both the reviewer and the author of the book on *Psycho-Social History and the Unconscious* everything that both the reviewer and the author . . . of the book on *Demythologizing and the Synoptic Gospels* took for granted was a tissue of exploded fantasy. . . . It wasn't that people can think at once confidently and oppositely about almost everything that matters—though that, too, can sometimes be a sobering reflection. It wasn't that they disagreed. I wished they did. What was biting me was the fact that *these minds never met at all*.[3]

In *Russell Kirk: A Critical Biography of a Conservative Mind* I hope to demonstrate not that Kirk was a man of undivided mind in his writings across disciplines—that perhaps goes without saying—but rather *the extent* to which there was an undergirding unity of worldview that informs all his work. To continue Barfield's metaphor, there may have been discipline-related "compartments" in Kirk's mind, but there was a sluice-gate open between each one, with certain key concepts playing a consistent part in filling them. The reader who accesses Kirk's works by way of any particular discipline, whether it be social criticism, horror fiction, economics, or whatever, will find the same philosophical underpinning supporting the thought expressed in one discipline as in another.

There is another purpose, also. I consider Kirk one of the greatest minds this nation has produced during the twentieth century and make no secret of my admiration of him, though that admiration is not uncritical. He was not a "man with a message" or any other such ideologue or sanctimonious bore. He was, rather, a quiet, wise, and gentle man whose spoken and printed words reflect imaginatively and memorably the wisdom of many great Western thinkers who have gone before him. Thus, I wish to share with interested readers something of my own high regard for Kirk's thought, believing that others might see and understand, even if they do not agree with his worldview.

So I encourage you to venture forth into the pages that follow, for I believe you will discover an interesting man whose beliefs, writings, and way of life speak pertinently to the needs and issues of our time. Readers who expect to find in the following pages an exercise in hero-worship will find nothing of the sort; they will, though, find a sympathetic perspective that looks *along* Kirk's life and works rather than *at* them, for it is by sighting along the light of knowledge by which he lived that one can see clearly (and thus better understand) his purposes and actions.

ACKNOWLEDGMENTS

In doing this, I am indebted to many persons whose assistance made this book possible. First and foremost, I must thank the wise and gracious Annette Y. Kirk, whose immense generosity in terms of time and patience informed and enhanced my research enormously. While visiting in her home less than a week before Russell died, I told Annette that she and her husband were two of the most extraordinary people I had ever met. At the time, she very graciously turned aside my intended compliment. I believe still in the substance of that compliment, and this book is, in part (I hope), a written vindication of that judgment. I am especially grateful for her allowing me extensive access to the correspondence and diary of her late husband. All excerpted quotations from the private papers of Russell Kirk are reprinted by permission of Annette Kirk as executrix of the literary estate of Russell Kirk, as are most of the photographs that appear between these covers.

To understand conservatism in general and Kirk in particular, there are two indispensable resources at which any scholar must begin, those being George H. Nash's *The Conservative Intellectual Movement in America since 1945* (1996) and Charles C. Brown's *Russell Kirk: A Bibliography* (1981). I profited immensely from reading these works and am grateful for the skill and intelligence that went into their crafting.

Others need to be acknowledged, as well. I wish to thank Mr. Ray Bradbury for granting permission to reprint his letter of September 16, 1974; Mr. John Chambers for allowing me to reprint a portion of a letter from his father, Whittaker Chambers; Mrs. T. S. Eliot for kindly authorizing me to quote from two of her husband's previously unpublished letters, to which correspondence she retains copyright; Ms. Madeleine L'Engle for granting permission to reprint a letter written to Arkham House Publishers in 1979; Mr. Thomas Howard for permission to reprint the contents of a note he wrote to Kirk in 1984; Mr. Peter Kreeft for permission to reprint a portion of a letter to Kirk dated July 16, 1985; David Higham Associates for permission to reprint several lines of poetry from Dante's *Hell* and *Paradise*, edited and translated by Dorothy L. Sayers and Barbara Reynolds, published by Penguin Books; Mrs. T. S. Matthews for allowing me to use a short portion from a letter written by her husband in 1972; and Ms. Miriam Marx Allen for granting permission to quote from a letter of February 25, 1964 written by her father, Groucho Marx.

My understanding of many areas of Kirk's thought has been enriched through reading the essays of my good friend John Attarian, whose advice has been crucial to the completion of this book. The suggestions and intelligent conversation of Gleaves Whitney, Ian Crowe, Marco Respinti, Alan

Cornett, and Gerald J. Russello have also helped me, and I am grateful. Michael Curry very graciously allowed me to use his handsome photograph of Russell Kirk that appears on the dustjacket of this book, and I thank him for it. Thanks are also due to my friend Thomas Ligotti for the loan of two out-of-print Kirk books and for first bringing Kirk's short fiction to my attention a decade ago.

I am thankful to the staff of the Harlan Hatcher Graduate Library at the University of Michigan for their helpfulness in my research, and grateful to Alyssa Theodore and Dawn Stoltzfus of the editorial staff at Madison Books. My parents, James and Ellen Person, have encouraged me enormously throughout the course of my writing this critical biography, having first instilled in me, during my earliest years, an understanding and appreciation of the things that matter most. Finally, I would like to thank my wife, Lista, for "pushing the paper" on this project—proofreading, keying changes, indexing, and printing pages—and our children, David James and Rebekah Joyce, for their patience with me throughout the writing of this book, for which I write these final sentences on the fifth anniversary of Russell Kirk's death.

Any errors in fact or other shortcomings in the pages that follow are of my own making.

NOTES

1. From Buckley's introduction to Lee Edwards, *The Power of Ideas: The Heritage Foundation at 25 Years*, p. xix.

2. Chamberlain, review of *Eliot and His Age*, *The Freeman* 22, November, 1972, 702–3.

3. Barfield, *Worlds Apart*, pp. 9–10.

1

Memory and the Continuum of Time: Russell Kirk's Life

We shall not cease from exploration
And the end of all our exploring
Will be to arrive where we started
And know the place for the first time.
—from "Little Gidding," by T. S. Eliot

"Dr. Kirk, have we any hope?" the President asked the bespectacled man who stood beside him in the Oval Office. The two men gazed through a window to the scene being enacted outside the White House gates and throughout Washington. It was early April of 1972, and the capital of the United States was flooded with many thousands of young people protesting Richard Nixon's prosecution of the war in Vietnam. Their sheer numbers and loud, vulgar contempt for the president seemed to suggest the first stages of a mob revolt and the utter rejection of everything the two men valued in American culture. Outside the White House gates, these screaming people, seemingly the wave of the foreseeable future, surged through the streets. "Have we any hope?" the president asked again. There was a painful silence.

Russell Kirk finally spoke. "That depends upon public belief, Mr. President. Despair feeds upon despair, hope upon hope. If most people

1

believe the prophets of despair, they will seek out private hidie-holes and cease to cooperate for the common good. But if most people say, 'We are in a bad way, but we still have the resources and the intelligence and the will to work a renewal'—why, they will be roused by the exigency to common action and reform. It is all a matter of belief."

In the few minutes remaining in his audience with the president, Kirk spoke of how other cultures had existed for centuries, experiencing periods of decline followed by eras of reinvigoration. "No human institution lasts forever, Mr. President," he concluded, "but the United States is young, as great powers go; and presumably three-quarters of our existence at least, lies before us. Our present troubles may be succeeded by an age of greatness."[1]

Visibly comforted and encouraged by these words, Nixon told Kirk he had always believed this and that he was grateful for his visitor's words of confirmation. Kirk left the White House a short time later to prepare to return to his home in Michigan. That evening, he was surprised to learn that Nixon, accompanied by a small cadre of Secret Service agents, had abandoned his rigid schedule of activities and walked over to the Lincoln Memorial to talk with individual antiwar protesters one-on-one. There were no rope-lines, no screening of questions, only Nixon and his critics face to face. Presumably, he believed that by this action he could change minds through earnest dialogue. It all depends upon public belief, Kirk had said. Despair feeds upon despair, hope upon hope—even amid confusing and discouraging circumstances. The news media were astounded, reporting the president's dialogue at the Lincoln Memorial and wondering what had motivated him to do such a thing. Or possibly, who.

Indeed, just who was Russell Kirk? Adviser to presidents, editor, writer of a gothic novel and numerous ghost stories, lecturer on political, aesthetic, and economic matters, syndicated columnist, cultural historian, biographer—he was all this and much more, preferring to term himself a man of letters. Aside from these stark terms, how might he be best understood? Historian Gleaves Whitney, speechwriter for Michigan Governor John Engler, identifies seven essential facets of the man,[2] which I have adopted and elaborated upon below.

FOUNDER OF MODERN CONSERVATIVE THOUGHT

Kirk is best known as the founder of the post–World War II conservative movement in America, an honor he acquired through the popular and critical success of his 1953 study, *The Conservative Mind*. This work, having seen seven editions, traces and examines conservative thought as a recurrent element in British and American life from the era of Edmund Burke down through the example of John Adams, James Fenimore Cooper, Irving Babbitt, George Santayana, and T. S. Eliot, among others. It is considered a landmark work of intelligent scholarship, one that—along with *A Program for Conservatives, The Roots of American Order,* and several other books by his hand—laid the groundwork for the political triumph of conservatives real and so-called during the 1980s and beyond. As early as 1956, Flannery O'-Connor could write, "Mr. Kirk has managed in a succession of books which have proved both scholarly and popular . . . to make the voice of an intelligent and vigorous conservative thought respected in this country."[3]

FOUR DECADES OF LEADERSHIP

As Whitney has written, "Kirk was not just a founder; he was a builder. He guided the conservative movement to maturity." From the mid-1950s to the mid-1990s, he remained in the public arena, helping to shape conservative thought through numerous lectures and debates, books, and articles. A portion of Kirk's impact as a builder was due to the sheer volume of his published works: 32 books; 800 essays, book reviews, and articles; and more than 3,000 newspaper and magazine columns. Normally no piece of writing dates more quickly than columns written for periodicals, but not so in the case of Kirk, whose writings focused for the most part on first principles and perennial questions, or at least pointed back to them. In many of his works he examined such issues as order versus freedom, continuity versus change, and the state versus civil society.

Kirk was also the founding editor of two quarterlies of Western culture, *Modern Age* and *The University Bookman;* he edited the latter from 1960 until his death in 1994, enlisting a blend of established conservative writers and young newcomers to write for this slim review of books otherwise ignored, many of them, in other reviewing venues.

POLITICAL OBSERVER AND ADVISER

Having lived through and observed closely the cultural and political changes of twentieth-century America, Kirk wrote frequent, ruminative essays on the nation's politics, establishing himself as an articulate champion of ordered freedom. The balance between the claims of order and freedom is a recurrent theme throughout American history, and he aligned himself with one of his historical heroes, the Anglo-Irish statesman Edmund Burke, in championing "liberty under law" and holding that prudence is the chief virtue in checking the excessive claims of each. Still, given his many writings on the subject of politics, Kirk prudently saw far more to life than politics; he did not "chew the newspapers," for he believed with the English novelist George Gissing that "Politics is the preoccupation of the quarter-educated." He was thus far more than an advocate for conservative politics and politicians. With Burke, he assigned a definite role and purpose for politics and government action. This made Kirk something of an odd-man-out to America's more politically absorbed conservative figures during the Reagan years; he did not believe "government is the problem," according to the popular perception of Ronald Reagan's widely quoted phrase. Rather, Kirk believed that government at the state and federal levels should stay within constitutional bounds rather than "press the envelope" of those bounds; he applauded federal legislation to protect certain waterfowl, for instance, believing this a legitimate piece of conservative legislation as it ensured future generations of humanity the timeless pleasure of hearing the cry of the loon at evening and preventing the bird's destruction, something far from certain were such a law not in place. (Trained as a historian, he was recognized by many as deeply knowledgeable in matters of constitutional law and "original intent," and on several occasions he was called to serve as an expert witness in court cases related to church/state relations.)

This said, Kirk early recognized that the twentieth-century American penchant for looking perpetually to government to solve social problems is culturally debilitating. As Whitney wrote, "His study of British and American culture led him to the conclusion that, in the absence of coercion by government, society could heal its own ailments. Society spontaneously and repeatedly generates its own order, and does so through both the self-interested and other-directed activities of its members. Burke pictured all the voluntary associations of civil society as 'little platoons,' to which we give our allegiance and in return for which we maintain a just and tolerable order." Indeed, Kirk adhered to a localist philosophy, believing that the small, voluntary associations of church, community group, guild, friends, and family (the "little platoons") make life livable, lovable, and interesting—as opposed to bland, predictable, and boring, the hallmark of the standardized "masses" with their internationalist vision. Believing that ideology and utopian schemes for entire nations lead to tyranny, he was fond of advising his readers and listeners to "brighten the corner" in which they live, with a nod to an old hymn popular during his boyhood, "Brighten the Corner Where You Are." He was thus no friend of governmental intrusiveness, legally coerced standardization, excessive taxation, or other agencies and actions that strain and (in time) destroy the voluntary associations of community. In one pithy statement included in *Prospects for Conservatives,* for example, Kirk wrote, "Taxation, taken to the limit and beyond, has always been a sign of decadence and a prelude to disaster." Decadent and a prelude to disaster because the onus of neighborly responsibility that inheres in the little platoons is removed and replaced by a program, a department, a handout from on high, the fruit of this being plain to see in any culture in which statism is pervasive. In such cultures, people will (for example, as observed by American prisoners of war in North Vietnam) let an entire building collapse from moisture damage rather than replace a single missing roof shingle, this being universally considered the government's responsibility. Kirk thus believed that the desire to lawfully shake free of governmental regulation and benevolence programs was not an exercise in "greed and selfishness," the progressive mantra of the 1980s against conservatism. Rather, it was a legitimate effort to keep government from interposing itself inappropriately, so that right relations between people in voluntary association might be restored and communities strengthened through the "centering" of individuals living in right relation with the transcendent and with each other.

PATHBREAKING SCHOLARSHIP

As many writers have noted, when Kirk burst on the scene with *The Conservative Mind* in 1953, the very phrase "conservative mind" was considered a contradiction in terms. It was accepted as secular dogma that the American tradition is a liberal tradition, meaning given to advocating freedom verging into license in some matters and pervasive statist control in others, and that conservatives were simply out-of-touch cranks and heartless, rich capitalists who resented the New Deal legacy of Franklin Roosevelt. In 1950 literary scholar Lionel Trilling had confidently written, "In the United States at this time liberalism is not only the dominant but even the sole intellectual tradition. For it is the plain fact that nowadays there are no conservative or reactionary ideas in general circulation."[4] He added that "the conservative impulse and the reactionary impulse do not, with some isolated and some ecclesiastical exceptions, express themselves in ideas but only in action or in irritable mental gestures which seek to resemble ideas." Trilling was partly right, for at the dawn of the 1950s the New Deal and Keynesian legacy had been enshrined in the popular imagination as a glowing success and the future of American economic policy. What the American people needed and wanted, it was believed, was an ever-growing, ever-more omnicompetent central government dedicated to the belief that ever-higher taxation and public sector activism would lead to prosperity for all, progressing toward the day when no American citizen would have to worry about personal cash shortages, unemployment, costly medical care, or lack of retirement benefits. At the same time Trilling wrote his often-quoted words, conservatives were generally seen as the laughably out-of-touch children of wealth and privilege who wanted to turn back the clock of history to the days of the Robber Barons.

As *National Review* senior editor Richard Brookhiser described it, *"The Conservative Mind* appeared at a time when the very title seemed a paradox. The American right wing was an intellectual rag-tag, about as coherent as the Iranian parliament: robber barons and free-enterprisers; Communists turned Americans; America Firsters turned McCarthyites; Midwestern Republicans and Confederates; with Peter Viereck on the sidelines whispering all the while that the True Prince was Franklin D. Roosevelt."[5] The conservative was routinely depicted in editorial cartoons in both Marxist journals and major newspapers as a top-hatted hog walking on its hind legs while wearing a tuxedo and smoking a fat cigar. As American liberals learned in time and to their dismay, the great danger of thinking in slogans is complacency; for the conservative "outsiders" made inroads toward gaining a voice in American culture singly during the late 1940s through the mid-1970s, and in waves from the late '70s onward. Kirk's *The Conservative Mind* made a huge impact toward this end in 1953.

ADVOCATE OF CLASSICAL LIBERAL ARTS EDUCATION

From the mid-1940s when he began teaching college courses to freshmen who had just returned from military service overseas until his death in 1994, Kirk was a strident advocate of a classical, liberal arts education in America and an enemy of educational fads of every sort. The educational system he urged upon the American republic was one common to an earlier day but found operating in increasingly fewer districts and campuses as the twentieth century progressed: systems that support the inculcation of wisdom and virtue as the chief end of education, from grade school through university. Such an education, he believed, is ever relevant, focusing students' minds, through normative literature, upon the best that has been said and written throughout the ages rather than the here today–gone tomorrow intellectual fashion of the moment. As Whitney has written, "The goal of the liberal arts is simply to make sure that each generation of students develops an understanding of and fluency with some of the most important ideas communicated through some of the most important books ever produced." He adds that a sound education in the liberal arts—which are really the thinking arts, as opposed to technical branches of knowledge—should enable one to understand and articulate what it means to be (for example) human, Western, American, and modern/postmodern.

Opposed to this vision is the current world of American education, dominated by a national teachers' union less interested in education than in wielding political power and willing, in great measure, to give classrooms over to an agenda of grade inflation, equality of results, denigration of Western culture in general, and other ideological pursuits. Kirk agreed with the observation made by many others that this agenda is carried out largely by administrators who speak in an obscure, pseudo-scientific jargon understandable only to other adepts: a dense, plodding vocabulary largely incomprehensible but pleasant-sounding to the tax-paying public. The depraved administrator Wither, from C. S. Lewis's novel *That Hideous Strength*, might have cobbled together some of the pronouncements issued to support such ideological initiatives as "self-esteem education" and Kirk's personal "favorites": college courses in golf and degrees in "packaging." Lewis's demonic creation "Screwtape," a "senior tempter" among Hell's elite, articulates the gist of many such modern educationists, in advice to a young trainee in the infernal realm:

> The basic principle of the new education is to be that dunces and idlers must not be made to feel inferior to intelligent and industrious pupils. That would be "undemocratic." These differences between the pupils—for they are obviously and nakedly individual differences—must be disguised. This can be done on various levels. At universities, examinations must be framed so that nearly all the students get good marks. Entrance examinations must be framed so that all, or nearly all, citizens can go to universities, whether they have any power (or wish to profit by higher education) or not. At schools, the children who are too stupid or lazy to learn languages and mathematics and elementary science can be set to doing the things that children used to do in their spare time. Let them, for example, make mud pies and call it modeling. But all the time there must be no faintest hint that they are inferior to the children who are at work. Whatever nonsense they are engaged in must have—I believe the English already use the phrase—"parity of esteem." An even more drastic scheme is not impossible. Children who are fit to proceed to a higher class may be artificially kept back, because the others would get a trauma—Beelzebub, what a useful word!—by being left behind. The bright pupil thus remains democratically fettered to his own age group throughout his school career, and a boy who would be capable of tackling Aeschylus or Dante sits listening to his coeval's attempts to spell out A CAT SAT ON A MAT.[6]

Such a system at once feeds upon and encourages envy, and it is ventured in the name of a higher good that cannot be questioned, much less opposed, by the lesser breeds who foot the bill for such nonsense through their tax dollars. Leveling is always a leveling down, and Kirk opposed this tendency vigorously, most notably in his biweekly column "From the Academy," which he contributed to *National Review* from 1955 to 1980, and in his book *Decadence and Renewal in the Higher Learning* (1978).

MAN OF LETTERS

Kirk was one of a very small number of people who have earned their living by writing in a variety of genres and lecturing. He crafted works on conservative cultural and political issues to be sure; but he also wrote novels and short stories, an economics textbook, book reviews and literary criticism, familiar essays, newspaper columns, essays on education, and other works. With his novel *Old House of Fear* (1962), he brought about a renaissance of interest in the writing and reading of Gothic literature. His critical biography *Eliot and His Age* (1971) was named one of the two essential studies of the great poet by no less a critic than Allen Tate. Several of his historical works, notably *The Roots of American Order* (1974), as well as a textbook he wrote on "the dismal science" of economics, have been used in high school and college classroom settings. Then there are the ghost stories. Kirk wrote numerous such stories, some of which have been highly acclaimed, notably "There's a Long, Long Trail a-Winding." He was also a great teller of ghost stories, drawing upon the lore surrounding the old house he lived in for much of his life, Piety Hill, in the village of Mecosta, Michigan.

CULTURAL CRITIC

In certain matters, Kirk was almost predictably "conservative" as that term is popularly understood. On other matters, his thought went against much of the contemporary American grain—including the conservative grain— and it did so in two different ways. As historian Wilfred McClay has written:

> In the first place, he was an intellectual genuinely at ease in America. He may have fancied himself a Bohemian Tory, but he was never that most tiresome of bores, "the alienated American intellectual," a restless species that grazes in herds of independent minds. He knew he was fortunate to live in a country free and prosperous enough to permit him a career as an independent writer, and he never forgot that fact. But at the same time, he was never an uncritical celebrant of American culture. He loved his country, but he did not idolize it. Instead, he held it accountable to a transcendent standard, against which he often found it seriously wanting.
>
> In particular, Kirk lamented the deification of progress, the cult of absolute equality, the advance of the Leviathan state, the licentiousness of the autonomous self, the transvaluation of values, and other such modern abstractions that have transformed and eroded the American republic. While he vehemently opposed ideology in all its forms, including conservative ideology, he at the same time lamented Americans' fixation upon short-term, practical, problem-solving, results-oriented, and utility-maximizing thinking in place of a deeper reflection upon the proper ends of things. Kirk, then, was trying to do something characteristic of traditionalist conservatives: fight on two fronts at once. He was defending the American way of life against its cultured despisers—while at the same time challenging many elements of that way of life by holding it up to its classical and Judeo-Christian antecedents. He comforted

the afflicted and afflicted the comfortable—and sometimes they were the same people.[7]

A hard man to pigeonhole, this Russell Amos Kirk.

KIRK'S LIFE

Kirk was born in the railroad town of Plymouth, Michigan, on October 19, 1918, in his grandfather's bungalow just a few yards from the train tracks. He was the son of Russell Andrew Kirk, a railroad engineer, and Marjorie Rachel (Pierce) Kirk, a homemaker and the daughter of the local bank president, in whose house he was born. From his mother young Russell acquired his facial features and gentle personality, and from her father, Frank Pierce, his love of good books (particularly imaginative literature), long walks, and intelligent conversation. In truth, Kirk grew up in an environment straight out of Ray Bradbury's *Dandelion Wine*: a small town of domestic good humor, a tinge of danger, boyish adventure, and normality—excepting a serious childhood bout of nephritis that nearly killed the boy. In his youth Russell and his neighborhood friends spent their time exploring the grounds near the railroad roundhouse and the woods adjacent to an old millhouse on nearby Wilcox Lake, where his family rented. He had no religious upbringing to speak of, though his mother presented him with a Bible during his teens, inscribing it "To Russell Kirk Jr." (He was called Junior by his mother until her death in 1942.) Life in Plymouth, some twenty miles west of Detroit, was quiet but not dull, especially since his beloved grandfather's house, a short distance from young Russell's house, was directly across Mill Street from the now-vanished Nelson Hotel, a stopping place for rail passengers, which doubled as a speakeasy and, over the years, sank into ever-more squalid decay. Kirk and the other neighborhood children were directed away from the Nelson, devoting their energies to games of "Prisoner's Base," "Kick the Can," and other outdoor games.

Russell spent his summers upstate in Mecosta, a town founded by one of his great-grandfathers, Amos Johnson, who had also built an imposing white house on a rise of ground just west of town, at the corner of Main and Franklin Streets. That white clapboard house, in which lived two elderly great-aunts during Russell's boyhood, had a reputation as a haunted house and a colorful history as the scene of spiritualist meetings and ghostly visitations dating from Mecosta's founding during the heyday of lumbering in upper Michigan. What with the house's inhabitants being Swedenborgians and spiritualists, the long-vanished lumbermen had given the old Johnson place the nickname "Piety Hill," the stronghold of the godly, and the name stuck. Russell spent his summers there doing nothing but what he loved to do best: reading, listening to his elders tell stories—ghostly and otherwise—of days gone by, and taking long walks. Back in Plymouth during the school year, he attended Starkweather School, a few blocks away from home, eventually moving up to Plymouth High School, a mile away from the millhouse. Long an avid reader, having read deeply in his grandfather Pierce's volumes of Edmund Burke, Samuel Johnson, Fenimore Cooper, Nathaniel Hawthorne, and others, he soared academically. His schoolfellows considered him bookish and smart, someone who was going to "do something with his life," as one schoolmate remembered him many years later. He graduated from high school in 1936, and in the fall of that year, having won a scholarship to continue his education, he began attending Michigan State College of Agriculture and Applied Science (now Michigan State University) in East Lansing. While at State he began contributing essays on history to various academic quarterlies. The Kirk family never having been wealthy, Russell needed to support himself in college by entering all manner of writing contests with cash prizes. Facing this need, he entered every such contest he could and often won. During summer breaks, he worked as a tour guide at Henry Ford's Greenfield Village in Dearborn, actually meeting the aging founder of the automotive assembly line on one occasion. In 1940 he graduated from Michigan State with a B.A. in history, then moved on to Duke University in the fall. In another year he had received his M.A. in history from Duke, having written his master's thesis on the fiery Virginian statesman John Randolph of Roanoke. This work was published eleven years later, becoming Kirk's first published book.

Kirk was drafted into the U.S. Army a few months after the Japanese attack on Pearl Harbor and the beginning of America's involvement in World War II. For the duration, he served in the army's Chemical Warfare Service and was stationed at the Dugway Proving Ground in Utah. He endured a fairly uneventful time in the service, spending much of his time simply reading, writing letters, and thinking on the meaning of things, when not on duty. By war's end, he had attained the rank of staff sergeant and had absorbed most of the work available in English by the author who, by Kirk's own admission, came to exercise the greatest impact upon his outlook, Marcus Aurelius.

Mustering out of the service in 1945, Kirk was appointed an assistant professor of the history of civilization at Michigan State the following year. In addition, he and a friend opened a secondhand bookshop in East Lansing that struggled for two years before closing. Kirk taught one semester per year at State until 1953. Those portions of the academic year not spent at East Lansing were spent in Scotland, where he pursued doctoral studies at St. Andrews University. In 1952 St. Andrews conferred upon Kirk the degree of Doctor of Letters, the highest arts degree of the senior Scottish university. He was the first (and, to date, only) American to earn this degree from St. Andrews.

His doctoral paper, a study of Anglo-American conservatism, was brought to the attention of several American publishers, eventually reaching the maverick publisher Henry Regnery in Chicago. Regnery immediately accepted it and published it in 1953 as *The Conservative Mind: From Burke to Santayana.* This work received many favorable reviews, notably one by Kenyon College president Gordon Keith Chalmers in *The New York Times Book Review. Time* magazine devoted the entire book review section of its Fourth-of-July issue to *The Conservative Mind,* with many critics sensing—though nobody could fathom the extent of its influence—that here was a landmark in twentieth-century letters. *The Conservative Mind,* now in its seventh edition, went on to become one of the most widely discussed works of political theory written in the twentieth century.

The year 1953 was a red-letter year for Kirk in other respects, as well. That year, while attending the Edinburgh Festival, he met T. S. Eliot, whose play *The Confidential Clerk* was set to debut. Kirk was present to review the play for *The Month,* while Eliot, an editorial director at the English publishing firm of Faber & Faber, had arranged to bring out the British edition of *The Conservative Mind* and sought to meet the work's author. After reading Kirk's appraisal of his play, Eliot wrote to commend the younger man's skill at "penetrating so far into the play merely on what he has seen at one stage performance, without having been able to read the text." The two got along cordially, by letter and in face-to-face meetings and dinners, establishing a polite friendship that lasted until Eliot's death thirteen years later, addressing each other in their correspondence as Mr. Kirk and Mr. Eliot, never Russell or Tom.

In 1953 Kirk also resigned from the faculty of Michigan State, moving into Piety Hill to establish himself as a full-time writer. To Kirk, it was plain that the administrators at his college were single-mindedly bent not on academic excellence but on State's becoming bigger, more populous, and better at collegiate sports than the nearby University of Michigan—an assessment the college administration took few pains to deny. A parting of the ways had been long brewing, with Kirk being quite vocal about the grade inflation and lowering of standards at State; and when the break came he was glad to be out of the toils of the college administrators and State's president, John Hannah. A man who had earned his bachelor's degree—and nothing higher—in poultry science (a "chickenologist," Kirk called him), Hannah didn't think much of this young, fault-finding hotshot, however high his reputation as a rising force to be reckoned with in the world of cultural criticism.

The next forty years of Kirk's career have been covered in detail in his memoir, *The Sword of Imagination,* and what follows can for the most part be found at greater length in that work (though some details appear here that are absent in Kirk's book). Over those decades, while finding time to serve as a justice of the peace for Morton Township (which envelops Mecosta) and take long walking trips through Scotland, Southern and Eastern Europe, and North Africa, Kirk published biographical and philosophical studies of Robert Taft and Edmund Burke, six volumes of literary and social essays, four volumes of supernatural fiction, an economics textbook, and several other works, notably a colorful historical survey, *The Roots of American Order*. With each passing year since his days at St. Andrews, it seemed, his interest increased in the culture of his ancestral Scotland, and his occasional writing took on a mildly Scottish or archaic flavor, with sentences beginning typically with such phrases as "Turn we now to a study of," "Wondrous to relate," "In the fullness of time," and "Aye, just so." This was done not out of affectation; rather, it was a reflection of his stylistic preferences grounded in a lifetime of reading in the works of earlier centuries, evidence of his own thought being rooted in something deeper than the style and catchphrases of the passing hour.

As noted earlier, he was the founding editor of two influential quarterlies, *Modern Age* and *The University Bookman*, the latter edited with the aid of college student assistants at his library, a converted toy factory a few hundred feet down Franklin Street from Piety Hill. For a quarter century, from 1955 to 1980, he contributed a regular column on the state of American education, "From the Academy," to *National Review*, associating himself from the time of the magazine's founding with William F. Buckley Jr., Frank Meyer, William A. Rusher, and the rest of the writers and editors surrounding that conservative biweekly. For years he also wrote a syndicated column, "To the Point," which appeared in many major newspapers throughout the country, notably the *Detroit News*, the Baltimore *Sun*, the *Los Angeles Times*, and the New Orleans *Times-Picayune*. During the 1950s, Kirk learned that the John Birch Society had publicly accused then-President Dwight Eisenhower of being a communist. Borrowing a quip from columnist George Sokolsky, Kirk wrote, "Ike's no communist—he's a golfer."[8] In these six, widely publicized words, Kirk stated a phrase for which he is widely known today, and at the same time punctured a reckless accusation with his characteristically dry humor. He had no interest at all in tolerating extremists of the left or the right, nor did he march in lockstep with other conservatives on the issues of the day. Regarding the central issue of American dissent during the 1960s, Kirk believed American military involvement in Vietnam was a huge mistake, though he supported American troops and believed the United States and the South Vietnamese ought either to adopt a strategy to win the war quickly or else quit the field with as little loss of life and dignity as possible—not simply fight a long, costly war of attrition. Years later, he was one of the few conservative writers to oppose the Persian Gulf War of 1991, believing it little more than a war over Western access to Middle Eastern oil masked as a war against murderous and unappeasable expansionism.

A longtime adherent to a stoic view of the world, modeling his life on the example of his grandfather and the authors he admired most, Kirk converted to Christianity in 1964, the year he married a lively, devout Thomist, Annette Yvonne Cecile Courtemanche. He had met her while in New York in 1960, when she, then a nineteen-year-old junior at Molloy Catholic College for Women on Long Island, spoke on one of his books, *The American Cause*, at a conservative event. Kirk, himself forty-two years old at the time, was smitten by her loveliness and intelligence, and spent the next few years writing long letters to her—though he never would have believed that Annette would someday consent to marry him. As for the faith he embraced in 1964, Kirk later claimed to have grown into Catholicism, having long found the ancient faith congenial to his own way of looking at life and truth. He prayed daily and observed church feast days, and was for many years a regular attendee of mass, though he stopped attending regularly during the mid-1970s. His reasons were twofold: First, like his friend Richard Weaver, the distinguished Southern-born social critic, Kirk felt he needed only occasional experiences in corporate worship to last him for long periods. Second, during the 1970s and '80s, his local parish church was torn by a severe internal dispute that created bitter factions within its walls, and was led by priests whose services tended to focus less upon man's relationship to God and more upon the iniquities of American foreign policy in El Salvador and elsewhere. Saddened by the rift within his church and not being one who enjoyed being hectored weekly by secularized clergy who presumed to speak on matters they little understood, Kirk stayed home most Sunday mornings and slept, maintaining throughout his life a daily schedule of staying up until 3:00 A.M. reading and writing, and then sleeping till mid-morning. (Indeed, he kept very "British" hours, rising late in the morning, eating each meal later than the American average, and retiring every night well after midnight.)

In time the Kirks welcomed four daughters into their lives: Monica, Cecilia, Felicia, and Andrea. They were educated in local Catholic schools and grew to young womanhood in a most unusual household; for at Annette's behest (with Russell's encouragement), their home in Mecosta also served as a refuge for homeless immigrants in need of job and language skills, unwed mothers in need of acceptance and help, and half-reformed burglars in need of shelter and work. Former South Vietnamese Captain Nguyen Tan An and his family of ten, displaced by the communist takeover of 1975, lived with the Kirks for two years, as did Rett Ludwikowski, a Polish

professor whose political incorrectness had earlier landed him in potentially deadly trouble with the communist authorities in his native land. A
young female prostitute from nearby Grand Rapids was given shelter from
her brutal boyfriend for several days, but she soon left quiet Piety Hill, preferring the risks of life on the streets. An unmarried mother-to-be was taken
aboard long enough to go into labor; then, the doctor being delayed, Annette stepped in to deliver the young woman's healthy baby. As late as
1984, the Kirks were still providing such help to a great number and variety of displaced persons, with Kirk writing to his friend Peter J. Stanlis, "We
have with us at Mecosta four Croats, four Poles, one Italian, one Swiss, one
Scot; we had two Ethiopians recently; also a congeries of Americans: A
summer household of twenty-four, in all, ranging from eight years of age
to ninety-three."[9] Throughout the many years of this activity, room was
somehow found to accommodate all who came. And in the midst of it all,
Kirk continued to find the time to write well-received books, departing
from Mecosta periodically to serve as a guest lecturer at numerous colleges
and universities throughout the United States and Europe.

A large, brick Italianate annex was built onto the old wooden house to
accommodate the Kirks' growing family and their many guests. Some of
these visitors came for a few days, and some stayed for several years. One
such guest was a hobo Annette spotted begging money outside her church
door one snowy Sunday in late 1966. This was Clinton Wallace, a man of
approximately fifty years, who had been wandering the less-traveled roads
of America since his mid-teens. From his many hours spent sitting in town
libraries and Christian Science reading rooms, he had read and memorized
a great number of poems from the Western canon; to potential benefactors,
he would recite lengthy passages from memory in exchange for meals and
shelter. Clinton, a tall, simple man with a booming voice and a long history
of odd jobs, petty thefts from church poor boxes, and short stays in prison,
was invited to lunch at Piety Hill that winter day, thus beginning an
eleven-year association with the Kirks. He lived at the Old House with the
family for six of those years, being paid out of Russell's pocket for setting
the table, pouring out wine at supper, and answering the front door. His
job skills being meager, Clinton enjoyed this work as the first "real job" he
had held in his long life. But every year or so he would get upset over some
small matter or simply be overtaken with wanderlust; then he would unexpectedly disappear from the Kirk home for several months, after first pil-
fering some small but valuable household item to be pawned to pay for
food and lottery tickets. At those times, Kirk would vow to all present that
Clinton Wallace would never again be allowed across the threshold of
Piety Hill. However, upon the hobo's inevitable return, Clinton, deeply
and invariably sorry for all the trouble he had caused, would be welcomed

back with open arms—with a beaming Russell Kirk standing at the head of the line to greet him at the front door. Kirk's affection for and fascination with Clinton and his wealth of true stories of life on the open road transcended even the fact that the man's overzealousness in tending the fireplace one winter night in 1975 led to the Old House catching fire and burning to the ground. (The brick annex withstood the flames and was soon remodeled to become a large residence in its own right, the new Piety Hill.) Clinton eventually qualified for Social Security benefits, at which point he moved into a small apartment of his own in nearby Grand Rapids. He died not long after leaving behind the only family he had known since boyhood. He was one of the most intriguing (and, at times, exasperating) persons Kirk met during a lifetime of meeting the great and the lowly, and the world-traveled writer spent hours listening to the hobo-butler relate tales from his colorful life story. Eventually he worked the basic details of Clinton's life into what became his best-known short story, "There's a Long, Long Trail a-Winding," and its sequel, "Watchers at the Strait Gate."

The new Piety Hill, a brick Italianate structure, took its full shape in mid- to late 1975, and was built in part with remnants salvaged from the remains of other interesting buildings that had fallen victim to the wrecking ball. "You possibly may have heard of our disastrous fire of Ash Wednesday last, which utterly destroyed my ancestral house here; only a single tiny ancient saucer was found in the ashes," wrote Kirk in an invitation to Malcolm Muggeridge in October 1975. "But you would be comfortably enough lodged here," he added,

> for the modern massive brick wing which survived the fire, a kind of Italianate tower, has plenty of bedrooms. We have begun to rebuild, both at our house and at my separate library-building. From the jaws of the Urban Renewers of Grand Rapids, we have snatched various curiosities which will embellish our restored house: two immense terra-cotta lions' heads from the demolished Isis Theater, a travertine lion's head from the quondam Morton House Hotel, eight bronze griffins from a demolished bank, a wealth of panelling from a demolished Anglican church, etc., etc. The crowning glory, being lifted to the top of our surviving house this very day, is a big Italianate cupola, with eight sides, from the vanished hospital for the aged of the Little Sisters of the Poor, Grand Rapids. . . . "These fragments I have shored against my ruin."[10]

As it had in the years immediately before the Ash Wednesday fire, Piety Hill attracted college students eager to study with Kirk in the solitude of his 10,000-volume library and gain publishing experience by helping edit *The University Bookman*. The students, some of whom arrived on scholarships provided by the Marguerite Eyer Wilbur Foundation, were in some cases admirers of Kirk, sometimes not; and most of them were scholarly, though a rare few were not. One individual was asked to leave Piety Hill after spending his days sleeping and his nights performing with a rock group in Grand Rapids. In the mid-1960s, another young assistant wrote an arrogant rejection letter to an aspiring *University Bookman* contributor who went on to found a very influential magazine of the right. (Never having read this letter before it was mailed, Kirk was embarrassed to behold it after finding a copy of it in his files many years later.) The students were for the most part conservative, but not straitlaced by any means. Studying in the Kirk library in the wee hours of a winter night, two student assistants got into a good-natured disagreement that escalated to the point that they began throwing small objects at one another; the fight ended when one of them threw a small bottle of white liquid type-remover at the other. It bounced into the fireplace and then, there being a fire blazing at the moment, the bottle exploded, splattering the library from floor to ceiling. The two students spent the remaining hours till dawn scrubbing the library's floor, mantel, ceiling, and prized statuary with cleaning rags and toothbrushes—under the firm direction of Annette Kirk. Among the students who studied with Kirk were Michael Henrie, an accomplished essayist and editor; Marjorie Haney, a skillful teacher and writer; Christopher O'Brien, an attorney of note; Robert Kamphuis, today a successful businessman; and Andrew Shaughnessy, a quiet young Scotsman who is also an essayist and trusted associate editor of *The University Bookman,* as well as Kirk's right-hand man during the final months of the older man's life.

Kirk good-naturedly tolerated, but did not encourage, the sobriquets that came to be heaped upon him over the years, including "the Sage of Mecosta," "the American Cicero," and other such honorifics, though he took a boyish delight when referred to as "the Wizard of Mecosta." (When one visitor piped up at supper one night at Piety Hill and said he was "in awe" of his host, Kirk responded quickly, with a glint of humor in his eye and struggling to keep a straight face, saying, "As well you ought!"—and then led the laughter at his own self-mocking remark.) In person, he was a quiet-spoken man, bashful, preferring to let others do the talking. If there were two virtues Kirk possessed in abundance, they were humility and generosity, he being one of the least self-absorbed intellectuals one might ever meet. Even on the rare occasions that he was roused to express anger at someone, he was short-spoken and to-the-point—and then the storm was over. (With Kirk, as with many people, shyness and quietness could be sometimes mistaken for signs of arrogance by certain first-time observers. A little over a year before his death, he confided to his diary, "My chief failing throughout life has been a painful shyness. It goes back before adolescence, to perhaps the eighth or ninth year."[11]) Upon being asked questions at table, he would give fairly short, humorous answers, though he could be drawn out after patient inquiry and then hold forth at modest length. When asked to tell a ghost story, he could go on for hours, but in most other circumstances he held his peace. His wife Annette, in contrast, is high spirited and loquacious: discerning, energetic, witty in the neo-classical sense of being quick to see connections (often humorous) between like-sounding words and concepts, and playfully but deeply respectful of her husband. Trained by exacting, old-school Catholic teachers of philosophy and rhetoric at Molloy, she possesses a razor-sharp mind; and while friendly and generous, she is a serious and prudent steward of the grant funds that enable students to study at Piety Hill, and nobody to underestimate or trifle with. On the few occasions when guests in her home have dared to be bluntly rude to her or disdainful of her husband, she has set them straight deftly and in no uncertain terms. She is a Thomist, given strongly to the interior life of reason; Russell was Augustinian in temperament, relating to explorations of truth as it is apprehended through rational thought as well as sources outside the human capacity to reason. Together they made what Annette called a team, each coming to depend upon the other to supply portions of the intellectual, spiritual, and material needs of each day in their married life.

During the last years of his life, Kirk stayed busy delivering lectures and then compiling these texts into books. A longtime smoker, he was stricken by a mild heart attack in 1980 and subsequently warned by his doctor to cut back to no more than one cigar per day. Kirk, having for years taken long walks in Scotland, the European Continent, and Northern Africa covering thirty miles on any given day, regardless of the weather, now confined his walking to the environs of Mecosta, often planting trees on these outings. His brief forays into the world of politics—he had campaigned energetically for Barry Goldwater in 1964 and been on friendly terms with Presidents Nixon and Reagan—came to an end in 1992 when he served as general chairman of Patrick Buchanan's Michigan primary campaign. In 1993 his health took a noticeable downturn, marked by a decided loss of appetite: having once been fairly burly and healthful in appearance, he now lost a great deal of weight and looked decidedly frail. A two-day conference in early October to celebrate his seventy-fifth birthday and the fortieth anniversary of *The Conservative Mind*'s appearance, followed by a long series of lectures across America extending into late November, left Kirk physically (though cheerfully) spent, and he was confined to bed for a month on doctor's orders. On the eve of Ash Wednesday, 1994, he was informed by his doctor that he had congestive heart failure and only a few months to live. Shortly after this diagnosis, Kirk put the finishing touches on his essay "Is Life Worth Living?" the final chapter in his long-anticipated memoir, *The Sword of Imagination*. (His answer to that question is an eloquent "Aye, just so.")

During the last weeks of Kirk's life, his daughters were just down the hall from his bedroom to help Annette attend to his few needs. His long-time assistant Andrew Shaughnessy was also on hand to converse with, to bring books over from the library for him to read, and to maintain a fire in the bedroom fireplace. Bedridden now, Kirk summoned to his side his four daughters—now grown, two of them married, all but the youngest living away from Piety Hill, but all together under one roof for the last time in their father's life. Kirk spoke with them of many things, telling them that if they would be wise they ought to read and reread four specific writings informed by the moral imagination: *The Little Fir Tree*, by Hans Christian Andersen; *The Pilgrim's Regress*, by C. S. Lewis; "The Golden Key," by George MacDonald; and *Tree and Leaf*, by J. R. R. Tolkien.

Kirk slept poorly during these final weeks and ate little, but kept himself busy indexing a forthcoming book, *Redeeming the Time*, and reading. On April 23, Annette hesitated to bring to his room the day's issue of *The Grand Rapids Press*; the banner headline and subheading read: "Nixon Dies—Daughters at His Bedside." She eventually decided to show him the paper; he read the story calmly, saying a few words of praise for his de-parted friend. (Nixon had disappointed Kirk by his decisions related to the Watergate coverup, which had cost Nixon the presidency, but the two men remained on cordial terms.) Five evenings later, before going to bed, he asked Andrew to step over to the library and bring over one of Shake-speare's plays, for he wanted to read that night. Annette arranged that a radio be placed in the bedroom and tuned to Blue Lake Public Radio, a lo-cal music and news station originating at the nearby Blue Lake Music Camp, for Russell wanted to switch on the radio first thing upon awaken-ing to hear the morning news. The night passed without incident, though Kirk slept little. At about 6:30 the next morning, he called for Annette. When she awoke, Russell told her that he had just learned from the radio news that Pope John Paul II had badly injured his leg, and that they must remember the pope in their prayers that day. He then asked for breakfast, which—for the first time in weeks—he ate hungrily and finished. For an hour or so, he and Annette talked of numerous things, mostly concerning books he had read, upcoming lectures he had been invited to make, grants they needed to procure for deserving students, and other matters. At a lit-tle after 10:00, Annette noticed that Russell was silent and unresponsive. She ran out into the hall and called for her daughters to come quickly. Joined by Monica and Andrea, she turned back to Russell, who had now closed his eyes. Kirk's oldest and youngest daughters then stood at their father's bedside, held his hands, and began to softly sing the lilting song that he had long ago sung to awaken them, "School Days." After a minute, Kirk opened his eyes one last time, smiled gently, and then closed them for the last time, a single tear rolling down his face. On the table at his bedside lay the Shakespeare play he had read the night before, *All's Well That End's Well.*

KEY CONCEPTS

To understand the life and work of Russell Kirk, it is helpful to review the six "canons" of conservatism outlined in *The Conservative Mind* as well as the six general principles articulated in his introduction to *The Portable Conservative Reader.* To better understand these principles, it is essential to grasp several key elements of Kirk's vocabulary and worldview.

The Permanent Things

In one of his favorite books, Eliot's *The Idea of a Christian Society* (1939), Kirk encountered a phrase and a concept that came to recur in his own writings: "the permanent things." In its context, Eliot had written:

[Without a] firm assurance of first principles which it is the business of the Church to repeat in and out of season, the World will constantly confuse the right with the expedient. In a society based on the use of slave labour men tried to prove from the Bible that slavery was something ordained by God. For most people, the actual constitution of Society, or that which their more generous passions wish to bring about, is right, and Christianity must be adapted to it. But the Church cannot be, in any political sense, either conservative, or liberal, or revolutionary. *Conservatism is too often conservation of the wrong things: liberalism a relaxation of discipline; revolution a denial of the permanent things.*[12] [Emphasis added]

To conserve, then, not "the wrong things" but "the permanent things" is the goal of those who possess imagination and a conservative inclination. Gleaves Whitney has succinctly described the permanent things as "time-tested principles." More specifically, they are mores or norms that transcend the world's cultures, though there may be degrees of difference in the way such mores are understood and practiced. In one culture, for example, it is expected that a man will marry no more than one wife; in another culture, a man may have three, four, or five wives: nevertheless, in each culture, it is believed that marriage is good and altogether preferable to lives of random sexual encounters, the resultant coarsening of culture, and the begetting of illegitimate children. In another of Kirk's favorite books, *The Abolition of Man* (1947), C. S. Lewis outlined numerous such norms that are observed across world cultures, inside and outside of religious societies, including what he termed the law of general beneficence, duties to parents, elders, and ancestors, duties to children and posterity, the law of good faith and veracity, the law of mercy, and several others. The permanent things thus include such mores as honor, courage, and character. There are others, as shown in the following illustration.

Thomas Howard, a writer and scholar Kirk highly respected, used to give his college English literature class an exercise in the permanent things at the beginning of each term. He would give the class a list of the following words: majesty, magnanimity, valor, courtesy, grace, chastity, virginity, nobility, splendor, ceremony, taboo, mystery, and purity. The class's reaction to this list was invariable: "either a total blank, embarrassed snickers, or incredulity," he wrote, adding:

> The entire list of words land in their laps like a heap of dead basalt meteorites lately arrived from some other realm. They don't know what to do with them. They have never encountered them. The words are entirely foreign to the whole set of assumptions that has been written (or should I say televised) into these students' imaginations for the whole of their lives. Majesty? The man must be mad. Valor? What's that? Courtesy? What a bore. Virginity? Ho-ho—there's one for you![13]

Howard's young charges apparently reason that if it can't be experienced through the five senses, it must not exist. Of what value can such things be? After acknowledging his students' reaction, Howard points out to them that "this awful list of words names an array of qualities that any Jew, any pagan, and any Christian, up until quite recently in history, would have not only understood, but would have extolled as being close to the center of things." But are the terms "relevant?" For his part, Kirk addressed this issue by writing that only by "proper attention to prudent reform—effected by holding to the enduring norms—may we preserve and improve a tolerably ordered, just, and free society."[14]

These norms, apprehended through the illative sense (defined and discussed below), are not *values*, Kirk hastened to add. (Indeed, during the last years of his life, he cringed at the way the two terms were used interchangeably by politicians and pundits who, then as now, trafficked in "family values," "values in education," and other high-toned terms with no certain meaning.) In *Enemies of the Permanent Things*, Kirk defined these two terms, so essential to his thought that he is worth quoting at moderate length:

> A norm means an enduring standard. It is a law of nature, which we ignore at our peril. It is a rule of human conduct and a measure of public virtue. The norm does not signify the average, the median, the mean, the mediocre. The norm is not the conduct of the average sensual man. A norm is not simply a measure of average performance within a group. There is a law for man, and law for thing; the late Alfred Kinsey notwithstanding, the norm for the wasp

and the snake is not the norm for man. A norm exists: though men may ignore or forget a norm, still that norm does not cease to be, nor does it cease to influence men. A man apprehends a norm, or fails to apprehend it; but he does not create or destroy important norms. . . .

When I write of a "norm," I do not mean a "value" merely. A value is the quality of worth. Many things are worthwhile that are not normative. When most writers nowadays employ the word "value" as a term of philosophy, moreover, they mean "subjective value"—that is, the utility of being worthwhile, of giving pleasure or satisfaction to individuals, without judgment upon the intrinsic, absolute, essential merit of the sensation or action in question; without reference to its objective deserts. In the subjective sense, going to church is a value for some persons, and taking one's ease in a brothel is a value for others. A norm has value, but has more than value. A norm endures in its own right, whether or not it gives pleasure to particular individuals. *A norm is the standard against which any alleged value must be measured objectively.*[15] [Emphasis added]

Observed norms make for custom, continuity, and healthy prescription. A significant element in maintaining continuity, Kirk argued, concerns the sense of *place* that is often associated with Southern culture. *Place* involves setting down roots and soaking up local culture. Kirk set his face against rootlessness, his attitude being similar to that of novelist Wallace Stegner in this regard, Stegner having once written: "Our migratoriness has hindered us from becoming a people of communities and traditions. . . . It has robbed us of the gods who make places holy. It has cut off individuals and families and communities from memory and the continuum of time. It has left at least some of us with a kind of spiritual pellagra, a deficiency disease, a hungering for the ties of a rich and stable social order. Not only is the American home a launching pad, as Margaret Mead said; the American community . . . is an overnight camp."[16] Little wonder then that Kirk stressed the importance of place throughout his life, admiring the likes of Wendell Berry and Andrew Lytle for farming ancestral ground and, for his part, always returning to his own land and home in Mecosta. "If you don't know who you are or where you come from, you will find yourself at a disadvantage," declared Lytle in his ruminative family history. He added:

The ordered slums of suburbia are made for the confusion of the spirit. Those who live in units called homes or estates—both words do violence to the language—don't know who they are. For the profound stress between the union that is flesh and the spirit, they have been forced to exchange the appetites. Each business promotion uproots the family. Children become wayfarers. Few are given any vision of the Divine. They perforce become secular men, half men, who inhabit what is left of Christendom.[17]

Today, given the marked decline in apprenticeships within families and communities, and that members of the American workforce "go where the jobs are," fewer Americans than ever can identify their family's "old home place," much less live on ancestral grounds over the course of several generations. This gives rise to a gibe issued by several hostile critics, who have claimed that Kirk was an advocate of a way of life straight out of Sir Walter Scott's Waverly novels, with generation after generation living at a family estate.[18] In truth, Kirk did no such thing. He did, however, point to the salutary benefits inhering in a way of life common to many Americans until well into the twentieth century and say, in a manner echoing the Southern Agrarians of the 1930s, *Do you really want to give up all of this? What will be lost if you do?*

The Moral Imagination and the Illative Sense

The words "the moral imagination" appear often in Kirk's writings across disciplines. He gleaned the phrase from a section of Edmund Burke's essay *Reflections on the Revolution in France*, in which Burke sardonically explained the intent of the French revolutionaries in their designs upon remaking society: "All the decent drapery of life is to be rudely torn off. All the superadded ideas, furnished from the wardrobe of a moral imagination, which the heart owns, and the understanding ratifies, as necessary to cover the defects of our naked, shivering nature, and to raise it to dignity in our own estimation, are to be exploded as a ridiculous, absurd, and antiquated fashion."[19] Kirk understood the moral imagination to be that human facility and process that envisages men as beings who are flawed but at the same time responsible for their moral choices, beloved by God, and meant for eternity. "Human beings, after all, are created in the image of God," wrote Kirk in 1988. "The moral imagination expresses what Pico della Mirandola called 'the dignity of man.'" Vigen Guroian has engaged with the idea of the moral imagination in his study *Tending the Heart of Virtue: How Classic Stories Awaken a Child's Moral Imagination* (1998). A friend and admirer of Kirk, he has written that the moral imagination

> is not a *thing*, not even so much a faculty, as the very process by which the self makes metaphors out of images given by experience and then employs metaphors to find and suppose moral correspondences in experience. The moral imagination is active, for well or ill, strongly or weakly, every moment of our lives, in our sleep as well as when we are awake. But it needs nurture and proper exercise. Otherwise, it will atrophy like a muscle that is not used. The richness or the poverty of the moral imagination depends on the richness or the poverty of experience.[20]

Defined in such terms, the moral imagination contrasts sharply with what Kirk identified as the "idyllic imagination," which is essentially the same vision espoused by Jean-Jacques Rousseau and modern-day hedonists, and which sees humankind as basically good but hampered from achieving happiness on earth because of society's conventions and the influence of others within society. In the passage from *Reflections* quoted earlier, Burke saw the French Revolution hurtling toward the Terror as men embraced a bloodless, empirical rationalism, stripped of all moral elements; his *Reflections* were written, in part, to warn Britain from following a similar course, which invariably leads to tyranny and depravity. The moral imagination stands at stark odds, also, with the "diabolical imagination." This worldview, embraced by the Marquis de Sade, Friedrich Nietzsche, and Josef Stalin, sees humanity in the same way a farmer views an overabundance of rabbits: a nuisance to be thinned, bred, killed, consumed, or otherwise used, but not to be considered anything more than a biological aberration—certainly not a special creation of any divine being.

Kirk made a point of adding that by *imagination* he did not mean *intuition*, being uneasy with the claims for intuition and knowing that his own creative imagination did not spring from private revelation or prophetic seizure. As he said of T. S. Eliot, the great poet's imagination was no "Inner Voice" of the private conscience:

> Nay, in large part, his remarkable imagination amounted to what John Henry Newman called the *illative sense*, which we may vulgarly term the jigsaw-puzzle capabilities of the intellect, a multitude of little evidences falling into place gradually, so that in the end one discovers "powerful and concurrent reasons" for belief, even though one cannot consciously trace the intricate process by which conviction was brought about. Intuition had a part in that imagination, of course, as it has in the perception of every man of genius. A passage in André Maurois's little book *Illusions* may help us here.
>
> Maurois describes the visit of Saint-John Perse to Albert Einstein at Princeton. The physicist had invited the poet there (both having received Nobel Prizes in the recent past) to ask him a question.
>
> " 'How does a poet work?' Einstein inquired. 'How does the idea of a poem come to him? How does this idea grow?' Saint-John Perse described the vast part played by intuition and subconscious. Einstein seemed delighted: 'But it's the same thing for the man of science' he said. 'The mechanics of discovery are neither logical nor intellectual. It is a sudden illumination, almost a rapture. Later, to be sure, intelligence analyzes and experiments confirm (or invalidate) the intuition. But initially there is a great forward leap of the imagination.' "
>
> As Maurois adds, an intuition by a scientist "perhaps stems from an unconscious statistical recollection or from the sudden glimpse of an analogy." Similarly, the talented poet's "intuitions" may be the work of the reproductive imagination, or of the illative sense, rather than unique and inexplicable glimpses of transcendent reality.[21]

Kirk knew that the "Inner Voice," more often than not, is simply a gilded justification of the subject's own desires. It is a voice of wishful thinking, which, in the average sensual man—typified by his friend Eliot's creation Apeneck Sweeney—"breathes the eternal message of vanity, fear and lust." The illative sense, then, denotes a method of reasoning beyond strict logic. It consists of knowledge that is borne in upon the mind from a source deeper than one's conscious and formal reason, combining intuition, instinct, imagination, experience, and much reading and meditation: a "supra-logical judgment," as Newman called it, in his *Essay in Aid of a Grammar*. It is summarized in Blais Pascal's succinct—if much-abused—phrase, "The heart has reasons that reason does not know."

In *The Sword of Imagination*, Kirk describes his long hours of thinking and meditation upon his readings during World War II while in the Utah desert. There at Dugway Proving Ground, he gave much thought to why the cold logic of H. G. Wells and Leonard Woolf gave him no satisfaction, though, as a modern skeptic he should have, by rights, embraced it. He found, instead, that his innermost being had long been far more attuned to the writings of Burke, Samuel Johnson, Samuel Taylor Coleridge, and Paul Elmer More, all of them ethicists if not believing Christians. In the writings of the stoic Marcus Aurelius, whom Kirk deeply admired, he found reference to the man who stands fast in the face of life's troubles and is then "translated indeed to Islands of the Blessed." Kirk wondered, "The Islands of the Blessed—were there such, hereafter? If the Islands were but a fable, was not Kirk the most miserable of men? Did there really exist a community of souls, joining the dead, the living, and those yet to be born? A community transcending time and space?"[22] One of the things that attracted Annette Kirk, a strong "cradle Catholic," to the former "Stoical Sergeant" was their shared interest in "discussing the essential questions . . . such as the metaphysical understanding of 'being,' the proofs for the existence of God, and the meaning and purpose of life." In a short memoir, she adds:

> While he agreed that what made man unique was his ability to reason and to know the difference between right and wrong, Russell also believed that pure reason had its limits and that logical proofs were not needed to validate religious truths. He persuaded me that even if a transcendent order were denied in the realm of reason, evidences of every sort—proofs from natural science, history, and physics—demonstrated that we were part of some grand mysterious scheme working upon us providentially.[23]

Russell Kirk remained stoical throughout his life, though his meditative and reserved nature was in time subsumed by Christian belief—a transformation he always referred to as an "intellectual conversion" rather than (as is often the case) a response to heartbreak or personal trauma. "What Kirk had been seeking was not so much consolation as understanding: knowledge of the source of authority in faith and morals," he wrote, referring to himself in the third person. "By what principles are we to live here below? And how are we to know that those principles, or norms, or doctrines, or dogmas, are true, and were true, and will be true?" The writings of Newman, read while he prepared to write his doctoral thesis, introduced him to the "complexities and assurances of Authority," apprehended by the illative sense. In his essay on John Keble, Newman had written, "Conscience is an authority; the Bible is an authority; such is the Church; such is Antiquity; such are the words of the wise, such are hereditary lessons; such are ethical truths; such are historical memories, such are legal saws and state maxims; such are proverbs; such are sentiments, presages, and prepossessions." Such truths are borne in upon the receptive mind, "falling into place most intricately," according to Kirk.

Contrary to what one may imagine, the illative sense operates widely across the world's cultures. In those societies in which the illative sense is lacking, cold and logical efficiency leads in the direction of exterminating unwanted or uncooperative people—H. G. Wells had politely but firmly advocated this course of action in his extended essay *Anticipations* (1901)— as well as a "why-not?" mentality in regard to everyday moral choices. The governments of Nazi Germany, Imperial Japan, and Stalinist Russia thrust aside the illative sense and the moral imagination in favor of cold, dialectical materialism, and history has shown the dire results. No wonder, then, that Kirk's conservatism counseled prudence as the highest virtue, believing that the best mindset is one that combines a willingness to change with a habit of mind for conserving custom and convention, thus enhancing healthy cultural continuity.

It may be mildly surprising to those who think of the word imagination only in terms of literature to learn that Kirk spoke of the moral imagination as applying to contexts across disciplines and outside the world of letters. On one occasion, he addressed a group of businessmen on the moral imagination, only to have one spectator arise during the subsequent question-and-answer period and loudly retort, "We don't need any imagination: We're practical." The substance of Kirk's reply found its way into one of his essays, "The Recovery of Norms": "When the moral imagination is enriched, a people find themselves capable of great things; when it is impoverished, they cannot act effectively even for their own survival, no matter how immense their material resources."[24] From at least the time of *The Conservative Mind*'s appearance, Kirk saw himself and his vocation as that of pointing the way to first principles and normative truth, these being sometimes neglected or forgotten but vital nonetheless.

The Contract of Eternal Society

"Did there really exist a community of souls, joining the dead, the living, and those yet to be born?" Kirk had reflected during his years reading

Marcus Aurelius. "A community transcending time and space?" Again drawing upon Newman, Burke, and other writers of the past, Kirk came to believe that each generation is linked intimately with the one that preceded it and the one that will follow. This he called *the community of souls* or *the contract of eternal society.* Our tradition, he believed—our moral, social, and artistic knowledge—form a patrimony from men and women long dead. "Tradition means giving votes to the most obscure of all classes, our ancestors. It is the democracy of the dead," wrote G. K. Chesterton, adding, "Tradition refuses to submit to that arrogant oligarchy who merely happen to be walking around."[25] The implication is that the living would be foolish to depend upon the small fund of knowledge acquired in a single lifetime, that we have much to learn from the past and therefore much to conserve; also, that we owe much to our children, including the transmission of sound mores and manners that make for an ordered soul, a clean and healthy environment, and an ordered society. A longtime admirer of Chesterton, Kirk often cited the famous Englishman's phrase "the democracy of the dead" to communicate that the past has an undeniable claim upon the present day; from our ancestors, we have inherited that which is maintaining and shaping our culture at present. "The past is never dead. It's not even past," says a character in William Faulkner's later fiction. Kirk would readily agree with this remark, though his supporting quotation on the subject would typically come from Eliot, words from "Little Gidding" that are today carved upon his own tombstone: "the communication / Of the dead is tongued with fire beyond the language of the living." Kirk's friend Andrew Lytle warned of the danger of ignoring the fiery communication of the dead:

> If we dismiss the past as dead and not as a country of the living which our eyes are unable to see, as we cannot see a foreign country but know it is there, then we are likely to become servile. Living as we will be in a lesser sense of ourselves, lacking that fuller knowledge which only the living past can give, it will be so easy to submit to pressure and receive what is already ours as a boon from authority.[26]

Kirk scorned utterly those who would break this "covenant binding upon us all," writing, "No man has a right to abridge that contract at will; and if we do break it, we suffer personally and all society suffers; and we are cast out of this civil social order . . . into an 'antagonist world' of total disorder—or as the New Testament has it, into the outer darkness, where there shall be wailing and gnashing of teeth." Echoing Bernard of Chartres, Kirk was fond of quoting, "We are dwarfs mounted upon the shoulders of giants," and he considered the Emersonian concept of each generation learning afresh the lessons learned painstakingly by earlier generations utter folly. Paraphrasing Burke, he wrote that we moderns

> tend to be puffed up with a little petty private rationality, thinking ourselves wiser than the prophets and the law-givers, and are disposed to trade upon the trifling bank and capital of our private intelligence. That way lies ruin. But though the individual is foolish, the species is wise; and, given time, the species judges rightly. The moral precepts and the social conventions which we obey represent the considered judgments and filtered experience of many generations of prudent and dutiful human beings—the most sagacious of our species. It is folly to ignore this inherited wisdom in favor of our own arrogant little notions of right and wrong, of profit and loss, of justice and injustice. Burke, though the most prophetic man of his age, never thought himself taller than the giants from whom came his strength.[27]

To pass along a tolerable heritage to the rising generation, Kirk strongly advocated an education in virtue and wisdom as well as a healthy environment. While many self-styled conservatives today readily identify with the need for educational reform, the latter is seen as something that separates Kirk from the conservative (really, the neoconservative) mainstream. For Kirk was a diligent conservationist. His home in upstate Mecosta, Michigan, some two hours north of Lansing by automobile, lies in the middle of the state's "stump country": land once covered by virgin pine forests that were clear-cut during the late nineteenth century and then left, after the loggers departed, a ruined landscape of stumps and fields badly damaged by soil erosion. Of course, Michigan's forests have come back since that time, and in a small way Kirk contributed to this, as he spent considerable time every year of his adult life planting trees on his property and on land throughout the village of Mecosta. "There is nothing more conservative than conservation," he wrote on one occasion,[28] a sentiment that stands at stark odds with the libertarian quip that the best thing about a tree is what you can do with it after you kill it. Granted, this and similar cultural pronouncements are often made with tongue firmly in cheek; still, this remark reflects accurately the belief system of many neoconservatives and right-leaning libertarians throughout America, who promote what Richard Weaver called the "reduction of human striving to material production and consumption," seeing no higher value in life than getting and spending, and policical influence as the primary measure of an individual's worth.

All these concepts Kirk considered essential to conservative philosophy. With this background in place, the reader is better prepared to understand Kirk's written work across the several disciplines in which he worked. May what follows prove fruitful to those who fare forward to the remaining short chapters of this study.

NOTES

1. Kirk recorded his recollections of this meeting with Nixon in several of his written works, most notably his memoir *The Sword of Imagination*.

2. See Whitney, "Seven Things You Should Know about Russell Kirk: The Origins of the Modern Conservative Movement in the U.S." *Vital Speeches of the Day* 63, June, 1997, 507–11. References to the text of Whitney's speech appear throughout this chapter.

3. O'Connor, Review of *Beyond the Dreams of Avarice*, in Leo J. Zuber and Carter W. Martin, eds., *The Presence of Grace, and Other Book Reviews*, p. 23. This assessment originally appeared in O'Connor's diocesan newsletter, *The Bulletin of the Catholic Laymen's Association of Georgia*, July 21, 1956.

4. Trilling, preface to *The Liberal Imagination: Essays on Literature and Society*, p. vii.

5. Brookhiser, "Hail to the Chief," *National Review* 33, October 30, 1981, 1263.

6. Lewis, "Screwtape Proposes a Toast," *The Screwtape Letters*, pp. 166–67.

7. McClay, "The Mystic Chords of Memory: Reclaiming American History," *Heritage Lecture*, no. 550, n.p.

8. Quoted in the PBS documentary *The Conservatives*, 1988.

9. Stanlis, "Russell Kirk: Memoir of a Friendship," in James E. Person Jr., ed., *The Unbought Grace of Life: Essays in Honor of Russell Kirk*, p. 49.

10. Letter from Kirk to Malcolm Muggeridge, October 10, 1975.

11. Diary entry, January 28, 1993. Kirk kept diaries periodically during his life, and this particular entry is taken from the last such journal he chose to keep.

12. Eliot, *Christianity and Culture*, p. 73.

13. Howard, "The Peal of a Thousand Bells," in *The Achievement of C. S. Lewis: A Reading of His Fiction*, p. 15.

14. Quoted in James E. Person Jr., "The Sharpening of the Conservative Mind," *Modern Age* 36, summer, 1994, 373.

15. "The Recovery of Norms," *Enemies of the Permanent Things*, p. 17.

16. Stegner, *Where the Bluebird Sings to the Lemonade Springs: Living and Writing in the West*, p. 72.

17. Lytle, *A Wake for the Living: A Family Chronicle* (Nashville, 1992), p. 3.

18. See, for example, Harvey Wheeler, "Russell Kirk and the New Conservatism," *Shenandoah* 7, Spring, 1956, 20.

19. Quoted in Russell Kirk, ed., *The Portable Conservative Reader*, p. 22.

20. Guroian, "Awakening the Moral Imagination," in *Tending the Heart of Virtue: How Classic Stories Awaken a Child's Moral Imagination*, p. 24.

21. Kirk, "The Christian Imagination of T. S. Eliot," Message at First United Methodist Church of Plymouth (Michigan), October 16, 1988. I am indebted to James Como's remarks upon Newman and the illative sense, from the epilogue of his *Branches to Heaven: The Geniuses of C. S. Lewis* for a portion of the remarks that immediately follow this quotation.

22. "A Stoical Sergeant in the Waste Land," in *The Sword of Imagination*, p. 69.

23. Kirk, "The Conservative Heart: Life with Russell Kirk," *Heritage Lecture*, no. 547, n.p.

24. "The Recovery of Norms," in *Enemies of the Permanent Things*, p. 17.

25. Chesterton, "The Ethics of Elfland," *Orthodoxy*, p. 48.

26. Lytle, *A Wake for the Living*, p. 4.

27. "The Recovery of Norms," p. 29.

28. "Conservation Activism Is a Healthy Sign," *The Sun*, Baltimore, May 4, 1970, A17.

2

A Reminder and a Challenge:
The Conservative Mind

Change is the means of our preservation.
—Edmund Burke

When it is not necessary to change, it is necessary not to change.
—Lucius Cary, second Viscount Falkland

The able statesman is one who combines with a disposition to preserve an ability to reform.
—Russell Kirk

In 1948 Whittaker Chambers, a longtime American spy for the Soviets who had turned with loathing against his controllers, accused former State Department official Alger Hiss of being a Soviet agent before the House Committee on Un-American Activities. This commenced an intense and protracted public controversy that was at its height in 1953 when Kirk published *The Conservative Mind*, which was not a Cold War document, but rather a conservative history of ideas. The time could not have been better for the appearance of a book that articulated the hitherto unexplored history of conservative thought in England and America while focusing upon the key figures on both sides of the Atlantic who had contributed to the mind of conservatism.

The reason for the book's timeliness was that the "irritable mental gestures" of the American Right that Lionel Trilling had written of in *The Liberal Imagination* seemed to be settling into something resembling genuine thought, and that of a sort that was markedly at odds with the progressive-minded spirit of the age. In the case of Chambers, an intelligent, articulate man had descended into the abyss of self-deception and murderous duplicity that is communism and returned to tell a fascinating story. Arthur Koestler later remarked that Chambers had not returned from hell empty-handed.

Historian Peter J. Stanlis has written, "As he noted in *Witness*, the harrowing account of his spiritual and political odyssey, Chambers had defected from Stalinist Communism in 1938, after a long struggle with his conscience, but *before* the Nazi-Soviet Pact of August 23, 1939, together with Stalin's purge trials, had converted many Stalinist Marxists into Trotskyist anti-Soviet Marxists."[1] The differences between these groups were jurisdictional rather than philosophical; and to many Trotskyites and sympathizers on the American Left, Chambers's testimony against Hiss was simply a cowardly betrayal of a good man who, regardless of his guilt, was on the correct side of history. Worse, Chambers made it emphatically clear that the successful penetration of the uppermost reaches of American government had been made possible because, as he saw it, liberalism and Marxism are blood relations in their shared vision of humanity as perfectible through education and state-guided behavior modification, their rejection of belief in Original Sin (and thus that humanity has a natural bent toward selfishness, self-centeredness, violence, and other sins), their drive for economic leveling through appeals to envy masked as appeals to compassion, and their contempt for tradition. To the American liberal, especially the anticommunist liberal, Chambers's claims were inflammatory and intolerable, regardless of their accuracy. After Hiss was convicted of perjury and sent to Lewisburg Penitentiary in 1951, Diana Trilling wrote famously and with a stunning disregard for the irony of her words, "Alger went to jail for all our sins." Battle lines were drawn for a philosophical war to the knife. The publication of *Witness* a year after Hiss's conviction intensified hostilities between the American Left and Right, with liberals in the American government, press, and academy expressing a grudging respect for *Witness* but unremitting contempt for the heavyset, awkward Chambers while claiming the suave, handsome Hiss as a political martyr, all evidence to the contrary notwithstanding. (As late as 1984, Fred J. Cook, a frequent contributor to the hard-left *Nation*, could describe Chambers, in somewhat frantic terms, as "a pathological liar who uttered more untruths than a computer can count."[2])

As the Left fired away at Chambers's iniquities in news conferences and periodical articles, conservatives found themselves with little ready to hand for a measured response. There were no nationally respected magazines of the Right, though there existed the monthly *American Mercury*, grown somewhat cranky and long in the tooth since its founding by H. L. Mencken and George Jean Nathan thirty years earlier; as well as the upstart weekly *Human Events*, and the monthly *Freeman*, each with a small readership, and that primarily among men and women of the Right. There were also precious few respected books by conservatives, though Friedrich A. von Hayek's *The Road to Serfdom* (1944) had fluttered liberal dovecotes upon its appearance by stating strongly the case for the market economy as against the statist economy, which over time stakes an ever-larger claim upon the liberty and private lives of tax-paying citizens. To those who had grown accustomed to the numerous federal make-work programs, rationing of goods and services, and extensive regulation characteristic of Franklin Roosevelt's presidency, and who saw state paternalism as part of America's future, Hayek's arguments were strange though thought-provoking. But there was yet no intelligent tracing of conservative roots or ruminative statement of conservative philosophical principles. "Incredible as it may seem," wrote William A. Rusher, "in 1950 the great intellectual tradition properly described as 'conservative' had no recognized interpreter or spokesman."[3]

At the same time, many American conservatives believed themselves compelled by historical necessity to embrace or at least grin-and-bear the reckless and, in time, tiresome behavior of Wisconsin Senator Joseph McCarthy, with his accusations of communists behind every ash-can.[4] For the time being, then, it seemed that all the "best" people were those who embraced the legacy of the New Deal and Harry Truman's Fair Deal, while the American Right, as commonly perceived, was little more than a largely inarticulate amalgamation of "aginners," anticommunist witch-hunters, and out-of-touch lost souls.

Yet all was not cool confidence among America's progressives. In 1951 *God and Man at Yale* had appeared out of the blue courtesy of maverick publisher Henry Regnery of Chicago. This work critically examined the role and status of religion and economics at Yale University, finding the general assumptions of the university's faculty anti-Christian and economically collectivist. It was written by a coltish recent graduate of Yale named William F. Buckley Jr., in a manner reminiscent of a debate team master charging triumphantly through his final, crushing summation. Although it did feature an introduction by the nationally respected book reviewer John Chamberlain, the book could still have been easily ignored by the mainstream press. But in publishing *God and Man at Yale*, and particularly by stating his case in a pointed, aggressively argued manner reminiscent of Hilaire Belloc at his best, Buckley had managed to irritate something long quiescent: a confluence of intellectuals unused to having their ways and assumptions challenged, especially by an articulate young know-it-all who (quite plainly) needed to be slapped down—and hard. To assess the book, *The Atlantic Monthly* tapped McGeorge Bundy, at the time a liberal associate professor of government at Harvard (who would one day become a principal architect of the American military involvement in Vietnam), who wrote a 2,900-word review of Buckley's hateful book, declaring at the outset, "As a believer in God, a Republican, and a Yale graduate, I find that the book is dishonest in its use of facts, false in its theory, and a discredit to its author and the writer of its introduction."[5] Bundy's review was eloquent and (in many quarters) convincing; it was also inaccurate in certain particulars and overheated, an "apoplectic denunciation," wrote Dwight Macdonald, himself no conservative by any means. Macdonald quipped that the Yale authorities responded to Buckley's book "with all the grace and agility of an elephant cornered by a mouse."[6] *The New Republic*'s Robert Hatch sniffed that Buckley was no credentialed authority on theology or economics, and therefore "his position is of no great general interest"[7]; while *The Saturday Review of Literature* ran two reviews of *God and Man at Yale*, by Seldon Rodman and F. D. Ashburn. The latter saw in Buckley's scrappy broadside something mightily sinister, enough so as to be worthy of the tarbrush. Ashburn likened Buckley to Torquemada and wrote that his book "has the glow and appeal of a fiery cross on a hillside at night. There will undoubtedly be robed figures who gather to it, but the hoods will not be academic. They will cover the face."[8] Clearly, conservatism was not yet worth the attention or respect of America's best and brightest.

Half a year later, in May of 1952, Chambers's *Witness* was published and immediately named a Book-of-the-Month Club main selection. To America's intellectual element, this was something more threatening than even Buckley's book. It was all very well for a young upper-crust Yalie to hold forth about the shortcomings of his schooling, but here was an older man, a former writer for the legendary *New Masses* magazine, a former communist operative, a writer of moving prose, with a sad and powerful story to tell. But he was also a latter-day Judas, the betrayer of the man who "went to jail for all our sins," Alger Hiss. A handful of major reviewers, notably Irving Howe and Brendan Gill, weighed in sourly and dismissively about *Witness*, but most major reviewing sources found it powerful and persuasive. Writing in *The New York Times Book Review*, leftist Sidney Hook called *Witness* "one of the most significant autobiographies of the twentieth century," though he could not, alas, find in it "an intelligent guide to victory or even survival" against communism.[9] But Harold Phelps Stokes of *The Yale Review* spoke for many readers of *Witness* when he declared, "It is written with extraordinary intensity and power. It is filled with the drama of action, scene, and soul. It contains passages of rare eloquence. Dealing with the raw stuff of history and the mounting crisis of our times, it offers a challenge to the Western world to find in its own freedom and faith a 'reason to live and reason to die' at once more valid and more potent than the Communist's."[10]

When *The Conservative Mind* appeared exactly one year after *Witness*, the third conservative book to achieve national attention in three years, it must have seemed to some liberal readers that the philistines were coming over the wall.

AFTER THE GREAT DIVIDE

In May 1953 Kirk was a little-known instructor in the history of civilization at a little-known Midwestern college. But he was a man who—*pace* Robert Hatch—was the only American to have earned a doctorate in history from St. Andrews, Scotland's oldest university, and thus could not be brushed off by critics as just another wrong-headed right-wing upstart. His doctoral study, polished and published as *The Conservative Mind* by Regnery, revealed a discerning mind, one given to circumspection, weighing, and analyzing, and articulating truths little discussed and a philosophy worth considering. He could write in elegant, convincing prose. Here, readers saw, was no mere Americanized Colonel Blimp saying that what's good for business is good for the good ol' U.S.A., but rather a man of wisdom and worth attending. With *The Conservative Mind* Kirk came to national attention, for the book was reviewed widely and for the most part favorably, or at least respectfully.

The genesis of this book had come about during Kirk's postwar years as an instructor at Michigan State. Having already written his master's thesis on the fiery reactionary John Randolph of Roanoke, he reflected that there was available, to date, no full-length study of American conservative thought. For a time he considered assembling and then publishing an anthology to be called *The Tory's Home Companion*. Wisely, this idea was shelved—wisely if only because it was not the right time for such a book and because the very term *Tory* was a devil-word in America, being associated in the popular mind with spoiled, snuff-sniffing revolutionary-era sympathizers with King George III. Kirk continued to think about some sort of project on conservatism while pursuing doctoral studies at St. Andrews, where he decided to write his doctorate on the thought of Edmund Burke and Burke's influence upon British and American culture. That lengthy study on Burke brought Kirk his degree and was of such quality that he decided to seek a publisher for it, under the proposed title *The Conservatives' Rout: An Account of Conservative Ideas from Burke to Santayana*.

Kirk first sent his manuscript to Alfred A. Knopf, who liked the book immediately but wanted the author to trim his text by one-half. Kirk thought this a foolish idea and asked that Knopf return his manuscript, which was grudgingly sent back. He next approached conservative publisher Henry Regnery, who also liked the manuscript and wanted to publish it, but considered the title too gloomy and off-putting. The book, published as *The Conservative Mind: From Burke to Santayana*—the title was Regnery's idea—appeared in May 1953, almost exactly one year after Chambers's *Witness*. (Before publishing the London edition of *The Conservative Mind*, T. S. Eliot of Faber & Faber mentioned to Regnery that he did not believe George Santayana [with whom he had been on cordial terms] to possess sufficient stature as a conservative thinker to merit the inclusion of his name in the subtitle. Upon learning of Eliot's reservations, and having grown to respect Eliot's own cultural conservatism, Kirk subtitled his second edition, and all succeeding editions, "From Burke to Eliot." For his part, Eliot published the British edition of *The Conservative Mind* without a subtitle altogether, in 1954.) "In this and subsequent books, Kirk revived the basic principles of conservatism, in particular as laid down by Edmund Burke, and applied them to modern America. Within five years, together with the principles of free-market economics, they had become the warp and woof of conservatism as we know it today," wrote Rusher.[11] Every book Kirk wrote thereafter contained thematic echoes harking back to *The Conservative Mind*.

What did Kirk set out to accomplish in this well-received history of ideas? To trace the theme of conservatism as a living philosophy within the English and American tradition, in a line running from Burke to Santayana and Eliot, Kirk believing that conservatism may be apprehended reasonably well by attention to what leading writers and politicians, generally called conservative, have written and accomplished. Kirk worked inductively from the thought of many thinkers—political, literary, and historical—some of them opposed, attempting to find a common conservative philosophy running through Burke, John Adams, the later Samuel Taylor Coleridge, John Randolph of Roanoke, Alexis de Tocqueville, James Fenimore Cooper, John Henry Newman, Benjamin Disraeli, James Fitzjames Stephen, Paul Elmer More, Irving Babbitt, and many others. Joseph Sobran has written, "Kirk was too sensible to chase after liberalism, refuting it point by point, and too wise to suppose that even a view he rejected could be totally wrong. His approach was, rather, to demonstrate that there was simply another, ancient way of looking at the life of politics and society, as embodied in the writing of scores of prescient authors, some of them unjustly forgotten. Thanks in part to him, they are now remembered. He helped mightily in restoring the prestige of Edmund Burke, now generally recognized as the greatest conservative to have written in the English language."[12]

Who would understand Russell Kirk must read Burke. Burke represented the beginning of the Anglo-American conservative tradition, for he wrote at a time when the old order was breaking apart on the European continent, a time concurrent with the victory of the revolutionists in France. As Kirk saw it, almost all of our arguments and much of our political terminology originated in the years during and immediately after the French Revolution, when Burke wrote his best-known work, which Kirk cited frequently, *Reflections on the Revolution in France* (1790). This was the era of what C. S. Lewis, in his address *De Descriptione Temporum*, termed "the Great Divide," a breaking apart of an epoch that separated the true "Old World" from modernity, Christendom from Western civilization. Arguably the Great Divide was greater even than the fall of Rome; for as historian Sheldon Vanauken has written, "Seneca and Dr. Johnson, though separated by 18 centuries, have more in common than Dr. Johnson and Freud, less than a century later."[13] People who lived before the Great Divide and thus shared its norms and adherence to the permanent things Lewis specified as "Old Western Man." But like the long-drawn-out roar of the receding ocean described in Matthew Arnold's poem "Dover Beach," symbolizing the decline of the age of faith, this later, Greater Divide is gradual, and Old Western Man has lived on in unaffected communities, even to this day. Lewis himself claimed to be a specimen of Old Western Man; Kirk was certainly one also. In Kirk, Lewis would have found a kindred spirit, though where Lewis identified the Great Divide as falling at about the end of the Napoleonic Wars, Kirk placed it a bit earlier, to the time when revolutionary change made the rise of Napoleon possible. The rise of democracy, the growth of industrialism, the elevation of abstract reason above reason informed by faith, the de-Christianizing of Western society, the decline in axiomatic acceptance of natural law, the development of ideology—these and a raft of other issues and difficulties arose during the French revolutionary era; their effects had been stunningly felt throughout the world between 1939 and 1945, and throughout the Cold War.

"Among the sentimental, calculating and soulless tyrannies which have infected the world since Burke's time, it is difficult to estimate which has been most destructive of the certitudes of traditional Christianity," wrote Stanlis in review of *The Conservative Mind*. He added,

> Mr. Kirk notes the general tenets of radicalism since 1790 include belief in "the perfectibility of man and the illimitable progress of society," based on a denial of original sin, a "contempt for tradition" involving attempts to establish "a variety of anti-Christian systems," and finally, political and economic levelling carried through on utilitarian principles by a multi-functional, all-powerful and non-spiritual state. Our urbanized iron age is indeed a wilderness of shattered mirrors, reflecting back fragments of many secular systems. Which

branch of philosophical radicalism has done the most to bring about our age of innovating state planners, benevolent Robin Hood politicians, levellers of the rich, the industrious, the competent, to a pauperized equality of condition? Benthamite utilitarianism receives the most severe censure, yet Mr. Kirk knows that no person or school of thought can be held responsible for the worst features of modern civilization. His book reveals that a congruence of many radical theories and the frequent failure of conservatives have brought us to our present condition.[14]

To better delineate the essential causes, historical and philosophical, of humanity's disillusionment with secularism and liberalism, as well as the positive principles of mature conservative thought, Kirk had written *The Conservative Mind*. Conservatism, wrote Kirk, "is something deeper than mere defense of shares and dividends, something nobler than mere dread of what is new." As Stanlis wrote, it is "a complex and mature philosophy of life involving principles which consider God, man, and nature, dealing in practice with the origin, nature and destiny of man in the universe." This said, conservatism cannot be adequately represented by any mere definition or formula or even in a particularly systematic manner. However, in his opening chapter Kirk distilled six "canons of thought" that he deemed fundamental to defining conservative thought. (Almost thirty years after first publishing *The Conservative Mind*, Kirk wrote the introduction to *The Portable Conservative Reader*; and in it he restated his six canons of conservatism in the form of six "general principles upon which most eminent conservatives in some degree may be said to have agreed implicitly." These general principles serve, to some extent, as restatements and glosses upon the original six canons, though there is no one-for-one correspondence.) The six canons are as follows:

1. *Belief that a divine intent rules society as well as conscience, forging an eternal chain of right and duty which links great and obscure, living and dead. Political problems, at bottom, are religious and moral problems. . . . Politics is the art of apprehending and applying the Justice which is above nature.* It was no accident that Kirk placed this item first in his short list of canons. In later editions of *The Conservative Mind*, he changed the words "a divine intent" to "a transcendent order, or body of natural law," recognizing that the truths of the *tao* remain true regardless of whether the people of a particular culture are theistic. Being no historicist, he believed that a transcendent order (or, to the theist, God) is at work in the lives of men and women through the decisions they make and the actions they take every day, however humble, however great. This transcendent intent is not clearly discernible in its particulars, for the problem of evil is real, not illusory. Rather, Kirk believed that the good and ill men accomplish in this life, like the light and dark threads that form

a tapestry, cannot be understood in full for now; they can only be seen in the light of eternity. The divine strategy may be couched in terms of natural law or may assume some other expression; but with few exceptions, mentioned below, conservatives recognized the need for enduring moral authority.

There is thus an integral moral element in Kirk's vision of conservatism. Between cultural conservatives, among whom he counted himself, and the so-called neoconservatives and rightward-leaning libertarians Kirk saw this crucial difference: The neoconservatives and libertarians, he believed, have at best a secondary interest in the permanent things. The libertarians he considered philosophical anarchists who would like to abolish or at least cripple government; more to the point, they show no awareness of, or concern for, the moral or spiritual crises of modern times. The permanent things are either unimportant in their view or needless fetters upon free individuals. He perceived the neoconservatives, who live and publish their magazines in New York City and Washington, as conservatively inclined individuals interested primarily in economics and American foreign policy. The true conservative, Kirk believed, is a person who is, in a manner of speaking, a guardian of the permanent things. During the Middle Ages, the title of "conservator" was given to guardians of the laws in the major cities of Europe, especially in Italy. In England, justices of the peace were designated *custodes pacis,* or conservators of the peace. In his poem "The House of Fame," Geoffrey Chaucer uses the word "conservatif" in the same sense, appertaining to security and custodial protection. The term "conservative" began to acquire its modern usage, related closely to the older usage, during the period of the Great Divide, early in the nineteenth century. The conservatives who immediately followed the age of Burke were designated as such in recognition of their role as conservators of the permanent things against the advance of revolutionary thought. As Kirk said in an interview in 1993, "There are certain permanent things in society: the health of the family, inherited political institutions that insure a measure of order and justice and freedom, a life of diversity and independence, a life marked by widespread possession of private property. These permanent things guarantee against arbitrary interference by the state. These are all aspects of conservative thought, which have developed gradually as the debate since the French Revolution has gone on."[15]

Because "the permanent and the transitory have to be distinguished afresh by each generation," as Eliot wrote, it is crucial that generation link with generation, that the contract of eternal society not be broken; for it is by the passing along of customs, stories, rights, duties, and the truths of faith that the individual and the community are made whole. The opposite of this—human beings without a history, their relatives scattered to the four winds by choice or indifference, their past a mystery, their future discerned as a grave only—causes alienation in the individual, consigns his heirs to their own future of rootlessness and despair, and increases the likelihood of their succumbing to demagogues.

The permanent things and the political realm interpenetrate. Politics may be the art of the possible, as Kirk was fond of saying, but as one discerning admirer of Kirk has written, the time comes when it is necessary for the politician to decide if what is possible is also right and acceptable.[16] (Kirk saw and embraced this distinction, as will be seen shortly.) Many today who call themselves conservative subscribe to the doctrine that politics is something of a necessary evil—and perhaps an unnecessary evil. To Kirk and traditionalist conservatives, there is a definite and laudable, though limited, role for politics in American culture. In one striking passage he once wrote,

> Politics is the application of ethics to the concerns of the commonwealth. Politics cannot be apprehended properly without reference to biographical and historical models for order, justice, and freedom; nor without reference to theory, which is not at all the same thing as ideology. Any community, great or small, is knit together by belief in certain enduring norms or principles. When knowledge of those norms dwindles, the fabric of society wears thin. Lacking a knowledge of the permanent things, a people become interested chiefly in immediate self-advantage or pleasure. Then things fall apart. And good-natured, unambitious men, as George Bernard Shaw put it, "stand by in helpless horror."[17]

At the time *The Conservative Mind* appeared, good-natured, unambitious men and women in America, and their leaders, beheld with foreboding the expansionist might of Stalin's Soviet Union, the nation whose master, pipe-smoking "Uncle Joe," had been a key ally against the Axis Powers in the recent world war. This concern was prominently in the politically focused review of Kirk's book by Gordon Keith Chalmers, president of Kenyon College, whose favorable assessment in *The New York Times Book Review* reached many readers. He found Kirk "as relentless as his enemies, Karl Marx and Harold Laski, considerably more temperate and scholarly, and in passages of this very readable book, brilliant and even eloquent." Kirk's style, tone, and substance, to Chalmers, aid him in addressing a very real and present danger. "All American thought, whether religious, political, literary, or ethical, should now be preoccupied with the recent intellectual blunder of this learned nation: the mistake in judging the nature and intentions of the present Russian Government," he wrote, adding:

> This mistake was made so consistently for two decades that when our politicians in the Nineteen Forties had to decide whether and how to deal with the Russians, they went wrong simply because they had learned too well the lesson taught by the most vocal and most heeded of the scholars. The seed of the

intellectual mistake lie deep—fully fifty years deep, perhaps a round hundred. Russell Kirk's able and timely book examines the values and ethical illusions which produced the blunder.

Against the Hegel-Marx-Laski axis, he analyzes and describes the affirmative tradition of Burke, de Tocqueville and Irving Babbitt. This is not a book about anti-communism, but about anti-pre-communism.[18]

To comprehend and face down the foe would require resolve, courage, and the willingness to stand up militarily to the aggressor. But first and foremost, Kirk deduced, intelligent conservatives must solve "the problem of spiritual and moral regeneration; the restoration of the ethical system and the religious sanction upon which any life worth living is founded." Historical events proved Kirk right on this score; for as Barbara von der Heydt demonstrated in her book *Candles Behind the Wall*, written forty years after *The Conservative Mind*, people of faith in Eastern Europe played a major role in undermining and bringing down communism in Russian and Warsaw Pact nations.

Kirk was no utilitarian. He knew that the spiritual element in the life of humanity cannot be regarded as merely the handmaiden of social improvement at home and effective foreign policy abroad. As he declared in the first of the six "general principles" of conservatism outlined in his introduction to *The Portable Conservative Reader*: "First, conservatives generally believe that there exists a transcendent moral order, to which we ought to try to conform the ways of society." Through ideology, some five-year plan of sorts, through which everyone will become A Better Person? No, for Kirk held with H. Stuart Hughes that "Conservatism is the negation of ideology." Society is "conformed" to the transcendent moral order through the virtuous citizen living, working, and exerting his influence in the small circles of fellowship in which he lives, through myriad ways: raising children in a manner by which generation links cordially and wisely with generation; voting intelligently; and performing the hundred-and-one small acts of consideration, service, and kindness by which family members, fellow townspeople, parents of local schoolchildren, fellow members of houses of worship, and other "little platoons" (as Burke called such groups) attend to helping and living in civility with each other.

2. *Affection for the proliferating variety and mystery of traditional life, as distinguished from the narrowing uniformity and egalitarianism and utilitarian aims of most radical systems.* Humanity can endure nearly anything except boredom. During the 1970s and '80s, Kirk's home, Piety Hill, was a living example of "the proliferating variety and mystery of traditional life," with the Kirk family taking in large numbers of refugees and scholars of all races, creeds, colors, and degree of social strata, housing them wherever a

spare room could be found, allowing them to stay for extended periods of time—sometimes whole years at a time—and in general turning the house into something straight out of the Kaufman and Hart play *You Can't Take It with You.* There is a gray dullness that comes with homogenization of culture, with people from every subculture throughout America parroting the same opinions, the same jokes, the same jargon and slang, these often provided through the medium of television. (Kirk detested television for this, as well as for the relentless vapidity of its programming and its potential as a vehicle of mass deception. He would not allow a television set inside Piety Hill until the last few years of his life—and then only to watch programs on videocassette.) Having traveled throughout much of the world on foot, he had experienced firsthand the color, the strangeness, the homeliness, the occasional fearsomeness of many different cultures, and he believed each of them worth conserving. In politics and in other aspects of culture, he opposed attempting to turn the various lands he visited into carbon copies of American society. However much we may honor it, the American Constitution cannot be exported, Kirk said often. (He treated satirically such ill-advised attempts to impose cultural hegemony upon other cultures in his novel *A Creature of the Twilight.*)

The cultures of the world's peoples have come about through centuries of custom, convention, and continuity. Kirk believed that far more damage—in the form of rootlessness, despair, envy, and resentment—is caused by seeking to homogenize the nations and the various cultures within nations than by leaving them to develop as they themselves see fit. As his fifth general principle of conservatism in *The Portable Conservative Reader*, Kirk affirmed that conservatives "pay attention to the principle of variety. They feel affection for the proliferating intricacy of long-established social institutions and modes of life, as distinguished from the narrowing uniformity and deadening egalitarianism of radical systems."[19] If who says A must say B, it follows that in regard to international relations, the conservative politician favors not an isolationist but a prudent approach toward intervening diplomatically or militarily in the affairs of other nations.

In his review of *The Conservative Mind*, chief editorial writer August Heckscher of the *New York Herald Tribune* seized upon the second of Kirk's six canons as defining "the quality which gives to a man like Chesterton so passionate an enjoyment of life, in all its waywardness and adventure; and which is for ever at odds with the rational uniformity sought by most reformers." Warming to his subject, he added:

American culture is shot through with the makings of such a conservatism. Here no ordered hierarchies impose settled values; but within the constant movement of our society, within the tendency to form groups and to agitate interests, there is mystery enough to satisfy a true conservative. To listen for the voices that emerge from this busy hum, to sense the nascent ideas and dawning perceptions is to become tolerant and tentative. The man who has gained this attitude will never fall into the error of thinking that consent can be manufactured by propaganda, or a people saved by a bright idea thought up by an advertising specialist.[20]

Such a concept of diversity stands starkly at odds with the vision of "openness" and "sensitivity to the other" that has prevailed for a generation, and that has been translated into masses of people wearing the same style of clothing, uttering the same sarcastic badinage, reading the same trendy periodicals, listening to the same pop music, adorning their automobiles with the same bumper stickers, frequenting the same fast-food restaurants and coffee shops, hating the same proscribed political and religious figures, "accepting" everyone else as worthy of respect and dignity (except people who live in mobile home parks, of course), and talking all the while of how free-thinking and open-minded they are. Opposed to this tendency is another, one more inclined to reflect and to adjure the crowd, but not in pride. There is at the heart of conservatism, as Kirk understood it, a sense of humility. As Eliot wrote in "East Coker," the only wisdom we are capable of acquiring is the wisdom of humility, for humility is endless.

3. *Conviction that civilized society requires orders and classes. The only equality is moral equality; all other attempts at leveling lead to despair, if enforced by positive legislation. Society longs for leadership, and if a people destroy natural distinctions among men, presently Buonaparte fills the vacuum.* On this point, it is important to distinguish between the terms "class" and "caste." By saying that civilized society requires orders and classes, Kirk was not stating that pigeonholes exist for the merchant caste, the ruling caste, and so forth; neither was he claiming that the mass of mankind was born with saddles on their backs, and that a favored few are born booted and spurred to ride them legitimately by the grace of God, to turn one of Thomas Jefferson's best-known quotations on its head. Himself the son of a railroad engineer, Kirk was well aware that there is much fluidity between social classes in America, and that it is possible to rise, given industry, talent, and ambition. (It is likewise possible to sink, given the absence of these qualities.) In this third canon of conservatism, he spoke of an aristocracy of talent and wisdom; specifically of those individuals within communities endowed with virtue, political acumen, trustworthiness, and imagination who are recognized by their neighbors as leaders. He considered it a sign of decadence when people elect as their leaders demagogues, smooth-talking makers of hollow promises, and, in general, people who move from political success to political success by force of personality rather than sub-

stance. This person may be no "Buonaparte"; he may be worse, or he may be (as is more often the case) a seedy, minor-league edition of Napoleon: a slickly packaged cad filled with a ravening lust for power, ruthless but beloved by society because he is "one of us." Such a society, Kirk believed, may prosper for a time, living on the inherited moral capital of earlier times, but—society being organic—it will sicken and die should it continue to embrace decadence. In a decadent society, a sneering envy, an "I'm-as-good-as-you" attitude, a desire to see the mighty fall and the charming rogue elevated, becomes the hallmark of its decline. In his memoir *Lanterns on the Levee*, William Alexander Percy recorded that racist, poor whites jibed at him with the remark, "Wal, the bottom rail's on top now and it's gwiner stay thar!" as they celebrated the victory of race-baiting James K. Vardaman over Percy's father, himself a good and true leader, in a Mississippi senate race earlier in this century. Today, wrote Percy in 1941, "the election of demagogues horrifies nobody. The intelligent are cynically amused, the hoi-polloi are so accustomed to victory they no longer swagger. The voters choose their representatives in public life, not for their wisdom or courage, but for the promises they make," an assessment that holds true to the present day.[21] Not every person is fit for leadership, nor is the voice of the people the voice of God. As William Henry Chamberlin noted in his review of *The Conservative Mind*, it was another Southerner, John C. Calhoun, who "maintained that liberty and equality, far from being inseparable are incompatible and backed up this belief with reasoning which can also be applied to the problems of our own times." He continues,

> It is this inequality of condition between the front and rear ranks, in the march of progress, which gives so strong an impulse to the former to maintain their position, and to the latter to press forward into their files. This gives to progress its greatest impulse. To force the front rank back to the rear, or attempt to push forward the rear into line with the front, by the interposition of the government, would put an end to the impulse and effectually arrest the march of progress."[22]

As to egalitarianism, Kirk—along with Jefferson—did not believe that all men are created equal in terms of talent, industry, and intelligence. Rather, he believed (as did Jefferson) that the only true equality, the only equality worth recognition as such, is equality before the bar of justice and in the sight of God.

Kirk's third canon of conservatism, then, was no nostalgic backward glance at an imagined past when "everybody knew his place—and stayed there." Rather, it was a statement reflecting the tradition and history of American society, for as he wrote (in terms I paraphrase, being unable to locate the exact reference), Americans certainly possess no state church, no

landed interest in the European sense, no squirearchy, no aura of true antiquity, no imperial pride; though they do retain the best written constitution in the world, the safest division of powers, the widest diffusion of
property, the strongest sense of common interest, the most prosperous
economy, an elevated ethical and intellectual tradition, and a strong spirit
of self-reliance unequalled in modern times.

4. *Persuasion that property and freedom are inseparably connected, and that
economic leveling is not economic progress. Separate property from private possession and liberty is erased.* Free community and the formation of small, voluntary associations related to neighborhood, place of worship, guild,
school, and family form the alternative to compulsive collectivism: a wise
government deciding who should live where and associate with whom.
The small associations, the "little platoons" Burke wrote of, form the
strength of any nation's culture. Let these be overridden by a government
or corporate entity working out of mixed humanitarian and profiteering
motives, and the products of community, notably civility and responsibility, dissipate. For example, new freeways that bisect long-established communities and turn cities into places to work in and (at day's end) escape
from, rather than places to live, contribute to this. When it is recognized
that the government is the first and last resource for maintaining order,
and that its responsibilities include all the higher functions of government
and down to such particulars as clearing roads and sidewalks of snow in
the winter, collecting rubbish, providing tax-funded entertainment, and a
dozen other tasks that neighborhoods once handled among their constituent citizens, then these tasks become "everybody's responsibility";
and as the old saw goes, everybody's responsibility very quickly translates
into "nobody's responsibility." The land of "nobody's responsibility" is a
harsh place to live, rife with boredom, where a volatile resentment at the
government, local or federal, for not providing more (or, really, for providing poorly for what it ought not to attempt to provide) is palpable. Kirk
remembered well the battle cry of the rioters in Detroit as they flung their
flaming Molotov cocktails into stores and houses in 1967, after a few years
of witnessing portions of their neighborhoods razed for the sake of free-
way construction and public housing: "Instant urban renewal!"

5. *Faith in prescription and distrust of "sophisters and calculators." Man must
put a control upon his will and his appetite. . . . Tradition and sound prejudice provide checks upon man's anarchic impulse.* It is common to hear well-meaning
people declare that they would like to see "the end of prejudice in America," prejudice being a devil-term today, signifying racism. But by *prejudice*
Burke and Kirk meant something very different from purblind bigotry. To

the conservative, prejudice is that virtuous habit of thought, grounded in morality, faith, and wisdom born of long tradition, by which the responsible person forms opinions, makes decisions, speaks, and acts. Burke wrote at length on the great value of prejudice, in his *Reflections on the Revolution in France*. Prejudice, he stated, "is of ready application in the emergency; it previously engages the mind in a steady course of wisdom and virtue, and does not leave the man hesitating in the moment of decision, sceptical, puzzled, and unresolved. Prejudice renders a man's virtue his habit: and not a series of unconnected acts. Through just prejudice, his duty becomes a part of his nature."[23] Almost everyone, including those who long to see "the end of prejudice in America," live by prejudice in some way; few reject everything that has been learned within family life and over the history of human experience in favor of learning everything afresh; Burke spoke truly when he wrote, "We are afraid to put men to live and trade each on his own private stock of reason; because we suspect that the stock in each man is small, and that the individuals would do better to avail themselves of the general bank and capital of nations and of ages."[24] Those who choose to learn everything the hard way, whether in the personal or public realm, choose the path of the fool and find that experience is a hard master. The individual is foolish, but the species is wise, Burke believed, though in times of cultural decadence even the species is no sure guide, and traditional normative standards must be consulted afresh and closely.

In his introduction to *The Portable Conservative Reader*, Kirk wrote as his third "general principle" of conservatism that "conservatives believe in what may be called the principle of prescription." Considering the importance of prescription—prejudice—to his thought, Kirk is worth quoting at length on this matter.

"The wisdom of our ancestors" is one of the more important phrases in the writing of Burke; presumably Burke derived it from Richard Hooker. Conservatives sense that modern men and women are dwarfs on the shoulders of giants, able to see farther than their ancestors only because of the great stature of those who have preceded us in time. Therefore conservatives very frequently emphasize the importance of "prescription"—that is, of things established by immemorial usage, so "that the mind of man runneth not to the contrary." There exist rights of which the chief sanction is their antiquity—including rights in property, often. Similarly, our morals are prescriptive in great part. Conservatives argue that we are unlikely, we moderns, to make any brave new discoveries in morals or politics or taste. It is perilous to weigh every passing issue on the basis of private judgment and private rationality. "The individual is foolish, but the species is wise," Burke declared. In politics we do well to abide by precedent and precept and even prejudice, for "the great mysterious incorporation of the human race" has acquired habits, customs, and conventions of remote origin which are woven into the fabric of our social being; the innovator, in Santayana's phrase, never knows how near to the taproot of the tree he is hacking.[25]

Given Kirk's elevation of wise prejudice, it is not surprising that Ralph Waldo Emerson, with his contempt for tradition and his wide influence, is examined and found wanting in *The Conservative Mind*. Kirk wrote "Reliance upon private judgment and personal emotion, contempt for prescription and the experience of the species, a social morality alternately and bewilderingly egocentric or all-embracing (the contradiction so frequently encountered in Rousseau)—the qualities of Emerson's thought gratified a popular American craving which ever since has fed upon Emersonian 'Self-Reliance' and 'Experience' and 'Nature' and his other individualistic manifestoes."[26] Kirk noted that despite Emerson's outward rejection of social atomism, there was in the Sage of Concord's philosophy a revolt against true voluntary community that nonetheless gave way to leanings toward social collectivism, "that dour substitute for free harmony, that solacing uniformity, which Tocqueville calls democratic despotism."[27]

Further, Emerson is reported to have remarked on his fifty-eighth birthday, "I never could give much reality to evil and pain," a sentiment that flourishes throughout his influential canon. To Kirk, the effect of Emersonian thought has been dire. "Few people have been so complacent about evil in their midst as have the Americans since the Civil War, and no people have been so ready to deny the very existence of evil. Twentieth-century America presents the spectacle of a nation tormented by crime, urban vice, political corruption, family decay, and increasing proletarianization; and amid this scene the commanding voice is not Savonarola's but the chorus of sociologists and psychologists and neo-positivists in pulpits, proclaiming that sin does not exist and 'adjustment' will heal every social cancer."[28] Lest anyone believe that Kirk laid the blame for all the nation's problems at Emerson's feet, he hastened to add that Emerson did not invent this ostrich-tendency of the American public, but that he was its most powerful and influential apologist. "If a foolish consistency is the hobgoblin of little minds, a fatuous optimism frequently is the damnation of expansive minds," Kirk concluded of Emerson. "As a social optimist ignoring the fact of sin, Emerson was a radical thinker, perhaps the most influential of all American radicals. Believing, with Rousseau, in the supremacy of benevolent instincts, he was ready to discard old ways of society so that ground might be cleared for the new edifices of emotion."[29]

Kirk added that among the most eloquent of the voices that opposed Emerson were those of Nathaniel Hawthorne and Orestes Brownson, the one a Calvinist in heritage, the other a Roman Catholic by choice. Against the modern spirit of the universal and absolute supremacy of man, these writers championed obedience to normative authority and prescriptive wisdom. They recognized that if the vision of modern men and women is clearer than that of their ancestors, it is only because of the great stature of those who have preceded them in time. They recognized also the substance of Kirk's sixth general principle of conservatism, that conservatives are chastened by the principle of human imperfectibility. Kirk wrote, "Human nature suffers irremediably from certain faults, the conservatives know. Man being imperfect, no perfect social order ever can be created. Because of human restlessness, mankind would grow rebellious under any utopian domination, and would break out once more in violent discontent—or else expire of boredom."[30]

6. *Recognition that change and reform are not identical, and that innovation is a devouring conflagration more often than it is a torch of progress. Society must alter, for slow change is the means of its conservation, like the human body's perpetual renewal; but Providence is the proper instrument for change, and the test of a statesman is his cognizance of the reality of Providential social forces.* The bare bones of Burkean thought, to anyone who has been exposed even briefly to Burke in historical survey, is that he believed society to be an organic entity, which grows, matures, suffers periods of sickness, and can in time die. As with the human body, violent alterations in society can damage or even destroy it. Change is necessary for growth, but change is not its own highest value. For that matter, to answer a question raised by numerous critics of Kirk and conservatism, neither is tradition its own highest value. In his study *Three Golden Ages* (1999), historian Alf J. Mapp Jr. took up the question of change, innovation, tradition, and prudence as they relate to science and the arts, arguing, "Creativity alone cannot save a society. Societies rich in creativity have fallen because of a lack of moral fiber. But neither can a society save itself solely by the cultivation of individual virtues apart from knowledge and creativity. Even the combination of virtue and creativity is not sufficient to save us without perspective. . . . We need to acquire perspective by studying the recurring patterns of vital communities whose creativity has enriched humankind."[31] And as Kirk wrote, the conservative working in any discipline, particularly the able conservative statesman, is one who combines with a disposition to preserve an ability to change and reform.

ON TRADITION AND CHANGE

One of the chief hallmarks of the conservative, then, is prudence, and that guided by the moral imagination. The fruit of prudent consideration is order, the bedrock of any society worthy of the name. Kirk's second and fourth general principles of conservatism outlined in *The Portable Conservative Reader* are together of a piece with this: Conservatives "uphold the principle of social continuity. They prefer the devil they know to the devil they don't know. Order and justice and freedom, they believe, are the artificial products of a long and painful social experience, the results of centuries of trial and reflection and sacrifice. Thus the body social is a kind of spiritual corporation, comparable to the church; it may even be called a community of souls. . . . Burke's reminder of the social necessity for prudent change is in the minds of conservatives. But necessary change, they argue, ought to be gradual and discriminatory, never 'unfixing old interests at once.' Revolution slices through the arteries of a culture, a cure that kills."[32] Further:

> Human society being complex, remedies cannot be simple if they are to be effective. The conservative declares that he acts only after sufficient reflection, having weighed the consequences. Sudden and slashing reforms are perilous as sudden and slashing surgery. The march of providence is slow; it is the devil who always hurries.[33]

On this matter of change, in a lengthy review-essay on *The Conservative Mind*, the distinguished literary scholar John Crowe Ransom, editor of *The Kenyon Review*, took up the issue of conservatives, particularly conservative politicians, as "trimmers" and accommodationists, prepared to give up trench after trench of one political or cultural position after another before the advance of their progressive opponents while claiming that the trenches now occupied by the enemy really concern matters that all reasonable people can agree upon, and that nothing was really lost after all. He focused upon one particular passage of *The Conservative Mind* in which Kirk had written that Burke and his disciples recognized that the duty of the statesman is "to reconcile innovation and prescriptive truth, to lead the waters of novelty into the canals of custom. This accomplished, even though he may seem to himself to have failed, the conservative has executed his destined work in the great mysterious incorporation of the human race; and if he has not preserved intact the old ways he loved, still he has moderated greatly the ugly aspect of new ways." "Evidently," wrote Ransom, "the badge which the conservative wears must have two faces. One is resistance to the new event; this is the fighting face, the one that ordinarily we choose to know him by. The other is acceptance after the event, permitting the expectation that when once the new ways are shaken down and become old ways they too will be loved." This, the critic added,

> looks like a mechanical service, or at least a rather menial one, if the party is to offer itself simply as a brake against alteration; it is hard to discover in that role enough of specific intelligence to qualify it as a religiosity of high grade.

And when the alteration comes to pass nevertheless, is there a piety humanly capable of the enthusiastic reversal that is in order? For example, is it pious of Mr. Kirk to testify that change is beneficial though its aspect is ugly? Perhaps he means that change as change is mere becoming, therefore hideous, but change accomplished passes into true being and is fit for the contemplation of the blessed. But I think not. And to what benefit does he refer? It would seem as if the conservatives had declined on principle, even after the event, to identify the precise benefit, which would be as if they were confessing an error in their precedent piety. Or is the divine process so inscrutable that the best of men cannot be sure of understanding it? In that case they might have presented their views with greater moderation.[34]

Ransom concludes that "it would seem risky to invoke theological sanctions for one's politics; it is a game that two can play at; better still, it is a game that does not have to be played at all." Overall, he concluded, such an invocation is "only a little less risky in Burke's time than in Mr. Kirk's and ours."

Risky indeed, answered Brainard Cheney in *The Sewanee Review*, but that is to misstate Kirk's point. It is a far cry from saying that God is on "our" side as opposed to saying that there is some form of divine sanction over the society in which one lives. On this issue Cheney crossed swords with his old teacher, finding Ransom's "an essentially distorted view of the conservative position and of history, and it seems to me that, in the context he gives it, it serves to place him in the same partisan camp with the utopian materialists—despite his having once championed more orthodoxy in Christian practice."[35] This light rebuke referred to Ransom's treatise *God Without Thunder* and to his days as one of the prominent members of the Agrarians, a group of conservative Southern writers who defended the culture of the agricultural South against the claims of the North's industrial culture. Ransom had played a major role in organizing and writing for the Agrarian's manifesto, *I'll Take My Stand: Essays by Twelve Southerners* (1930). Ironically, *I'll Take My Stand* was intended, in its own way, to accomplish something of what Kirk attempted in his "prolonged essay in definition," a purpose described succinctly by Louis D. Rubin Jr., who wrote that the Agrarians' volume "constitutes both a reminder and a challenge. *What are you losing that you once possessed?* it says. . . . *Are you quite sure that you want to discard it entirely?*"[36] Ransom had lost sympathy with, or at least faith in, reactionary Agrarianism over the intervening years, and now he wrote almost wistfully of conservatism as something essentially good but incompatible to the needs of the change-driven modern world, with industrialism triumphant and agrarianism in decline as a way of life in America. But the case for conservatism cannot be dismissed lightly, said Cheney, who wrote, "In *The Conservative Mind*, Mr. Kirk makes a monumental contribution toward clarifying the position of the conservatives in modern society, he presents them with a challenging cause, and he lists impressive social and political resources for them." Kirk may falter when he tries to relate conservatism to the modern world and its present predicament, said Cheney, but he speaks wisdom to modern America nonetheless, especially in warning of the need to assure sharp surveillance of the leviathan business, the leviathan union, and the leviathan state.

Citing Burke, Kirk noted that the able statesman is one who combines with a disposition to preserve an ability to reform. The conservative at large is of like mind. To use one example: Kirk could not resist the triumph of the automobile over the horse—he referred famously to the automobile as "a mechanical Jacobin"—but he traveled from place to place in cars (though he did not himself drive). There are no stables of horses on the grounds at Piety Hill. In such matters as this, Kirk accepted the inevitable, though without enthusiasm. (Not for him the modern televised car commercials inanely touting the "passion" of driving for the sake of driving.) There is a cost involved with automobile culture, mainly an increase in rootlessness and a corresponding decrease in the American family's sense of place, and Russell Kirk, long of Piety Hill in Mecosta, Michigan, rejected that culture. By Ransom's judgment, did Kirk compromise his principles, just like any nonconservative? It would be hard to assent, for Kirk was arguably unlike most Americans in regard to the automobile, using it only when absolutely necessary. And on other matters, he refused absolutely to accommodate: Until his death he remained a staunch supporter of the pro-life position in regard to abortion rights, long after *Roe v. Wade* (1973). When that alteration came to pass, there was no piety humanly capable of "the enthusiastic reversal that is in order." Here, Kirk did not testify that change is beneficial though its aspect is ugly, nor that change as change is mere becoming, still less that this particular change, once accomplished, passes into true being and is fit for the contemplation of the blessed. And while he would agree with Ransom's postulate that the divine process is sufficiently inscrutable that the best of men cannot be sure of understanding it, he would add that each man is responsible for working in the light of such wisdom as he possesses. Kirk's, then, was not the attitude of the historicist; and those who charge him with elevating tradition (however good or ill) to being an end in itself or accepting each cultural change as a conservative tradition in the making do so by reckoning without the moral imagination, which is guided by prudential wisdom. At one time, even our traditions were new, admits the traditionalist Tevye, in *Fiddler on the Roof*. Yes, but not every new thing ought to become a tradition. "Kirk's critics assume a doctrine of cultural inevitability, melioristic or otherwise, which he, quite validly, elects to reject," wrote Donald Atwell Zoll. "His main purpose is *conservation*, hardly a reactionary point of view. It may not be quite realistic to argue for the return of the horse and the abolishment of automobiles, aesthetic preferences aside, but it is surely rational and realistic to insist that automobiles be prevented from poisoning us to death. The continuity and preservation of artifacts are not quite the same as the conservation of values."[37]

What, then, is a conservative? Assessing *The Conservative Mind*, historian Michael Oakeshott profiled a conservative as a person "particularly disposed towards a certain exactness or frugality in conduct. And in the exercise of this disposition he tends to handle things with care, intent upon getting the most out of them without immediately wishing that the store were greater or other than it is." Oakeshott added:

> To snatch and to discard are equally foreign to his character. He is not worried by the absence of innovation, and is not inclined to think that nothing is happening unless great changes are afoot. Of course he recognizes change to be unavoidable, and like anyone else (except those who are infatuated with change) he may consider some changes to be improvements and others to be changes for the worse. But, because he perceives the loss in every change more readily than the gain, he is not apt to initiate change. He favours a slow tempo, and is averse from large or sudden changes which he considers to be unnecessarily extravagant. Decay he can often view with equanimity; what grieves him is the wanton dissipation of achievement and the destruction of what has no ground of dissolution within itself. He is cautious by temperament; if he is forced to gamble he will bet in the field rather than on some favoured animal. And, of course, like any other character, he is apt to suffer from the defects of his virtues. If he is of a reflective turn of mind he may cast about for some convincing intellectual support for his disposition, and he may even come to compose, or to adopt, a system of general beliefs about the world and about human conduct which he thinks to be appropriate. He will be mistaken if he supposes that these beliefs are in any proper sense the "ground" of his disposition, or that they afford any cogent "justification" of it; but in spite of their *ex post facto* character and the exaggerated symmetry they are liable to impart, they may serve to make his attitude more intelligible to himself and to others.[38]

Kirk would add, a bit more succinctly, that the conservative is that person who, generally speaking, holds by tradition and the wisdom of his or her ancestors, believing that there are normative truths that transcend dialectic, to the end that the permanent things are upheld for the cultural and spiritual health of the individual, the small community, and the commonwealth. What, then, had he accomplished by writing *The Conservative Mind*? In an important essay on Kirk's significance, neoconservative essayist David Frum described *The Conservative Mind* as "a romantic reading of the past for the purposes of the present" and declared that "Russell Kirk inspired the postwar conservative movement by pulling together a series of only partially related ideas and events into a coherent narrative—even, though Kirk objected to the word, into an ideology. Kirk did not record the past; he created it." *The Conservative Mind* is not history per se; rather, "it is a work of literature meant to achieve political ends," Frum claims. Which is not to say that the book is ahistorical, for discerning important, little-noticed threads in the tapestry of the centuries and presenting these findings in a compelling manner is part of the historian's role. Indeed, in this sense *The Conservative Mind* is an expression of history reminiscent in accomplishment to that of Christopher Dawson. Jeffrey Hart, professor emeritus of English at Dartmouth College, has written, "You encounter in Dawson names you have never heard of, connections and comparisons you have never seen before, scholarly vistas unthought of suddenly opening before you. His erudition, however, works in the service of a large central project: recovering the continuities of Western culture and reshaping in a dramatic way our sense of the history of Western civilization."[39] This is exactly what Kirk, on a narrower scale, accomplished in *The Conservative Mind*. Frum concludes:

> Yet if Kirk's great work cannot be counted as history, exactly, it ought to be esteemed as something in some ways more important: a profound critique of contemporary mass society and a vivid and poetic image—not a program, an image—of how that society might better itself. It is, in important respects, the twentieth century's own version of the *Reflections of the Revolution in France*. If Kirk was not a historian, he was an artist, a visionary, almost a prophet. As long as he lived, by word and example he cautioned conservatives against over-indulging their fascination with economics. He taught that conservativism was above all a moral cause: one devoted to the preservation of the priceless heritage of Western civilization.[40]

Acts of preservation, no matter how praiseworthy, can have about them the aura of taking the side of a losing cause. The passion for change, novelty, and the casting aside of established ways has a long history in Britain and America, and Kirk acknowledged that conservatives throughout the history of both nations have been beaten down socially and politically time and again. His original title for his masterwork, *The Conservatives' Rout*, was not chosen idly. Kirk refused, though, to give in to the belief that because something has been defeated it is therefore discredited, or that defeat is final. On this matter he was fond of quoting from T. S. Eliot's essay on Francis Herbert Bradley: "If we take the widest and wisest view of a Cause, there is no such thing as a Lost Cause, because there is no such thing as a Gained Cause. We fight for lost causes because we know that our defeat and dismay may be the preface to our successors' victory, though that victory itself will be temporary; we fight rather to keep something alive than in the expectation that it will triumph." Upon the book's appearance in 1953, one man who firmly believed himself to stand on the virtuous but losing side of history, Whittaker Chambers, recognized the significance of *The Conservative Mind* and urged editor Roy Alexander of *Time* magazine to see it reviewed properly, as he found it "one of the most important books that is likely to appear in some time." *Time* agreed and went so far as to devote its entire book review section of the July 6 issue to Kirk's study, with reviewer Max Ways writing, "Kirk tells his story of the conservative stream with the warmth that belongs to it. Even Americans who do not agree may feel the warmth—and feel, perhaps, the wonder of conservative intuition and prophecy, speaking resonantly across the disappointing decades."[41] For his part, Chambers wrote to Kirk early in 1954 to say, "I am rereading *The Conservative Mind*, which, like all really good books, gives something more at each reading."[42] The flamboyant poet Roy Campbell wrote to tell Kirk that he considered *The Conservative Mind* "one of the most important books of this century."[43]

In a review seldom noted by Kirk scholars, the brilliant libertarian-conservative essayist Frank Meyer praised Kirk for having "given us a deep, eloquent, and convincing restatement of the fundamental principles of conservatism." Kirk erred, though, by restricting his survey to the line of conservative thinkers descending from Burke while neglecting "so many of those who combine the firm reverence of the conservative outlook with equal devotion to the principle that political society exists to give the fullest possible liberty to the individual." Meyer cited Lord Acton, Herbert Spencer, and Thomas Jefferson (on the basis of his *Summary View of the Rights of British America*—"one of the most important conservative documents in our history," by Meyer's lights) as figures wrongly excluded from *The Conservative Mind*. "The book is rich and rewarding in the depth of its perceptions and in the warm sympathy with which Mr. Kirk explores the insights of the 18th- and 19th-century thinkers who express his concept of conservatism. It is perhaps because of his implicit repudiation of the American fusion of individualism and conservatism that he is more disappointing when he deals directly with contemporary men and situations," Meyer concluded. (The "fusion" Meyer mentioned at the last was to become an important element in his thought throughout the 1950s and early '60s—and the subject of future debates with Kirk.)[44]

Of course, there were some commentators to whom Kirk was simply a wrongheaded proponent of "right-wing ideology," a new landed squirearchy, and other questionable causes not found between the covers of *The Conservative Mind*. Reviewing the book for *The New Republic*, Francis Biddle wrote a respectful but negative assessment, finding much in the volume over which the American liberal might profitably ruminate—especially in Kirk's discussion of Alexis de Tocqueville, author of *Democracy in America* (1831), who saw the inculcation of virtue as the only saving grace of American democracy—though nothing much of value to the would-be conservative. "When we examine the content of most conservative thinking described in this volume the vagueness of its substance and the confusion of its ideal emerge with greater emphasis, set against this extraordinary Frenchman's analysis," Biddle wrote, though he declined to cite specific examples of the vagueness and confusion in his lengthy review.[45] Socialist Norman Thomas found Kirk's book "an eloquent bit of special pleading which is, in part, a false, and, in sum total, a dangerously inadequate, philosophy for our times," especially because Kirk's "opinions of trade unions, socialism, the income tax, the causes of wars, his uncertain grasp of economics, show failure to cope with reality."[46]

In every era, Kirk said, some will attempt to discredit and pull down the permanent things, and others will defend them manfully. Literally to his dying day, Kirk labored on behalf of the permanent things, by his words and actions. With the publication and widespread reading of *The Conservative Mind*, a rag-tag scattering of men and women of the right began to cohere into a movement. Writing less than two years after the appearance of Kirk's best-known work, social theorist and historian James Burnham hailed Kirk as "probably the leading spokesman of the New Conservatives, who are wheeling so formidably into position on our intellectual field."[47] In the coming years, the so-called "New Conservatives" (not to be mistaken with the neoconservatives of the 1980s and '90s) would establish influential magazines, found think tanks and foundations, conduct conservative-themed seminars on a scale ranging from the small to the gargantuan, and undertake many other activities, coming to affect American culture at large in a discernible way—to the point that the quiet-spoken man from Mecosta was sometimes forgotten as more politically focused, media-savvy conservative figures came to the fore in American society. But till the end he was remembered and honored by many admirers as America's preeminent cultural conservative. Having articulated the history of conservative ideas in *The Conservative Mind*, he accomplished still another noteworthy thing: As William Rusher noted in 1992, "Russell Kirk performed one other important service as well: He gave this great movement its name."[48]

NOTES

1. Stanlis, in Person, ed., *The Unbought Grace of Life: Essays in Honor of Russell Kirk*, p. 39.
2. Cook, "Freedom Medalist," *The Nation* 238, March 10, 1984, 277.
3. Rusher, in Person, ed., *Unbought Grace of Life*, p. 50.
4. I have no quarrel with McCarthy's belief that there were communists in high places in the American government. Several recent books based upon research into the recently opened Soviet intelligence archives—notably *The Haunted Wood: Soviet Espionage in America—The Stalin Years* (1998), by Allen Weinstein and Alexander Vassiliev—bear out the facts on this matter, that there was significant

penetration of American security by communist operatives. It is my belief, though, that McCarthy was to anticommunism what the Rev. Jim Bakker of "PTL Ministries" was to Christianity: a self-deceived, self-serving boor whose methods needlessly harmed innocent people and did far more to discredit a worthwhile cause than to advance it. This does not excuse the activities of McCarthy's enemies, who by their sanctimonious and relentless cries of havoc, as well as their exaggerated claims of McCarthy's damage to American culture, caused far more "hysteria" during the 1950s—and in the years since—than the Wisconsin senator ever managed on his own. Further, McCarthy damaged the cause of conservatism by what Lee Edwards, in his study *The Conservative Revolution* (1999), has termed his "often careless inquiries," which "allowed liberals to transform anticommunism into McCarthyism and hang it around the necks of conservatives for the next thirty years."

5. Bundy, "The Attack on Yale," *The Atlantic Monthly* 188, November, 1951, 50.

6. Macdonald, "God and Buckley at Yale," *The Reporter* 6, May 27, 1952, 36.

7. Hatch, "Enforcing Truth," *The New Republic* 125, December 3, 1951, 19.

8. Ashburn, " 'Isms' & the University," *The Saturday Review of Literature* 34, December 15, 1951, 45.

9. Hook, "The Faiths of Whittaker Chambers," *The New York Times Book Review*, May 25, 1952, 1.

10. Stokes, "Whittaker Chambers' Story," *The Yale Review* n.s. 42, Autumn, 1952, 126.

11. Rusher, in Person, ed. *Unbought Grace of Life*, p. 50.

12. Sobran, *"The Conservative Mind* Is Classic: So Is Author Russell Kirk," *The News-Herald*, Lake County, Ohio, May 6, 1982, 10.

13. Vanauken, "Old Western Man: C. S. Lewis and the Old South (and Other Dinosaurs)," *Crisis: A Journal of Lay Catholic Opinion* 11, December, 1993, 28. In an unrelated matter, but by a curious coincidence, the Kirk family's "burglar-butler," Clinton Wallace, collapsed and died at the door of his apartment after walking home from a nearby theater in Grand Rapids, Michigan, where he had viewed a motion picture titled *Across the Great Divide*.

14. Stanlis, "The Conservative Mind of Russell Kirk," *The Newman Review* 5, nos. 3–4, 1954, 24.

15. "Interview with Russell Kirk," *Continuity: A Journal of History* 18, Spring/Fall, 1994, 8.

16. See Joanne Emmons's remarks in Person, ed., *The Unbought Grace of Life: Essays in Honor of Russell Kirk*, p. 65.

17. *Decadence and Renewal in the Higher Learning: An Episodic History of American University and College since 1953*, p. 291.

18. Chalmers, "Goodwill is Not Enough," *The New York Times Book Review*, May 17, 1953, 7.

19. *The Portable Conservative Reader*, p. xvii.

20. Heckscher, "Toward a True, Creative Conservatism," *New York Herald Tribune Book Review*, August 2, 1953, 4.

21. Percy, *Lanterns on the Levee: Recollections of a Planter's Son*, p. 153.

22. Quoted in Chamberlin, "A Study of Conservative Thought and Its Progress in the Past Two Hundred Years," *The Wall Street Journal*, June 10, 1953, 6.

23. Burke, quoted in Kirk, ed., *The Portable Conservative Reader*, p. 26.

24. Burke, in Kirk, ed., *Portable Conservative Reader*, pp. 25–26.

25. *Portable Conservative Reader*, p. xvi.

26. Kirk, *The Conservative Mind: From Burke to Eliot*, p. 241. All quotations from *The Conservative Mind* are taken from this edition.

27. *Conservative Mind*, p. 242.

28. *Conservative Mind*, p. 244.

29. *Conservative Mind*, p. 244.

30. *Portable Conservative Reader*, p. xvii.

31. Mapp, *Three Golden Ages: Discovering the Creative Secrets of Renaissance Florence, Elizabethan England, and America's Founding*, p. 573.

32. *Portable Conservative Reader*, p. xv-xvi.

33. *Portable Conservative Reader*, pp. xv-xvii.

34. Ransom, "Empirics in Politics," *Poems and Essays* (New York, 1955), pp. 138–39. This review-essay originally appeared in *The Kenyon Review* in 1953.

35. Cheney, "The Conservative Course by Celestial Navigation," *The Sewanee Review* 62, winter, 1954, 154–55.

36. Rubin, introduction to the 1962 edition of *I'll Take My Stand: Essays by Twelve Southerners* (Baton Rouge, 1977), p. xxxii.

37. Zoll, "The Social Thought of Russell Kirk," *The Political Science Reviewer* 2, Fall, 1972, 134.

38. Oakeshott, "Conservative Political Thought," *The Spectator* 193, October 15, 1954, 472.

39. Hart, "Christopher Dawson and the History We Are Not Told," *Modern Age* 39, Summer, 1997, 211.

40. Frum, "The Legacy of Russell Kirk," *The New Criterion* 13, December, 1994, 14, 15, 16. Frum's is one of the most thoughtful essays written since Kirk's death on Kirk's accomplishment in general and *The Conservative Mind* in particular, though he and I must, I suspect, agree to disagree in respect to the question of conservatism as an ideology.

41. Ways, "Generation to Generation," *Time* 62, July 6, 1953, 88. This review was originally unsigned, as such was the policy of *Time* for many years; the critic has since been identified as Max Ways.

42. Chambers to Kirk, January 19, 1954. In fairness, it must be added that, in a letter to another correspondent, Chambers, who considered himself more a "man of the Right" than a conservative, wrote of *The Conservative Mind*, "If you were a marine in a landing boat, would you wade up the seabeach at Tarawa for that conservative position? And neither would I!"

43. Campbell to Kirk, undated, circa 1955.

44. Meyer, "Conservatism and Individualism," *The American Mercury* 67, July, 1953, 141, 142.

45. Biddle, "The Blur of Mediocrity," *The New Republic* 129, August 24, 1953, 17.

46. Thomas, review of *The Conservative Mind*, *United Nations World* 7, August, 1953, 34–35. In time, Kirk and Thomas developed between them a respectful friendship, which is recounted in Kirk's memoir *The Sword of Imagination*.

47. Burnham, review of *A Program for Conservatives*, in *The Annals of the American Academy of Political and Social Sciences* 298, March, 1955, 216.

48. Rusher, in Person, ed., *Unbought Grace of Life*, p. 50.

3

Virtue and the Historical Consciousness: Kirk's Writings on History

People will not look forward to posterity, who never look backward to their ancestors.

—Edmund Burke

We are people to whom the past is forever speaking.

—Bruce Catton

What good is history? Wouldn't we all be better off living life rather than reading about it? asks the perennial sophomore, more often as a taunt than a question. The answer, evident in Kirk's historical writings, is that historical knowledge has worth beyond measure: within the historical consciousness grows wisdom, a sense of spiritual rootedness, and through reading of and understanding the lives of the great, the knowledge of virtue. "The truths of history, the real meanings, are to be discovered in what history can teach us about the framework of the Logos, if you will: about the significance of human existence: about the splendor and misery of our condition," wrote Kirk in his essay "Regaining Historical Consciousness."[1] By "the framework of the Logos," Kirk meant that history is not a sequence of random events but the working out of Providential will over the course of time, in a manner barely discerned, if at all, from a mundane perspective. The person of a conservative mind thus views history as something of a tapestry of many-hued threads, indecipherable at present, as we are enmeshed in the skein, but intelligible at a future date when time and the timeless become one. Not now perceived as such, history is the grand design a-building. As much as possible, it is one of the hallmarks of the conservative mind to view the present from the perspective of eternity; and if this is difficult, to wait stoically for more information toward meaning, and not to succumb to despair.

This view of history as held by Kirk becomes apparent upon reading the history he wrote, especially *The Conservative Mind, The Roots of American Order,* and his studies of John Randolph of Roanoke and Edmund Burke. His historiographical method harks back to Christopher Dawson (1889–1970), author of such works as *The Age of the Gods: A Study of the Origins of Culture in Pre-Historic Europe and the Ancient East* (1928) and *Religion and the Rise of Western Culture* (1950). He contributed essays to T. S. Eliot's *Criterion* and was much admired by Eliot himself, who on one occasion called Dawson the most powerful intellectual influence in England. As a historian, Dawson was a lover of books—thousands of them. According to Jeffrey Hart, a senior editor at *National Review* and English professor at Dartmouth, "You encounter in Dawson names you have never heard of, connections and comparisons you have never seen before, scholarly vistas unthought of suddenly opening before you. His erudition, however, works in the service of a large central project: recovering the continuities of Western culture and reshaping in a dramatic way our sense of the history of Western civilization." It is precisely this that the reader encounters in Kirk's historical works, along with another specialty of Dawson: a deepened sense of the continuity of Western culture, its philosophical traditions and acts of heroism, from ancient times through to the present (along the way finding Europe's medieval era, the so-called Dark Ages, not a time of darkness but of cultural preservation: when there was, as Hart puts it, "an enormous effort on the part of beleaguered communities to preserve and add to the inheritance of religion, culture, and learning and to provide the basis for a revival of civilized order").[2]

In Dawson as in Kirk, there is a strong emphasis upon the role of religion as the seedbed from which culture arises. Culture arises from the cult, as Kirk wrote on many occasions, with a glance to Dawson. In its simplest sense, culture is that refined accumulation of ways, mores, values, customs, conventions, and manners practiced by a particular people living in a particular place at a particular time. Informed by ethics grounded in a transcendent order or faith in a deity, a culture produces the virtuous individuals, and the nonvirtuous, who are the makers of history. "The death of a man at a critical juncture, his disgust, his retreat, his disgrace, have brought innumerable calamities on a whole nation. A common soldier, a child, a girl at the door of an inn, have changed the face of fortune, and almost of Nature," wrote Edmund Burke. (He referred to specific historical figures here: The man who died at a critical juncture is the Athenian general Pericles, the man who retired in disgust is Prime Minister William Pitt upon his retreat from public life, the child is Hannibal, who vowed at age 12 to make war upon Rome, and the girl at the inn door is Joan of Arc.) Kirk was fascinated by such individuals, especially those who were cultural conservators, who worked to prevent cultural decadence. As Gerald J. Russello has noted in his essay "Time and the Timeless: The Historical Consciousness of Russell Kirk":

> Kirk explored in his work the tension in Western civilization between the individual and the community, and between respect for the past with concern for the future. Kirk knew that history is made by individuals: ever wary of abstractions, Kirk concentrated on specific persons who altered history through their actions, rather than making obeisance to abstract "History." Kirk saw the conservative's task as preventing this individual action from degenerating into neoterism or revolution, and only by understanding individual action within the broader canvas of history disciplined by authority and tradition can we prevent this degeneration. The historical figures Kirk puts forth for our consideration are those who were able to act within the bounds of history, even as they changed it.[3]

"Authority" and "tradition" are much maligned words in American culture at large at present; yet they are words that represent concepts vital for any culture to endure, for the citizens of any society to exist as anything other than the flies of summer. Kirk's friend Gerhart Niemeyer, longtime professor emeritus of government at the University of Notre Dame, praised tradition unstintingly as a reality of political existence and cultural creativity. He does not confound history and tradition, citing the latter as something paradoxically outside of and yet an integral working part of history, describing it in brief as "public memory—the stuff that Aristotle describes as 'civic friendship.'" According to Niemeyer, "Tradition implies awareness of being, along with awareness of history. Tradition is not only remembrance of ancestors, but also openness to God. Tradition results in appropriate humility of individual persons, while it denies not freedom of choice. Indeed, freedom of choice presupposes awareness of tradition." In words that might easily provide a commentary upon *The Conservative Mind* and other works of history written by Kirk, Niemeyer describes tradition as the basis for both authority and continuity, making possible the wise raising of children and a framework for myriad other decisions, "particularly those that have to be made without delay; it also provides the material for deliberation when time is available for that."[4]

Kirk's first book addressed the life and career of an outspoken champion of tradition and the authority of the American Constitution. *Randolph of Roanoke: A Study in Conservative Thought* (later revised and published as *John Randolph of Roanoke: A Study in American Politics*) began as the author's master's dissertation and was published in 1951 by the University of Chicago Press. It is the systematic study of one of the most extraordinarily brilliant conservative statesmen ever to grace the chambers of the U.S. House of Representatives and Senate, a Virginian whose fiery personality, appeals to normative truths, and strictly constructionist interpretation of the Constitution would arguably render him unelectable if his like were to arise today. In the life of John Randolph (1773–1833), the soft-spoken Kirk found a bold, eloquent spokesman for many of the same beliefs he held dear, Randolph being a champion of regionalism (as opposed to nationalism), agriculture and agricultural interests, economy in government, and freedom from foreign entanglements, both economic and military.

Randolph had begun his career as a fervent ally of Thomas Jefferson and a firm Democratic Republican, but had turned against the Sage of Monticello because he considered his fellow Virginian too much given to the political abstractions of the revolutionary-era French; he took English society and mores as his model and found that the influential Jefferson's embrace of natural rights theories, along with the increased presence of Napoleonic influence in what are now the southernmost United States, would prove harmful to the fledgling nation. Should America become unduly enamored of French influence, Randolph feared, she might take on the worst attributes of postrevolutionary France; a mobocracy driven by passion and inclined to worship abstractions (such as Reason bound by expediency alone), and ready—despite its cries for *égalité*—to embrace an emperor. (This mistrust was surely at the base of Randolph's break with Jefferson; their differences over the now widely forgotten Yazoo land deal controversy and the attempt of Jefferson and James Madison to acquire Spanish Florida in 1805 merely pushed Randolph the final distance away from his old leader.) Like Kirk, Randolph was no fancier of needless innovation, no nationalist (when he spoke of his "country," he meant not the United States, but the Commonwealth of Virginia), no believer in abstract rights cobbled out of sentiment and well-wishing, and no democrat, having complete contempt for the idea that the voice of the people is the voice of God. Heaping scorn upon "the all-prevailing principle that *vox populi, vox dei*," Randolph declared, at the Virginia State Convention of 1829, "I would not live under King Numbers. I would not be his steward, nor make him my taskmaster. I would obey the principle of self preservation, a principle we find even in brute creation, in flying from this mischief."[5] As a member of the House and Senate, he was virulently contemptuous of proposed legislation built upon humanitarian ideas; in considering any issue put before the legislature, his relentlessly recurrent question was in essence this: Is it constitutional? This, along with his prickly personality and eccentricities, which led some to consider him at least half insane, made him somewhat unpopular with his legislative colleagues, though somewhat more so with his constituents. As a statesman he served not as a delegate, but as a representative, of the men who elected him, standing upon the principle of traditional rights rather than natural rights and the popular whim of the moment. This was bound to make him one of those Kirkian heroes who belong to an aristocracy of talent and wisdom, who go forth often to battle but seldom to victory.

Kirk and Randolph shared the above-described mistrust of Jefferson, though, as historian Alf J. Mapp Jr. has demonstrated, there was much in Jefferson's thought congenial to their own, aside from the obvious shared vision of the United States as a voluntary union of states inhabited by self-reliant agrarians, loosely bound by a weak central government. Admittedly, according to Mapp, Jefferson "is not only the patron saint of a political party." He is also

the patron saint of a host of ideologists, most of them of the liberal persuasion. Many of them approach the task of telling Jefferson's life story as if it were that of a revered father. Each conservative thought attributable to this Founding Father is an isolated slip from grace. To reveal it to the public, they seem to feel, would be as disloyal and as pointless as exposing to general gossip the few instances in which a beloved parent, deservedly respected for sobriety, indulged too heavily in drink.[6]

As Mapp convincingly reveals in his *Thomas Jefferson: A Strange Case of Mistaken Identity*, Jefferson's slips from grace were far from isolated. What are we to make of Jefferson the revolutionist who, while serving on Virginia's Committee to Revise the Laws of the Commonwealth in 1777, opposed with Burkean stolidity Edmund Pendleton's proposal for a completely new set of laws, claiming that such a change could jeopardize the rights of property? This democrat who could refer to the mass electorate as "the swinish multitude"? This egalitarian who advised that a public education program should be so planned that "the best geniuses will be raked from the rubbish annually"? He also held to a Burkean concept of society as a compact between the dead, the living, and those yet unborn: the contract of eternal society. No heedless innovator, he believed that each generation owed to its ancestors the judicious preservation and use of their cultural legacy, and that future generations are in turn owed a sound and beneficial heritage. Jefferson admired tradition and the past, and sought, particularly in his taste in architecture, to appropriate the usable past for the benefit of

American culture. At the same time—though long associated in the public mind with leanings toward atheism, social leveling, and faith in the perfectibility of man—he strongly believed in God and in the vital role of religion in society (albeit a belief informed by a deep distrust of priestcraft and most reports of the miraculous), considered social equality an impossible goal, and was suspicious of both Utopianism and its agent, big government. However, for the very obvious and overarching influence of Francis Bacon, a man considered by many conservatives the father of modern scientism, and John Locke, a man Kirk considered "the grandfather of liberalism," Jefferson cannot be claimed wholeheartedly by American conservatives as one of their own. For each "conservative" thought Jefferson expressed, a correspondingly liberal one can be found—sometimes in the same document. Still, it is instructive to note that Mapp cited Kirk as one of seven conservatives who participated in a 1967 symposium and agreed to seven four-square conservative principles, five of which, Mapp argued, would find a whole-hearted champion in Jefferson, these five being:

> For the most part, a deep belief in God and a concern with religion in the daily affairs of men.
>
> A suspicion of big government and a reliance upon local administration of public affairs.
>
> A belief in the imperfect nature of man and a hostility to any scheme—political or social—that suggests a Utopian world.
>
> An admiration for tradition and the past.
>
> A respect for the importance of property and free enterprise in stabilizing society and spurring individual incentive.[7]

All of which made little difference to Randolph, who derided "St. Thomas of Can*ting*bury" as a man much too given to abstractions and not enough to the traditional rights and duties of America's English heritage, particularly as articulated by one of his favorite authors, Burke. "To call Randolph 'the American Burke' is no great exaggeration," wrote Kirk.

> Randolph's character was more like that of the elder Pitt, with "his intractable, incalculable nature, his genius tinged with madness." But Burke's theory of indivisible sovereignty, his contempt for abstract harmony in government, his impatience with questions of legal "right," and his advocacy of "expediency tempered by prescription and tradition," accompanied by his reverence for the experience of mankind—all these were the principles of Burke.[8]

Historian Peter Stanlis encountered *Randolph of Roanoke* in a bookstore soon after its initial publication while organizing a conference on Burke for the December 1951 meeting in Detroit of the Modern Language Association of America. Noting a statement on the flyleaf that cited Burke as the great "political exemplar" of Randolph, Stanlis, having recently submitted his doctoral thesis on Burke, opened a copy to discover that Kirk's grasp of Burke's significance and vision was well considered and well stated.

Although Kirk presented no sustained exposition of Burke's political thought, beyond a few paragraphs or brief statements, to my great surprise and joy I discovered that he was wholly on target in every important subject he dealt with, and frequently hit the bullseye. It was clear to me that Kirk had a far better understanding of Burke's politics than any of the many established experts on Burke that I had read during the past three years or more. Only Professor Ross J. S. Hoffman of Fordham University understood the importance of moral natural law in Burke, and he had not written on it. Unlike most eighteenth-century scholars, Kirk had even perceived that when Burke attacked revolutionary "natural rights" he did not thereby reject nature as a norm in favor of social customs, as practically all previous writers on Burke had assumed and argued. Although Kirk stressed legal prescription as most fundamental in Burke's politics, whereas I had argued that legal prescription was a vital derivative principle from natural law, nevertheless he was close to the essence of Burke's thought.[9]

I have heard this little-discussed book described by some admirers of Kirk as their favorite among the author's works. Certainly it lacks that faint odor of the midnight oil that hangs about other theses brought into publication, and there appear within this early effort strong glimmers of Kirk's mature style, as when he pauses at one point to ruminate, "No 'right,' however natural it may seem, can exist unqualified in society. A man may have a right to self-defense; therefore, he may have a right to a sword; but if he is mad or wicked, and intends to do his neighbors harm, every dictate of prudence will tell us to disarm him. Rights have no being independent of circumstance and expediency."[10] "It is doubtful whether a more concise study could have been made, which at the same time possesses as this does, so much felicity of expression," wrote George Green Shackelford of the Virginia Historical Society.[11] "Mr. Kirk has done a real service in resuscitating the ideas of our most profound conservative," claimed Anthony Harrigan.[12]

Perhaps Randolph of Roanoke was America's most profound conservative, as of the time of Harrigan's review, but as Kirk and Stanlis knew, there was a far greater conservative voice to heed and honor. In *Edmund Burke: A Genius Reconsidered*, first published in 1967, Kirk put his hand to the study of a longtime hero, the "enduring Burke," whose written works, he believed, played a major role in the ruminations of the early leaders of the United States and speak still to the discontents of the modern world.

Like the name of Locke, Burke's name does not appear in Madison's notes of the Constitutional Convention of 1787, nor in the *Federalist Papers*. This is not because the Framers had failed to read Burke, for he had been without doubt the most eloquent parliamentary opponent of George III's colonial policies as they affected British North America; he had also been a parliamentary agent for New York, his *Conciliation Speech* (1775) was known to every American with an interest in Anglo-American relations, and throughout the revolutionary era and beyond he had edited *The Annual Register*, arguably the world's most trenchant and trusted English-language source of information about public affairs at the time. During the Constitutional Convention, the delegates did not quote any living statesman in their deliberations, Burke included, as they would be able to respond should they disagree with interpretations of their words at the convention. After 1790, though, Burke's reputation came markedly to the fore in the United States, especially after the appearance of his *Reflections on the Revolution in France*. This work, a lengthy discourse upon perils of existence in a society bound not by reflective wisdom and tradition, but by the passions of the passing hour, was read and discussed by such Americans as John Adams, Alexander Hamilton, John Quincy Adams, and many of the fifty-five Framers. Among American jurists, John Marshall and Joseph Story were deeply influenced by Burke's words, Burke believing in what might be called the politics of prudence. This begins from the belief that politics is possible only with the belief that some things are permanent, transcending dialectic, and only if the desire for change is matched by the knowledge that establishing a terrestrial paradise is impossible and that the future is unknowable by man here below.

Standing at sword's point with the revolutionary doctrine prevalent in France, Burke strongly opposed speculative ideology built upon abstractions, namely primitivist theories of the social contract (stemming from the thought of Thomas Hobbes, John Locke, and Jean-Jacques Rousseau) and appeals to ill-defined natural rights, against which he placed traditional rights. Careful readers of Burke have discovered certain key principles and enduring concerns in his political philosophy. Among these, as listed concisely by Burke scholar Peter Stanlis, are: "moral natural law, prudence, legal prescription, limited power under constitutional law, normative appeals to Providence and religion, appeals to history and tradition as preceptors of experience and prudence, a defense of private and corporate property as essential to civil liberty, and respect for party government."[13]

Upon the appearance of *Edmund Burke* in 1967, Jeffrey Hart wrote, "Kirk's scholarship is wide-ranging—I do not in fact know of a contemporary writer who has his command of intellectual 'connection,' often exhibited in a passing allusion—and of course he brings to bear his close knowledge of the vast array of modern Burke scholarship."[14] In a discerning review of a later edition, George A. Panichas wrote that for Kirk, "Burke exemplifies how public life and the life of the mind interact in those unique and subtle ways that fuse insight and wisdom and that make Burke 'one of the wisest men ever to meditate upon the civil social order.' This short critical study, 'an essay in biography,' as Kirk terms it in a prefatory note, examines this process of showing how Burke 'speaks to our age.'" The critic goes on to speak of Kirk's depiction of Burke as a prescient social and political thinker, saying:

> Kirk thus sees Burke as "a modern man" who was concerned with "our modern perplexities." And beyond this, as Kirk shows throughout the book, Burke was a visionary, "our Tiresias." From a directly social and political perspective, Burke was a reformer who fought against "crooked politics," but also and above all he was a conservator who combined his burden of responsibility as a man of affairs in "the defense of civilization." Burke discerned, then, and warned against the dangers, if not the fateful consequences, of "the armed doctrine" and "metaphysical madness" perpetrated by radical innovators.[15]

"Kirk's biography tells the story of a remarkable statesman, of a remarkable society, and of a remarkable period of human history," wrote philosophical historian Roger Scruton in his foreword to the 1997 edition of *Edmund Burke*. "English readers will be gratified by the author's sympathy for our eccentricities, while American readers will learn much about the British Empire and its meaning. The book provides a clear and succinct guide to one of the great conservative thinkers of modern times. Kirk sees his subject as he was, and in terms of hopes and fears which he shares. Burke was engaged, he argues, in a continuous pursuit of justice, and valued order, tradition, and the conservative instinct largely because they prevent the massive injustices which ensue when men take it on themselves to manage their own destiny."[16]

Of primary significance to Burke's philosophy, to that of Alexis de Tocqueville, and to cultural conservatism in general, is the element of virtue as the chief goal in the life of the individual and the small community. "To the extent that we abandon our pursuit of virtue," wrote Bruce Frohnen in his invaluable study *Virtue and the Promise of Conservatism*, "we abandon the necessary link between ethics and politics, and between the transcendent and the material—between God and man—which is the basis of any truly good life." The virtuous life being of little worth to those who prate unctuously about the need for an envy-driven ethic of fairness and sentimental utilitarianism, virtue is not widely spoken of today without a sarcastic smirk. Even among neoconservatives and libertarians, it is of, at best, secondary importance behind economic and political concerns. This is no small matter, for as Frohnen pointed out:

> To promote affirmation in a time of cynicism, in a time during which iconoclasm has formed a new and intolerant intellectual orthodoxy, is to be truly "revolutionary." But such promotion is the essence of conservatism. We must understand and cherish whence we come so that we may determine in which direction we should travel in the journey of life. . . .[17]

The written works of Burke and Tocqueville, who figure prominently in Kirk's historical writings, give sustained, compelling philosophical arguments for the conservative "good life" (meaning the virtuous life, not a life with the promise of a winter home in Bimini). Burke and Tocqueville each defended his own and other societies on the ground that existing institutions, varied though they are in custom and convention, allow for a life that promotes service to the community: service given freely, out of affection for those with whom one has lived one's life.

For Burke and Tocqueville, as for Kirk, the good life can exist and human nature can be fulfilled only in the society whose citizens serve the existing social order because of uncoerced affection and belief in its goodness. "Contemporary conservatives who deny the existence or the need for accepting virtue in effect deny their own philosophical roots and the possibility of achieving their own inherent goal," wrote Frohnen. But the imperative of virtue has been obscured to much of the modern mind by the omnipresent stress upon egalitarian materialism, itself the poisonous legacy of Hobbes and others. But by brightening one's own corner, in the burden of the old hymn—that is, by renewing our commitment to the truths and life of the spirit while faithfully performing the acts of obligation, responsibility, and love within the little platoons to which one belongs in society—"we may," in Frohnen's words, "regain our understanding of God's will and our need to follow it if we are to live a good life." Conservative political philosophy, arising from wise tradition, recognizes that any good life "depends at least as much upon goodness of heart as upon brilliance of mind": that—to put it briefly—in the world of politics, for example, the content of one's character matters greatly, not just the ability to campaign successfully for the popular (if imprudent) cause of the hour.

Virtue is developed, learned and soaked up, really, within the small communities to which the individual belongs. Throughout the history of Western civilization, there has been a constant tension between the claims of the individual and the claims of the community and of society at large, between tradition and change, between the exigencies of the past and the demands of the future. These struggles have been borne out in the lives of notable men and women; the virtuous man or woman Kirk saw as standing in the breach performing a noble service: seeking to slow the advance of cultural decadence and spiritual entropy.

The Conservative Mind had provided a series of ruminative meditations upon the lives of many such individuals, including Burke, Tocqueville, Randolph of Roanoke, and others besides. "The conservative canon is stamped with the genius of Edmund Burke, who saw human society as an order appointed by Providence, growing slowly with the ages into maturity, carrying into the present the accumulated wisdom of generations, expressing itself in a rich diversity of social and economic classes each bearing its own unique burden, and all working together toward the common good: a good fulfilled and achieved only on the condition that each man, village, town, profession, and class maintains itself distinct and apart," wrote Frederick D. Wilhelmsen, in a review of Kirk's best-known work. He added, "The politics of prescription—Burke's trademark—grew out of a deep sense of veneration and reverence. Mr. Kirk indicates, with great penetration, how Burke's distrust for the abstract 'natural rights' of the Revolution was born of his love for the complexity and mystery of human life, and for the sacredness of the person."[18]

Elsewhere, Kirk identified Burke as one of four men of letters who dominated British and American political thought between the time of the "Glorious" Revolution of 1688 and the Jacobins' execution of Louis XVI and Marie Antoinette in 1793, the other three being John Locke, he of the "social contract" theory of society; the Baron de Montesquieu, philosopher of constitutional order; and David Hume, the empirical skeptic. He wrote that the powerful minds of these four still have much to teach those who will attend them. "They did not play the comic role in politics, even though this or that notion of theirs may seem absurd by hindsight. These are the giants on whose shoulders we moderns stand."[19] All four, whatever their differences, possessed a high degree of political imagination. In his essay "Tradition and the Individual Talent," Eliot wrote, "Some one said: 'The dead writers are remote from us because we *know* so much more than they did.' Precisely, and they are that which we know." Or as Kirk put it, in respect to the four men of letters under discussion:

> We discard Locke's theory of a primitive state of nature; but we can still profit from his arguments for reason in politics and religion.
> We discern difficulties in the application of Montesquieu's doctrine of separation of powers; but we are the beneficiaries of his endeavor to reconcile the claims of authority and the claims of freedom.
> We may be vexed by Hume's complacency, thinking him Mr. Know-All; but we would be intellectually poorer, were we deprived of his realistic analysis of human motives and his understanding of the foundations of the civil social order.
> We may reproach Burke for intemperate partisanship, much of his career; but we know that, as even Harold Laski put it, Burke's writings form "the permanent manual of political wisdom without which statesmen are as sailors on an uncharted sea."[20]

It may surprise some readers to see Kirk speak so favorably of Hume, given the high place of virtue in the philosophy of the former and the sometimes bumptious skepticism and impiety of the latter. But between the time Kirk wrote *The Conservative Mind*, in which the author had nothing favorable to say about Hume or his fellow Scotsman Adam Smith, and the publication of *The Roots of American Order* over twenty years later, he had read more deeply and carefully in the writings of both men and had come to hold a favorable opinion of each. Kirk came to see the obvious influence of Hume upon the Framers, notably Madison and Hamilton, and discovered that Hume possessed a penetrating understanding of the role of prescriptive order in maintaining society.

As for Kirk's understanding of Smith, Forrest McDonald has written that Kirk spent considerable time studying Smith's *Theory of Moral Sentiments* upon its appearance in a Liberty Fund edition in 1976. Through close study, Kirk came to understand that there is more to Smith than *The Wealth of Nations*—so much so that he was moved to include Smith as one of his "three pillars of order" in an essay by that title in 1981, the other "pillars" being Burke and Samuel Johnson. The significance of Kirk's new understanding of Hume and Smith, according to McDonald, was this:

> To bring the Scots into the pantheon was to give conservatism an even broader and firmer intellectual foundation than Kirk had provided before. Hume and Smith shared Kirk's (and Burke's) belief in a transcendent moral order, in social continuity, in the principle of prescription, in prudential and natural change as opposed to forced change on the basis of abstract theoretical systems, in variety and inequality, and in the imperfectability of man; but they went further. Rejecting the mechanistic model of society that was so fashionable in the eighteenth century, they viewed it instead as a living organism. From that premise it followed that society could not be tampered with or improved as an engineer might work with a machine, except at its mortal peril. It also followed—and this is crucial—that in the absence of coercion by government, society would heal its own ailments.[21]

THE ROOTS OF AMERICAN ORDER

During the Youth Movement of the mid-1960s to early 1970s, it was commonplace for young draft resisters and antiwar protesters in America to liken themselves to the various "rebels" and "nonconformists" of the revolutionary era in American history. Just as Patrick Henry, Samuel Adams, John Hancock, and other individuals had rebelled against the British "establishment," so did these latter-day rebels stand defiant against the "tyranny" of Lyndon Johnson and Richard Nixon—or so reasoned the people of the peace movement.

Certain of these men, notably Sam Adams, were radicals in the true sense. But in reality, the American Revolution, like Britain's "Glorious Revolution" of 1688, was "a revolution not made, but prevented" (as Edmund Burke styled the latter event). The events of 1775–83 did not, as did the French Revolution, signal the introduction of a whole new way of governing in America, nor a whole new way of viewing man in his relationship with others and with his God. It was, as Kirk interpreted it, a conservative reaction against intrusive innovations visited upon Britain's thirteen seaboard colonies by George III and Parliament. "The American Revolution was a conservative movement, resisting centralized usurpation from abroad. Some of our greatest political thinkers have been profound conservatives, and the average American clings to his basic institutions with a tenacity which impressed Lord Bryce and other foreign observers," wrote Richard M. Weaver in a review of one of Kirk's books. "To equate the American with the radical is ignorant, when it is not tendentious, as often seems the case today."[22]

Indeed, the thought, activities, and government practices by the American "radicals" of the late eighteenth century had roots deep in the history of England, Rome, Jerusalem, and Athens, as Kirk demonstrated in the "other" great book he wrote, which forms an historical counterpart to *The Conservative Mind: The Roots of American Order*. This ambitious, thick volume, several years in the writing and composed under the terms of a grant bestowed by Pepperdine University, represents Kirk's most ambitious piece of sustained writing in the discipline of history. In June 1970 Kirk wrote to Eric Voegelin to say that he intended to begin writing *The Roots of American Order* by the mid to late summer, describing his yet-unwritten work as one "which will draw heavily upon your works; it's to be used primarily in an experimental course in Christian colleges."[23] The completed work went somewhat beyond Kirk's stated scope.

The Roots of American Order is less a discourse upon American history than a prologue to the study of the constituent components of that record, providing needed context for apprehending it. Further, it offered strong evidence that America began not as an "experiment" that unfolded or an "idea" that developed, but as a nation of communities that had inherited long-established conventions and traditions and grew as such. The American Revolution and the founding documents associated with its progress and aftermath point not to a nation of legal and cultural innovators and rebels; if anything, as the Declaration of Independence makes clear, separation was brought about by British innovations deemed intolerable to a people who had established their own governance and commerce during the course of two and a half centuries on the North American seaboard. Historian M. E. Bradford called it "a Burkean preface to historical research *per se*, and a touchstone for understanding the specious eschatologies and mythologies which structure the narratives of our regnant historians." Bradford masterfully summarized Kirk's intent, writing:

Jerusalem, Athens, Rome, and London—the four great iconic cities for the Anglo-American and tropes for four distinctive structurings of social and political life, these plus an assortment of supporting figures who have made for our perception of these citadels as the sequence and a synthetic "given"—are the ingredients in Kirk's cultural dynamic. As a principle of order Jerusalem represents, of course, faith and pious submission. Athens signifies (apart from its force as a negative political example) reason and art: philosophy and the examined life. Rome [specifically the Roman Republic] is a simpler model. Rome is law and public order, a notion of the common good, of corporate liberty. After Rome comes Jerusalem again—the life, death, and resurrection of Christ. Medieval man sifted that first Jerusalem and Athens and Rome through the filter of the gospels, the fullness of God's revelation to His creation. And, most significantly for Americans, in and around the city on the Thames. Christianity taught of the integrity of the individual soul. In England that translated into liberty under law, in community. Kirk gathers up the threads as he goes. Mixed in with his discourse of cities and men is an account of certain habits and ideas, their slow and steady formation. And much church history. For the moral imagination has many of its roots there, as Kirk never allows us to forget, though the decorums which it nourishes take a prudential, secular form. These reverend patrimonies, religious and traditional, reach so far back into our composite past and have so nourished our identity that we are loath even to think of them unless they begin to lose their hold.[24]

Reviewers and other commentators were deeply impressed by the depth and fairness of *The Roots of American Order*, finding it not so much a work of philosophical partisanship as a fair-minded, insightful work of scholarship. In a letter to Kirk's publisher, Ray Bradbury wrote, "In these polarized and emotional times we need more thinkers of excellence on both sides in order to make fair decisions concerning our future. Russell Kirk is just such an excellent thinker. I hope his *The Roots of American Order* is read by fair-minded people of both left and right everywhere in our country."[25] Continuing in this vein, Hilaire Belloc's biographer, Robert Speaight, wrote that *The Roots of American Order* "is sober, objective, and erudite. In so wide-ranging a resumé [Kirk] puts his finger unerringly on the people who really matter. . . . All the quotations are pithy and relevant. This book should become a breviary for every educated person, and especially for those who are less well educated than they imagine. In taking us back to our beginnings it brings us up to date, often with a salutary jolt."[26] English pundit and man of letters Malcolm Muggeridge, reviewing the work in *Esquire*, wrote, "I cannot imagine how this so essential task of referring back to the origins of order as it has existed in North America could have been more lucidly, unpretentiously, unpedantically and yet informatively executed than by Professor Kirk. His book is exactly what people need to read, and he has made it easy, even pleasurable, for them so to do."[27]

Athens, Rome, Jerusalem, London: from these storied cities stem the roots of American order, particularly the fourth. In one of the last books he saw through to publication, *America's British Culture*, Kirk boldly stated a ruminative overview of the culture inherited from Britain by the people of the United States, writing, "Two centuries after the first United States census was taken, nearly every race and nationality [have] contributed to the American population, but the culture of America remains British." These are somewhat startling words to read in the multicultural late twentieth century, foolhardy words coming from anyone less learned than Kirk. By them he meant, simply, that though many ethnic and racial groups have contributed gloriously to the American mosaic, British culture has overshadowed and shaped American life in ways and to such an extent that only the uninformed and the hardened ideologue would deny the claim.

At the outset, the very term "culture" needed to be defined for Kirk's readers; after all, just a few months before the appearance of *America's British Culture*, the governor of New York, a man celebrated widely for his brilliance, asked in a public forum, "What do you mean by 'culture?' That's a word they used in Nazi Germany." Kirk made it plain that he held by T. S. Eliot's definition of culture as the preferences, mores, and customs of a people, sanctioned by recognized arbiters of such and by individuals of distinguished talents. Further, Kirk recognized with Eliot that culture arises from the cult, the organized human community having its matrix in the core religious foundation (or lack of it) of a people. American culture is, then, in Barrett Wendell's words, "that living body of customs and duties and privileges, which a process very like physical growth has made the vital condition of our national existence."

Having assumed a reasonable definition of the word "culture," Kirk allocates the rest of *America's British Culture* to examining four aspects of British culture that have permeated that of the United States. These are: literature and language, legal theory, form of representative government, and mores—which is to say, our moral habits and beliefs, social customs, intellectual inclination, and prejudices (for good or ill).

America's British Culture is by no means a call to reclaim a patrimony of master-servant relations or caste-conscious snobbery. Nor is it a call to look upon non-British cultures as "lesser breeds without the law," in Rudyard Kipling's phrase. Rather, as with *The Roots of American Order*, it is a quietly but powerfully stated affirmation of America's dominant cultural heritage, perceived by Kirk and many others as being endangered by the desire to ruthlessly level, centralize, and (inevitably if inadvertently) destroy. Writing of America's cultural heritage, Kirk concluded, "Fulbert of Chartres, in medieval times, declared that we moderns . . . are dwarfs standing upon the shoulders of giants: we see farther than do the giants, but merely because we are mounted upon their shoulders. . . . If we think to liberate ourselves from the past by leaping off those giants' shoulders— why, we tumble into the ditch of unreason. If we ignore the subtle wisdom of the classical past and the British past, we are left with a thin evanescent culture, a mere film upon the surface of the deep well of the past. Those who refuse to drink of that well may be drowned in it." "We do not listen to ancestral voices, or strive to hear, beneath the din of politics, the rumors sent down to us from former times, which tell us of our imperfection," observed Roger Scruton. "And until we listen, our future is in jeopardy."[28]

KIRK ON THE DECLARATION AND LINCOLN

Throughout his career, Kirk found himself periodically at odds with other historians regarding two particular issues: the significance of the Declaration of Independence and the question of Abraham Lincoln's stature as a statesman. To state it briefly, he believed the Declaration to be at once a document declaring American independence from British governmental control and a quiet instrument of sidelong appeal to influential eyes in France, written in the hopes of an alliance. Further, he believed Lincoln a great man, a great president, and a sound conservative, despite a long list of controversial policies enacted during the sixteenth president's first term in office that many twentieth-century conservatives have found beyond the pale— including the wartime suspension of habeas corpus along with the summary jailing of political opponents, the institution of the military draft, the clear if understated call for a servile insurrection with the Emancipation Proclamation (issued when many able-bodied Southern men were in uniform and away from their homes), the transformation of the United States from a voluntary union of states into an ironclad union of de facto provinces, the subsuming of the Tenth Amendment to the Constitution, and, through the sentiments expressed in the Gettysburg Address, the elevation of equality as the highest defining principle of American political culture, to name a few. Nevertheless, at one meeting of Southern conservatives, Kirk, pressed repeatedly to denounce Lincoln, declared, "He was a great man."

Ironically, this one statement forms Kirk's single-most intriguing point of agreement with a group of historians who otherwise stand opposed to Kirk on these two issues. These historians—notably Harry V. Jaffa, Walter Berns, and Martin Diamond—are the disciples of Leo Strauss, a man with whom Kirk sometimes disagreed but whom he respected. (Kirk founded the periodical *Modern Age* after becoming incensed at what he deemed an unfair review of one of Strauss's books in *Partisan Review;* what was needed, Kirk reasoned, was a new review, one less partisan and more intelligent. Thus *Modern Age*.) The Straussians, as they are called, tend to believe that the formative document of the American tradition is the Declaration, and that the equality clause is paramount. Given this, it follows that a strong nationalist government, such as Lincoln propounded and made real by military might, is required to uphold this vision of the principle of the "natural"—divinely endowed, by Jefferson's wording—equality of political right for all. As George H. Nash described it, "Straussian or classical political philosophy . . . was logically congenial with energetic government designed to improve the polis, inculcate virtue, and help man attain his 'natural' end. The nationalistic ideas of Union and of a powerful government determined to implement a 'proposition' ["that all men are created equal"] fitted in very well with Straussianism. For in that conception of politics the libertarian distinction between state and society, between individual and polis (Union), broke down."[29] The upholding of that "distinction" was crucial to the thought of Kirk, Richard Weaver, Frank Meyer, and other conservatives given more to traditional rights, recognition and acceptance of natural inequality among men in terms of all but matters of justice before magistrates and before God, regionalism and states rights, and the vision of America as a loose confederation of states such as existed before 1865.

From evidence recalled from personal experience, this latter grouping of conservatives would hold that it is a characteristic of the Straussians to argue in terms of personalities, to move obliquely from planted axiom to planted axiom, and to use historical evidence selectively (to their advantage). For his part, for years Kirk played the role of Rick Blaine, from *Casablanca*, to the Straussians' version of Peter Lorre's Ugarte: "You despise me, don't you?" accused Ugarte in the 1942 film, to which Rick replied, "If I gave you any thought, I suppose I would." Kirk chose not to become embroiled in debates with the Straussians, telling the few who asked him about it that he believed he had too many other, more important tasks and responsibilities at hand to be caught up in what the vast majority of Americans in general and conservatives in particular would consider a tempest in a teacup.

One of Kirk's more outspoken opponents among the conservative ranks was Jaffa, a historian grounded firmly within the Straussian tradition. In his essay "On the Education of the Guardians of Freedom," published in *Modern Age* in 1986, Jaffa undertook the "education" of Russell Kirk, citing a passage from the latter's introduction to a 1983 edition of Albert Jay Nock's *Mr. Jefferson* and then spending the remainder of his essay attempting to set Kirk straight. "What are we to think," Jaffa asked, "when we read, by a leading publicist of American conservatism, a brusque dismissal of the Declaration of Independence and all it stands for?" The first order of business, here, is to deflate the reputation of Kirk: By Jaffa's lights, he is no longer the founder of modern postwar conservatism, the author of the esteemed *Conservative Mind*; rather, he is merely "a leading publicist," an advertising man of sorts. The quotation from Kirk's introduction to *Mr. Jefferson* runs as follows:

Nock's little book has very little to say about the Declaration of Independence. That is as it should be, for the Declaration really is not conspicuously American in its ideas or its phrases, and not even characteristically Jeffersonian. As Carl Becker sufficiently explains, the Declaration was meant to persuade the court of France and *philosophes* of Paris, that the Americans were sufficiently un-English to deserve military assistance. Jefferson's Declaration is a successful instrument of diplomacy; it is not a work of political philosophy or an instrument of government, and Jefferson himself said little about it after 1776.

To this, Jaffa responded, "I do not think that there is another example, in the entire history of politics or of writing about politics, of more misinformation crammed into fewer words. That Kirk has studiously ignored everything that I have written on the Declaration over the past thirty years is certainly pardonable. He has distinguished company. But that he has ignored Abraham Lincoln—not to mention Calvin Coolidge—cannot easily be forgiven."[30]

To say the least, this is quite a statement by Jaffa and quite an accomplishment on Kirk's part, this having packed more misinformation into a short paragraph than can be found "in the entire history of politics or of writing about politics." That said, it might be offered that Jaffa himself has surely not ignored everything written since 1945 by and about a certain political regime in Central Europe built entirely upon misinformation and lies; surely his claim here is an overstatement not otherwise comprehensible. And for Kirk to ignore "Silent Cal" Coolidge! What was he thinking—and can he ever "be forgiven"?

In truth, Jaffa scores a point by catching Kirk out on his statement that Jefferson himself said little about the Declaration after 1776. As the Straussian demonstrates in his essay, Jefferson was sufficiently proud of the Declaration to mention it many times during the fifty years immediately after its composition, going so far as to state that he wished to be remembered to posterity as the father of the Declaration. However—and here Kirk gets his own back—by his own admission, Jefferson intended no radical interpretation of human equality, a concept that would have gone against the grain of his countrymen's habit of mind in 1776; "Men were not born equal physically or mentally, nor were they born with equal social opportunities. But they were born with an equal right to life and liberty and to the pursuit of happiness," commented historian Alf J. Mapp Jr. on the Declaration's most controversial point.[31] For two and a half centuries, since 1619, the people of Virginia had enjoyed their own representative government wielding legislative power, working under the terms of a charter secured by Sir Edwin Sandys, a man described in history as "the father of self government in America," he having introduced to England's first North American colony the concept that just governments derive their powers from the consent of the governed. Here Jaffa and Kirk find themselves in philosophically debatable ground, for on one hand, the Founders were harking to a longstanding tradition of self-government that antedated its most articulate spokesman, John Locke, he of the abstract "social contract" theory of government.

Was America, then, founded upon a tradition or upon an abstraction? In its language, the Declaration certainly had its roots in John Locke, who derived his own theory of just government from Richard Hooker, neither man "conspicuously American," the one being the father of American liberalism, the other a champion of orthodoxy. By his own reading in history, and upon the authority of other historians—such as M. E. Bradford and Carl Becker—Kirk considered the Declaration to possess elements of tradition but much abstraction, believing that government built upon theory rather than experience and prescriptive truths would grow into a despotism—which, thanks to the Constitution, America certainly did not achieve during its formative years, between the end of the War for Independence and the War between the States. As to the question of whether the Declaration was intended as a public relations instrument of a sort to entice France into an alliance, this is subject to much debate. The Continental Congress of 1776 discussed the possibility of an alliance with the French during their deliberations but had as much reason to fear an alliance between their own, predominantly Protestant, union of states and Roman Catholic France as it did to desire one. But as the saying goes, desperate times require desperate measures; and with Lord Howe's army uncomfortably within striking distance of Philadelphia during the summer of 1776, and with each delegate to Congress knowing that his life was forfeit by participating in an act King George would declare treasonous, they had much reason to seek an alliance. The strategy seems to have been to make *independence* an established fact first, before approaching France (or possibly Spain) in search of an alliance; and in the end, the Declaration seems to have been published primarily for domestic distribution, though a long-delayed copy was delivered to the government in Paris within a few months. Whatever the intent of Congress may have been aside from formally stating American independence from Britain, an issue that is subject to ongoing scholarly inquiry, alliance with the French did become a reality, though not at first in terms of the troop strength and materiel the long-suffering Continental Army needed. As a historian, Kirk saw no reason to change his position on this issue of potential alliance, knowing he was in company with other reputable historians, particularly his friend M. E. Bradford, by viewing the Declaration as a document of separation and a soft-pedaled plea to a potential ally, not as an instrument of governance.

And Kirk indeed ignored Lincoln's gloss on the Declaration, because he disagreed with Lincoln's interpretation of that document, believing that the sixteenth president wrenched the "equality clause" out of context and, for the sake of future generations, read into the Declaration a meaning the Continental Congress never intended, making it a blueprint for equality of outcome and social leveling. Kirk deeply admired Lincoln and considered him, on somewhat shaky grounds (I believe), a conservative, despite his expansion of federal powers and effective destruction of the old America known and beloved by Hawthorne, Henry Adams, and others among Kirk's heroes of conservative thought. Contrary to Jaffa's claim, Kirk had read Lincoln; he had simply not swallowed Lincoln whole, remembering that an examination of Lincoln's writings reveals a man who could be found on both sides of many issues, depending upon his audience—including the issues of secession and whether the conflagration of 1861–65 was a war for national union or for emancipation.

ON SENATOR TAFT AND *THE AMERICAN CAUSE*

Many conservatives have argued that, since the era of Lincoln, America's federal government has become a veritable leviathan in regard to issues of regulation and control of many aspects of life, intruding ever more surely into the lives and decision making of ordinary citizens. An heir of America's first well-known Republican, though one who never became president, was Ohio's Robert A. Taft, son of President William Howard Taft. Blunt-spoken and hard-working, he was the antithesis of the caricatured Republican of the mid-twentieth century: snobbish, bigoted, wealthy, a tool of business. No tool of anyone, Taft was something of a throwback to old Randolph of Roanoke, though without the Virginian's eccentricities. He believed that the role of the federal government was not to make lives comfortable, but to be "a keeper of the peace, a referee of controversies, and an adjuster of abuses; not as a regulator of the people, or their business and personal activities." Where the North Star of Randolph's political convictions was the issue of constitutionality, Taft's political compass insisted upon the question of whether a proposed act would serve to enhance or retard the liberty of the American people. Further, as historian Lee Edwards has stated, Taft

supported "equality of opportunity," whereby all men and women could rise from obscurity. Government, he said, must provide a floor through which no one should be permitted to fall. "The philosophy," wrote Taft biographer Robert Patterson, "was closer to the enlightened noblesse oblige of conservatives like Disraeli and Burke than . . . the probusiness materialism of his Republican admirers."[32]

To many conservatives, Taft was their shining hope for recapturing the White House from the New Dealers and Fair Dealers during the 1940s and early 1950s; to their chagrin, Taft was never the Republican nominee, losing out to Thomas Dewey and Dwight Eisenhower. When he died in 1953, conservatives were forced to acknowledge that their wilderness years were far from over, that though an avuncular Republican was in the White House for most of the 1950s, overseeing a caretaker government, conservative political hopes would have to wait. In the meantime, there were new conservative books to read, including one that appeared shortly before Taft's death, *The Conservative Mind*.

The author of that book greatly admired Taft. In 1967 Russell Kirk and James McClellan wrote and published *The Political Principles of Robert A. Taft*, a work that became perhaps most shakily received of all Kirk's books. In a work that is not so much a biography as a thematic examination of Taft's philosophy, the authors described a man guided in his political thinking by a commitment to liberty under law, an aversion to statism, a belief in a humane economy, and the elevation of prudence as the highest virtue. Kirk and McClellan "traverse the major episodes of Taft's career, demonstrating throughout the Senator's careful method of building up a practical political position in keeping with first principles.... In each case, Taft's major qualities emerge with clarity and force: high intelligence, hard work, fidelity to conviction," wrote M. Stanton Evans, in *National Review*.[33] "In praising Taft, Mr. McClellan and Mr. Kirk ignore important incidents," cautioned reviewer George Schoyer, in *The Library Journal*. Nevertheless, "on the whole, this is a good exposition of the views of a usually constructive Conservative leader."[34] Not so, wrote the anonymous reviewer for *The Times Literary Supplement*, calling the book "a pious panegyric that so tough-minded a man as Senator Taft could be expected to like," for Taft was an interventionist in domestic affairs "in a way that should have scandalized Professor Kirk and Mr. McClellan (or at any rate should have distressed a Goldwater supporter like Professor Kirk)." The critic concluded, "No series of quotation from Burke will make of Taft a serious conservative thinker."[35]

Kirk, who wrote panegyrics to nobody, especially to men he recognized as "tough-minded," brushed off the *TLS*'s criticisms and turned his mind to other matters. While he had not known Taft personally, he had followed the Ohioan's political career carefully during the late 1940s and early '50s, coming to recognize Taft's Burkean tendency of possessing the propensity to reform married to the inclination to look to tradition, reconciling what is most important in old customs and ancestral wisdom with the change society must undergo for the sake of growth and cultural life. Shortly before Taft's death, he was asked if he had read *The Conservative Mind*, to which he shook his head no and said, "You remind me of Thurber's *Let Your Mind Alone*. There are some questions that I have not thought very much about, but I'm a politician, not a philosopher."

Wisdom and tough-mindedness were very much an issue of national discussion at the time of Taft's death. For one thing, the recently ended Korean War had revealed that many American soldiers captured by the North Koreans and Chinese had proven woefully ignorant of American history and the nature of America's economy, religious institutions, relations with other world powers, and domestic policies; thus, under the skillful and brutal ministrations of their communist captors, they proved easy subjects of brainwashing, denouncing their country and its Korean mission in propaganda broadcasts and written statements.

To Kirk, this was highly disturbing, though not surprising. As a young instructor in the history of civilization at Michigan State after World War II, he had witnessed firsthand the declining standards of knowledge and scholarship demonstrated by the thousands of men and women who flooded the nation's institutions of higher learning under the provisions of the G.I. Bill. If a significant number of America's best and brightest saw historical knowledge as a frill to be disregarded if possible and gotten through if necessary, how much more so would American men fresh out of high school respond to the sly propaganda of those who despise America and all it stands for?

In response to the dismal performance of American prisoners of war at the hands of the communists, Kirk, in 1958, wrote *The American Cause,* a deceptively short work in which are condensed many truths about American political philosophy, the role of religion in American life, the proper relationship between the individual and the federal government, and many other topics. It is one of the least read but most valuable of Kirk's works. Reviewers were mixed in their assessments of the work, with one writer making the bizarre statement that, in it, Kirk seeks to rally Americans to "a cause in which he does not altogether believe."[36] A more balanced appraisal was offered by James J. Flynn, who wrote, "Mr. Kirk has, with a certain amount of success, presented a credo for all Americans to live by. . . . Whether the general reader—civilian and military—will profit from it is in the laps of the gods."[37]

Why learn history? Not simply to become steeled against the mind control of totalists. Kirk saw history as serving a noble purpose: to help the attentive reader grow in wisdom by learning that the experience of man upon earth is storied and built from long experience, learning as well the place and significance of humanity within time and in eternity. "The truth is this," wrote Robert E. Lee, near the end of his life: "The march of Providence is so slow and our desires so impatient: the work of progress is so immense and our means of aiding it so feeble; the life of humanity is so long, and that of the individual so brief, that we often see only the ebb of the advancing wave and are thus discouraged. It is history that teaches us to hope."[38]

NOTES

1. *Redeeming the Time*, p. 102.
2. Hart, "Christopher Dawson and the History We Are Not Told," *Modern Age* 39, Summer, 1997, 211.
3. Russello, "Time and the Timeless: The Historical Consciousness of Russell Kirk," *Modern Age*, summer, 1999, original manuscript. In this well-conceived essay, published shortly before the appearance of this book, Russello seeks to demonstrate the influence of not only Dawson, but also Eric Voegelin and John Lukacs upon Kirk's historiography.
4. Niemeyer, "In Praise of Tradition," *Modern Age* 36, Spring, 1994, 233.
5. *John Randolph of Roanoke: A Study in American Politics*, 4th ed., pp. 544, 567.
6. Mapp, *Thomas Jefferson: A Strange Case of Mistaken Identity*, p. 410.
7. Mapp, *Thomas Jefferson*, pp. 410–11. Mapp notes that of the remaining two principles, one, "An abhorrence of communism," antedates Jefferson, though he would undoubtedly have considered Marxism a form of tyranny over the minds of men; and the other, "A conviction that social equality is not, in and of itself, a desirable end," is an issue about which Jefferson's beliefs "probably must remain unknown." The symposium Mapp cites is described in Leonard Lief's *The New Conservatives* (Indianapolis and New York, 1967).
8. *John Randolph*, p. 43.
9. Stanlis, "Russell Kirk: Memoir of a Friendship," in Person, ed., *The Unbought Grace of Life: Essays in Honor of Russell Kirk*, p. 32.
10. *John Randolph*, p. 44.
11. Shackelford, review of *Randolph of Roanoke*, in *The Virginia Magazine of History and Biography* 60, January, 1952, 189.
12. Harrigan, "Great Conservative," *The Freeman* n.s. 2, May 5,1952, 512.
13. Stanlis, in Person, ed., *op. cit.*, p. 31.
14. Hart, "The Relevance of Burke," *National Review* 19, September 19, 1967, 1022.
15. Panichas, "The Inspired Wisdom of Burke," *Modern Age* 40, spring, 1998, 216.
16. Scruton, foreword to Kirk, *Edmund Burke: A Genius Reconsidered*, p. ix. In light of Scruton's brief but trenchant commentary, the words of Conor Cruise O'Brien, author of *The Great Melody: A Thematic Biography and Commented Anthology of Edmund Burke*, are puzzling, O'Brien writing, on page lxi of that volume of a revival of interest in Burke during the 1950s and '60s that was connected with "American politics and policies." O'Brien adds: "Some American scholars notably Peter J. Stanlis and Russell Kirk, drew upon Burke for arguments in the context of the Cold War, the Vietnam War, and the idea of America's imperial responsibilities. This revival produced some valuable detailed work, but as a whole the Burke of this revival was seriously distorted by its polemical and propagandist purposes, inflating the aspects of his career that suited those purposes, and deflating those that did not suit." Aside from scattered references to Burke in Kirk's only arguably

"Cold War" book, *The American Cause,* there exists nothing in the written record to support O'Brien's claim here as it relates to Kirk. If anything, Kirk was criticized periodically by some fellow conservatives for being too *non*-political in his conservative beliefs.

17. Frohnen, *Virtue and The Promise of Conservatism: The Legacy of Burke and Tocqueville,* p. 214. The other quotations from Frohnen's book are taken from pages 9, 11, and 41.

18. Wilhelmsen, "To Recover a Concept and a Tradition," *The Commonweal* 58, June 19, 1953, 278.

19. "Men of Letters as Statists: Locke, Montesquieu, Hume, Burke," in Person, ed., *Literature Criticism from 1400 to 1800,* p. xiii.

20. "Men of Letters as Statists," p. xviii.

21. McDonald, "Russell Kirk: The American Cicero," in Person, ed., *Unbought Grace of Life,* p. 17.

22. Weaver, "Battle for the Mind," *Chicago Sunday Tribune Magazine of Books,* October 24, 1954, Part 4, 3.

23. Kirk to Voegelin, June 20, 1968.

24. Bradford, "A Proper Patrimony: Russell Kirk and America's Moral Genealogy," in Person, ed., *Unbought Grace of Life,* pp. 72, 74.

25. Bradbury to Sherwood Sugden, September 16, 1974.

26. Speaight, "What Holds America Together?" *The University Bookman* 15, Autumn, 1974, 5.

27. Muggeridge, review of *The Roots of American Order,* in *Esquire* 82, no. 2, February, 1975, 20.

28. Scruton, in Kirk, *Edmund Burke: A Genius Reconsidered,* p. viii.

29. Nash, *The Conservative Intellectual Movement in America since 1945,* 2d ed., p. 209.

30. Jaffa, "On the Education of the Guardians of Freedom," *Modern Age* 30, no. 2, Spring, 1986, 136.

31. Mapp, *The Virginia Experiment: The Old Dominion's Role in the Making of America, 1607–1781,* 2d ed., p. 434.

32. Edwards, *The Conservative Revolution: The Movement That Remade America,* p. 9.

33. Evans, "The Triumph of Taft," *National Review* 20, April 8, 1967, 351.

34. Schoyer, review of *The Political Principles of Robert A. Taft,* in *Library Journal* 92, October 15, 1967, 3648.

35. Review of *The Political Principles of Robert A. Taft,* in *The Times Literary Supplement,* February 22, 1968, 176.

36. David Spitz, "Confusion of Principles," *The Nation* 186, April 12, 1958, 328.

37. Flynn, review of *The American Cause,* in *Annals of the American Academy of Political and Social Science* 316, March, 1958, 143.

38. Lee, quoted in Mapp, *Frock Coats and Epaulets: Psychological Portraits of Confederate Military and Political Leaders,* p. 222.

4

For Virtue and Wisdom:
Kirk on Education

> We make men without chests and expect of them virtue and en-
> terprise. We laugh at honour and are shocked to find traitors in
> our midst. We castrate and bid the geldings be fruitful.
> —from *The Abolition of Man*, by C. S. Lewis

Of the many hundreds of essays, articles, reviews, and books Kirk wrote
during his long career, he wrote most often about the state of American education. At the request of his friend William F. Buckley Jr., he wrote a twice-
monthly column on educational concerns, "From the Academy," for the
magazine Buckley founded and edited, *National Review*, carrying out this
responsibility for twenty-five years; and these essays form only a portion of
his total contribution to the ongoing debate. Kirk lectured widely on the
subject and published essays in many forums outside *National Review*, writing also two books that caused a stir upon their appearance a quarter century apart, *Academic Freedom* and *Decadence and Renewal in the Higher Learning*. (As Peter J. Stanlis has claimed, Kirk's best short statement of his
position on American education is his introduction to a 1986 edition of Irving Babbitt's *Literature and the American College*, part of Transaction's *Library
of Conservative Thought*, for which Kirk served as general editor until his
death.) In addition, he lent support to the work of his wife, Annette, when
she served as a member of the National Commission on Excellence in

Education, and whose 1983 report, *A Nation at Risk,* sounded the call for an educational reawakening.

Kirk's interest in what he viewed as the decline in American education, especially at the college and university level, had its roots in the years immediately following World War II. As he records in his memoir, *The Sword of Imagination,* American colleges and universities were flooded with returning servicemen who had come to take advantage of the G.I. Bill. When the great numbers of ex-servicemen graduated, around 1950, the institutions of higher learning employed a number of questionable measures to maintain the high numbers of faculty and administrators hired during the immediate postwar years. While serving as an instructor at Michigan State College (later Michigan State University) in East Lansing, Kirk was struck by the low level of basic knowledge and ambition he encountered among the students he taught. These students, part of an innovative program at State called "University College"—instituted by President John Hannah, designed to process through as many students as possible, and loathed by the faculty—were for the most part profoundly ignorant in regard to historical knowledge and blithely unconcerned about it, viewing their time at State and their hoped-for diploma "as a means to material ends: the way to practical success, social advancement and general jollity."[1]

Worse, he perceived that the administrators he encountered at State, notably President Hannah, viewed the purpose of education in exactly the same light, seeking to transform Michigan State from a small, respectable land-grant college into The Home of the Spartans: an educational behemoth with more students than the nearby University of Michigan, better athletic teams than the hated Wolverines, and classes purposely geared down and graded to ensure that the greatest possible number of students achieved high exam scores with the least demanding amount of work. Just think, Kirk was told on one occasion, how impressive State would look to outsiders beholding the high number of students on the dean's list—a bastion of academic giants! Kirk would have none of this, and complained about State's lowering of standards to any administrator who would listen, hoping that the school's leaders would see, at the very least, that there was something degrading about a college offering courses (and in some cases, degrees) in such fields of expertise as fly casting, "poultry science," golf, and packaging (as in wooden crates and cardboard boxes). With the exception of fly casting and golf, these goals and skills, valuable though they are, "may be achieved through *training* (as distinguished from *education*), through personal endeavor of a kind not scholastic, and through a state of mind like that of Democritus, the laughing philosopher. But these goals are not primary concerns of real colleges and universities," he wrote, years later.[2]

His concerns were pooh-poohed by everyone of significant influence at what he came to call "Behemoth University," and in 1953, not long after *The Conservative Mind* was published, Kirk left Michigan State for good and shifted his large personal library and few belongings to his family's ancestral home in Mecosta, a few hours journey northwest of Lansing. There he would be far from the bustle and noise of urban life, living just outside a tiny village where the cost of living was low—so low, in fact, that Kirk told Henry Regnery that he figured he could survive there fairly comfortably on five hundred dollars per annum—and there was plenty of time to read and reflect and ample opportunity to write. His decision to depart was cemented after he learned that at the outset of the 1953 fall term, a few months after his resignation, Hannah had taken it upon himself to denounce Kirk by name to an incoming class of freshmen, over the college's loudspeaker system. Outraged, Kirk gave Hannah his come-uppance that same year, publishing an article on American higher education in the *Collier's Encyclopedia 1953 Yearbook* that discoursed upon his former college's academic shortcomings and took Hannah to task in telling detail. Almost twenty-five years after leaving State, even after serving as distinguished visiting professor at numerous colleges and universities throughout the United States and Europe, the memories of his brisk treatment under Hannah's administration still rankled. In a letter to this writer, Kirk confided that his "early association with Michigan State was the least, and most distasteful," of his various academic experiences, and that he preferred it not be mentioned in a short vita to be included in a publication I edited at the time.[3] Kirk had friends aplenty within and without Michigan State, and he retained these friendships for the rest of his life, but he never ceased to consider State "a waist-high university, more enchanted with athletics than academics."[4]

A few years before he died, Kirk was asked by *The Detroit News* columnist Chuck Moss if he still considered Michigan State "waist high," to which he replied with a chuckle, "Yes, but a great many places have joined it . . . by trying to be all things to all men. There has been a vast lowering of standards which few have resisted."[5] Further, as Kirk noted, it is entirely possible for students to attend university for four years, attain a bachelor's degree, and not once attend a lecture by a senior scholar, lectures and discussions being handled by young graduate assistants. Kirk cited with approval remarks by his friend Peter Stanlis, who wrote:

> For the better undergraduates, these mass-production universities are a grave threat to meaningful individual freedom and to genuine intellectual development. The same applies to the better faculty members who are interested in teaching. Many of the best faculty yield to the pressure of the administration

policy of publish or perish. Like Dr. Faustus, they sell their academic souls for the temporal power of success and prestige for research. While in perpetual pursuit of scholarship, the best professors are removed from the most capable students, who otherwise could benefit from their superior knowledge and ability.[6]

"Then what do the professors profess?" Kirk asked in 1968, immediately answering his own question in terms as fitting at century's end as they were when written. "Well, they engage in 'research'—much of it trifling—and they publish. Much of what they publish is unreadable and not worth reading, but publication insures advancement. And it is so unpleasant to spend one's time instructing the rising generation, particularly when that generation is wretchedly prepared for college studies by most high schools, and when that generation is bored with the life of the mind."[7]

Kirk's concern, then, extended not only to higher education, but to secondary—and even elementary—schooling as well, which he perceived as fields increasingly inundated with unimaginative teaching designed less to inculcate knowledge and assure mastery of subject matter before advancement than to promote social adjustment above nearly all other considerations, the fruit of educational theorist John Dewey's emphasis. Opposing this, Kirk advocated adjustment to the norms and values observed by the small voluntary community of family, church, lodge, guild, and association, the engine of the contract of eternal society; with teaching devoted to skill development across disciplines, with special emphasis placed upon the reading and comprehension of history and imaginative literature, and character development, in a partnership between parents and teachers, in the primary and secondary levels. To be more specific, Peter J. Stanlis has written that Kirk

believed that the greatest single objective of genuine education was the highest possible inner development of students—their intellectual, moral, aesthetic, and social nature—and that schools, like the other basic institutions of civil society, were merely the necessary instrumental means to that ideal end. He regarded the liberal arts and humanities as the soundest form of education to fulfill that objective. Therefore, in essence he held to a modern practical adaptation of the Medieval *quadrivium* and *trivium*—the seven liberal arts of grammar, logic, rhetoric, arithmetic, music, geometry, and astronomy, plus the humanities—history, *belles lettres,* philosophy, politics, the ancient classics, the fine arts, languages, ethics, and science. He found in John Cardinal Newman's *The Idea of a University* (1852) the ideal modern expression of his own philosophy of education, and in Irving Babbitt's humanism its practical application in the twentieth century.[8]

Not surprisingly, given this, Kirk considered mere conformity to the herd, at the lower levels and in higher education, a grave error: "If the time is out of joint, conformity to vulgar errors is sin and shame," he wrote.[9]

This said, Kirk was more than a simple "aginner," snarling fashionably at modern educational follies. He documented and recounted numerous incidences of the excesses and foolishness promoted by administrative ideologues, warning that this confluence of benign indirection would in time bring about in America just what haunted Thomas Jefferson's darkest dreams. "If a nation expects to be ignorant and free, in a state of civilization, it expects what never has been and never will be," wrote the Virginian over two hundred years before Kirk began championing educational excellence. "I do not know where the last ditch in our educational war may be at the moment; but point it out to me on the trench-map and I will go to it," wrote C. S. Lewis, in his essay "The Idea of an 'English School.'" Sgt. Kirk followed Lewis into the trenches in the educational war and spent the better part of his career defending traditional American schooling against the inroads of ideologues and ignoramuses.

A BRIEF FOR ACADEMIC FREEDOM

"The subject of academic freedom has been so overdone in recent years that discussion itself has often become academic. Indeed, this freedom has been imperfectly apprehended by even the scholar, as well as the layman, and both have contributed to its adulteration," wrote George A. Panichas— not in 1999, as one might well suppose, but in 1955, upon the appearance of Kirk's study *Academic Freedom*.[10] Much has been said and written, now as then, about academic freedom. The questions that derive from this subject remain constant: Freedom to do what? And: Freedom from what?

At the outset of *Academic Freedom*, a work that served as his opening broadside in the "educational war" spoken of by Lewis, Kirk addressed those questions systematically, as well as the issues that naturally devolve from the very question of academic freedom. In doing so, he saw the need to clarify terms and make distinctions, ruffling feathers among educational progressives as well as conservative allies. Kirk defined academic freedom as "security against hazards to the pursuit of truth by those persons whose lives are dedicated to conserving the intellectual heritage of truth of the ages and to extending the realm of knowledge. It is the right or group of rights intended to make it possible for certain persons (always very few in number, in any society, when compared with the bulk of the population) to teach truthfully and to employ their reason to the full extent of their intellectual powers."[11] Commenting upon this, sociologist Robert A. Nisbet wrote, "This is an excellent definition, and what Mr. Kirk succeeds in doing is not merely to demonstrate the relevance, indeed, indispensability, of this freedom to Western culture, but to make plain also the source of the freedom and its institutional and intellectual contexts." By Kirk's definition, academic freedom belongs to those educators ("always very few in number"—this a lament, not a qualifying boast) whose lives are dedicated to extending the field of knowledge. As Kirk makes plain, and as Nisbet summarized, academic freedom is "not to be regarded as an easy refuge for the crass-minded, for the trivializer, for the crusader or fanatic, or for any individual whose prime commitment is sectarian or commercial," for "we cannot hope to maintain the tradition of academic freedom if we insist upon using it as a shield for every vocational fad, every popular fancy, or for every personal crusade."[12]

Kirk viewed the purpose of education as classical, with special acknowledgment to the educational theories of Irving Babbitt: to inculcate wisdom and virtue, with the understanding that learning is a lifelong process, not something from which to be liberated on commencement day. At one time, even the unschooled (or many of them) felt a reverence for learning, believing it the path to wisdom—and not worldly wisdom alone. Learning, they believed, was the means to orientation. By way of definition, Kirk wrote, "To orient, or orientate, is to settle, to find bearings; to locate one's self in one's environment with reference to time, place, and people; to determine one's true position."[13]

To gain one's bearings in the world is brought about through humane learning: the reading and rumination upon books, those books written by authors who possess the moral imagination. The reason why Johnny can't tell right from wrong, much less identify which century the Civil War was fought and between whom, is explained by the decline in humane learning and the reading of imaginative literature in a society gone slack-jawed by television and other "cool" media (to use Marshall McLuhan's terminology), which reduce many Americans into passive receptors of sensation, and subject to every fad, foible, and propaganda ploy of the day.

In *Why Johnny Can't Tell Right from Wrong* (1992), a work with which Kirk firmly agreed and saw reviewed in *The University Bookman*, William Kilpatrick traced the gradual replacement of traditional, character education in America's schools with the "decision-making" model, in which students participate in free-form classroom discussions wherein all viewpoints are to be considered equally valid and in which the only way a student can err is by showing intolerance to the expected mindset of moral universalism. In the decision-making environment, the student who in any sense holds by the permanent things is made out as a bigot, a Bible-thumper, an eccentric, or a crank. Kilpatrick notes that the decision-making method is modeled on therapy sessions designed for recovering drug addicts, and that it is designed to create self-esteem rather than self-respect. With its "Who are you to judge?" overriding premise, it is an environment in which the devil-may-care partygoer is in his element, and where the student possessing principles is entirely on the defensive. In such an atmosphere, the only upward moral gradation inevitably takes the form of a variation upon Mammy Yokum's dictum: "Good is better than evil 'cause it's nicer"—assuming that such terms as "good" and "evil" aren't hooted out of the dialogue. Of such an educational model, Kirk was fond of quoting the Fool in *King Lear:* "A mad world, my masters."

Kirk's concern about the state of American education enfolded the leveling down of academic expectations and the abdication of character development as part of everyday school life. According to George Panichas, in his review of *Academic Freedom,* Kirk "believes that perhaps the greatest crisis affecting the entire educational system in the country, and one that gnaws at the roots of academic freedom, is the great leveling process of the doctrinaire educationists, who seek to water down standards and make education palatable to the masses. Mr. Kirk, of course, is not preaching or advocating an aristocratic theory of education, under which only those with ability are educated as potential leaders. Rather, he is decrying the fact that education without the proper mental disciplining is no education at all, and at most one in which a 'servile intellect,' happy and adjusted in mediocrity, is the end result."[14] Happy and adjusted was indeed the end result Kirk witnessed and detested at Behemoth University in its many manifestations throughout America: a combination of educational utilitarianism, owing much to the influence of Bacon and Jeremy Bentham, and sentimental humanitarianism, with its hallmark blaming of all society's ills on systems and sociopolitical structures rather than the choices made by individuals, all owing much to Jean-Jacques Rousseau.

Kirk saw much value in prudent dialectic for learning, once writing, "Not all learning comes from books: good conversation, judicious experience of the world, and contemplation count for as much or more; a learning purely bookish is a frail reed. Yet if a people cast aside the Law and the Book, speedily they find themselves condemned to what Edmund Burke called 'the antagonist world' of madness, despair, and unavailing sorrow. We Americans have been sinking into the perilous condition of knowing the price of everything and the value of nothing. The first step toward redemption is to confess that we have been stumbling about complacently in a pit of ignorance. To acquire the cardinal virtue of prudence, nearly all of us need a cordial acquaintance with books."[15]

"I am a bookman," wrote James Russell Lowell long ago, and Kirk could say the same of himself. To him, the development of character, the inculcation of wisdom and virtue in the student, sprang in large part from the reading of intelligent books, especially works of imagination. As the chapter on Kirk's literary criticism demonstrated clearly, his taste in literature steered far clear of puerile works of didacticism that are offered earnestly by some parents to their children as "good, clean literature" and just as avidly avoided by those same children. Kirk particularly loathed certain books of this sort designed for young readers, such as the boring and interminable "adventures" of Dick and Jane, and sterile books about upright student athletes and prim student nurses. He joined with Dr. Johnson in advocating literature that pleases and instructs, advocating the reading of Robert Louis Stevenson, Jacquetta Hawkes, Rudyard Kipling, William Morris, C. S. Lewis, G. K. Chesterton, James Boswell's *Life of Johnson*, Simone Weil, Fenimore Cooper, and a host of others.

In *Academic Freedom*, Kirk examined and, for the most part, found wanting, the beliefs of two schools of thought on the subject: those on the political right, whom he named the "indoctrinators," whose number included his soon-to-be friend and ally William F. Buckley Jr.; and those of the left, which he dubbed "the social reconstructionists," who were doctrinaire liberals and included Henry Steele Commager and Robert Hutchins, among others. In painstaking detail, he sought to demonstrate "that the partisans of the first camp would undo academic freedom, in its political aspect, by excessive regulation," and "that the partisans of the second camp would leave academic freedom naked unto its enemies, in its political aspect, by tolerating license."[16]

The critical response to *Academic Freedom* was mixed—and, in some cases, puzzlingly inconsistent. On one hand, historian Walter P. Metzger, writing in the *Political Science Quarterly*, dismissed the book's "factual errors and loose ratiocinations" but nevertheless declared that "this book should be widely read."[17] On the other hand, Henry M. Wriston, a historian and former president of Brown University, found not "factual errors and loose ratiocinations," but great precision instead: "When dissecting an opponent, even some he 'admires,' the author uses a scalpel. He points out words used loosely, he seizes upon flaws in logic with avidity—in criticism he is a precisionist." Nonetheless, Wriston deemed *Academic Freedom* a deeply flawed and untrustworthy guide to its subject, because Kirk, despite being a "precisionist," was "carried away by passion into dogmatic assertions and examples that do not fairly illustrate."[18]

Undoubtedly one of the most interesting reviews was that published by Buckley, in *The Freeman*. Having been firmly, but politely, criticized for his position on academic freedom as expressed in *God and Man at Yale*, wherein Buckley stated the case for firm control of hiring and curriculum at the college level by the alumni, Buckley pulled his own punches in writing a negative review of *Academic Freedom*, a reflection of his deep respect for Kirk. (At about the time he wrote this review, Buckley visited Kirk in Mecosta to ask the older man if he would write regularly for a new conservative magazine he hoped to launch soon, called *National Review*. Kirk agreed to do so, with little convincing.) In *Academic Freedom*, Kirk had seized upon Buckley's belief that university faculty ought to promulgate two doctrines: faith in Christianity, and individualism. Of this Kirk wrote, "I personally agree that the first of these is a good thing, and I think that Mr. Buckley knows what he means by it. I do not agree that 'individualism' is a good thing, and I do not think that Mr. Buckley knows what he means by it. In truth, any professor who attempted to indoctrinate his students in both Christianity and individualism would be hopelessly inconsistent; for individualism is anti-Christian. It is possible logically to be a Christian, and possible logically to be an individualist; it is not possible to be the two simultaneously."[19] Here and in the rest of his discussion, Kirk's basic emphasis was that Buckley, though well intentioned, had not clearly thought through the ramifications of his statements should they be enacted as he desired.

In his review, Buckley found Kirk's study one that is so unfocused and deals in such generalities that "no one could conceivably refer to this book as a reasoned statement of a coherent position on academic freedom."[20] The fuzzy nature of *Academic Freedom* stems, Buckley believed, from Kirk's surprisingly imprecise use of language, especially in the case of such terms as "Truth" and "the Word." For example, in his book Kirk stresses repeatedly that teachers merit certain immunities and privileges in their work, for they are "bearers of the Word" and purveyors of "Truth." But, Buckley inquired, "What Word? The Word of Christ? Kirk must think so, for he says elsewhere that the beginning of Wisdom is the fear of God. In that case, where would Sidney Hook, a persistent God-baiter, get off asking for academic freedom for himself?" Such troubling questions led Buckley to declare, "The point is that the doctrine of academic freedom cannot be defended on the premise that those who defend truth are entitled to certain immunities because to do so requires the identification of truth and the social discrimination that would follow against those who believe in error."

Despite these cautionary words, Buckley and Kirk shared fairly similar beliefs in the matter of retaining teachers in light of what individual teachers believe; neither believe that the hiring and retention of faculty should resemble a Rousseauesque open marriage—entirely nonjudgmental about everything except judgment—or that everyone with an ed-school degree or an all-hallowed doctorate and who can hold the attention of students is fit to teach. To be blunt, both Buckley and Kirk could well imagine instances in which "social discrimination" would be not only the natural response to untruthful teaching, but practically the required response. One need not cite extreme cases, such as professors in German universities during the 1930s proclaiming the necessity of "weeding" the human race of "lesser breeds," or (a more specific and recent instance) the professor occupying a tenured chair at Princeton's Center for Human Values who professes the belief that parents of children born with birth defects should be allowed to lawfully kill those children anytime between birth and their twenty-eighth day of life—all for the sake of their happiness (that of the parents, not the children).[21] There are other examples wherein the need for such differentiation might well apply: the divinity school professor who believes in no divinity, the journalism teacher who advises her students to cover religious news by first pigeonholing the subject's politics and, from that point, basically making up the rest of the story from whole cloth, as the "journalist" sees fit; the math department head in an urban school system who advises his faculty that correct answers in accounting exercises and tests aren't important, but that the issuance of a large number of passing grades is; the history or social studies teacher whose emphasis is less upon accurately describing the history of one world culture than in systematically and explicitly denigrating another. Should these individuals be held accountable for the beliefs they attempt to inculcate into their students, and if so, by whom? It is not clear whether Kirk believed such individuals should be held accountable by humanistic peers and administrators and possibly cashiered or simply have their doctrines blazoned forth to the world for all to see and steer around if they so choose; but it is clear that neither he nor Buckley believed in the philosophy that holds "Let a thousand flowers bloom": let all ideas and philosophies be accorded like respect and acceptance, and let the students choose what they want to believe.

Students will choose what they want to believe without the help of philodoxers and fanatics; therefore Kirk believed, with Babbitt, that education should be humanistic, with a strong grounding in normative literature, affirming traditional beliefs while allowing for gradual changes in matters of form and emphasis. Kirk urged the reading of imaginative and historical literature, appropriate to age, at the elementary and secondary levels, and the teaching of humane letters at the college level. He did not view character development as the domain or concern of prigs and latter-day Puritans. The boredom and restlessness that result from an upbringing in which the imagination is neglected were cause for grave concern, he believed. Mincing no words on this matter, using terms many parents of young children refuse to utter, Kirk once wrote, "To the permitted brat with the permissive parents, few appetites are denied, and he grows up ignorant of the norms of human existence. Never learning in childhood that certain things exist which we ought to fear, he slides into physical maturity, bored, flabby in character, and moved by irrational impulses toward violence and defiance, the consequence of a profound disorder in personality."[22] Consequently, as medical educator David C. Stolinsky has put it, "The reason we fear to go out after dark is not that we may be set upon by bands of evangelicals and forced to read the New Testament, but that we may be set upon by gangs of feral young people who have been taught that nothing is superior to their own needs or feelings."[23]

If this is intolerant or reactionary, Kirk believed, so be it; for a body that cannot "react" to adverse stimulation is a corpse, or one of the living dead. With Buckley, he perceived that truth is discernible if not entirely knowable here below, even among nonbelievers like Babbitt, George Santayana, and Sidney Hook. In the months that followed the release of *Academic Freedom* and Buckley's review of it, Kirk agreed to contribute a bi-weekly column on American education to Buckley's *National Review*, which was then a weekly magazine. The fact that a cordial working relationship between the two men flourished for twenty-five years indicates that Buckley saw much merit to Kirk's mordant commentaries on the state of American education, more than his review of *Academic Freedom* would suggest.

ON *DECADENCE AND RENEWAL IN THE HIGHER LEARNING*

Alexis de Tocqueville wrote that Americans tend to neglect the general for the particular, to shy away from theory. "A pragmatic attitude dominated the United States before the term 'pragmatism' was coined among us," wrote Kirk. "When a people achieve great power and corresponding responsibilities, nevertheless, there occurs urgent need for reference to first principles. That time is upon us. No longer do all Americans take for a sign of health the impulse for compelling young people to 'adjust' to modern society, without reflection. If the time is out of joint, conformity to vulgar errors is sin and shame."[24]

Robert Frost once said famously that writing free verse is like playing tennis without a net. Kirk saw attending or working at the university of mid century, with few exceptions, to be akin to playing tennis without a net, equipment, court, or rules. To him, little had changed for the better in American higher education in the twenty-three years since he first began writing on the world of academe. By 1978, when *Decadence and Renewal in the Higher Learning* appeared, he had seen the nation's colleges and universities sink to levels of standardless egalitarianism, mass thinking, and pseudointellectual extravagance he had foreseen, but had hoped against, many years earlier.

In *Decadence and Renewal*, Kirk set his face against the "academic barbarism," which he perceived as having taken the traditional goals of higher education, the inculcation of wisdom and virtue, a concept that the American public, by and large, had forgotten or else never knew. This "Episodic History of American University and College since 1953" is a year-by-year detailing of a progressively downward spiral away from the classical understanding of higher education, culminating in the academy acquiescing to student terrorism on campus during the late 1960s and early 1970s. Kirk saw

something of a leveling off after that time and a few hopeful signs for renewal, but the events of America's flirtation with academic anarchy in 1968
and the years immediately afterward haunted him profoundly. "At the
source of our educational troubles, Kirk avers, is our loss of contact with our
religious and philosophical heritage," wrote M. Stanton Evans in a favorable
review. "Because we no longer know what we believe, or what we are supposed to do, we are unable to conduct the business of education in proper
fashion. If we have no sense of direction for ourselves, then we obviously
cannot convey a sense of direction to others. Hence the use of 'decadence'
in the title—to mean specifically 'the loss of an object.' "[25]

But *Decadence and Renewal* is something far more thought-provoking and
constructive than a 354-page grouse about how awful everything is in the
academic world, for in Kirk's criticism of education, as in his social criticism,
a glimmer of cheerfulness breaks in. He writes approvingly of those small
colleges he had come to admire—Hillsdale, Rockford, Hampden-Sydney,
and Aquinas, among others—at which high standards have been maintained and the struggle against leveling, utilitarianism, secularism, and collectivism has been successful. With such examples at hand, he declared that
decadence "is not inevitable, so long as a tolerable number of men and
women retain the elements of reason and the will to survive." He added:

> Has the higher education in America been a democratic triumph or an egali-
> tarian disaster? Neither, as yet—although in recent decades we have been slid-
> ing toward the latter consummation. If the choice had to be made, Eliot wrote
> once, it would be better to educate well comparatively few people than to
> school everybody shoddily; for in the former circumstance, at least we should
> possess some competent leadership. An egalitarian disaster has not yet oc-
> curred in this country only because in fact we have not yet wholly abandoned
> the older understanding of education as an intellectual means to an ethical end.
> No democracy can endure if it rests upon intellectual apathy and indifference.[26]

A judgment ecclesiastical in its hope amid gloom, but anything more
would be dishonest. Indeed, in his final educational column for *National
Review,* in 1980, Kirk wrote that he had seen discouragingly little progress
in American education at all levels during his many years of writing on the
subject, declaring bluntly: "From kindergarten through graduate school,
American education is an extravagant failure." In a quarter-century of con-
tending "against the dominations and powers of Holy Educationism" he
confessed himself "beaten down, horse, foot, and dragoons."[27] Yet ages of
decadence in any civilized nation can sometimes give way to ages of renewal, as with Augustan Rome. Nothing being inevitable except death,
hope for renewal lives in the choices of a people whose numbers are salted
by men and women possessing intelligence, vigor, and respect for the permanent things. "We Americans possess the resources for such a fullness of

the higher learning as bloomed in the age of Augustus, and for more than that. Either we will become Augustans in the dawning age, I suspect, or we will take the road to Avernus."[28] Of necessity to our becoming Augustans, he believed, is the recovery of the higher learning.

The Augustan Age lasted only six decades, noted Richard B. Hovey in a thoughtful review of *Decadence and Renewal* in *Modern Age*. Claiming "I go along with Russell Kirk, say, eighty percent of the way," Hovey notes what several reviewers of the book believed of it: that while Kirk makes many telling points in *Decadence and Renewal*, and while his overarching vision is sound, he is perhaps too sweeping in his condemnations, overstating the severity of professorial tergiversations and the slackness of the teaching and learning at America's colleges. (Certainly, for many Americans who were college students during the 1960s and 1970s, the work required to obtain a degree in any discipline was no walk in the park.) In his most telling criticism, Hovey writes that Kirk "leads us to an almost abysmal dichotomy." That being:

> He posits a powerless professor: "Freedom and power stand in eternal opposition." Nor am I garbling by quoting out of context. For Dr. Kirk defines the scholar as "a man who professes to have given up the claim to power over men in favor of the service of truth." How in the academic-bureaucratic power-structure such a person is to prevent being squashed, to secure conditions adequate for meeting his responsibilities, and to speak out the truth, Russell Kirk does not say.[29]

At one time, many years earlier, Kirk himself had been in that position; he had escaped being "squashed" by resigning, taking up his battered typewriter, and writing essays and books on education that, over time, gained a select audience among professors, administrators, and students. In this role, he was far more influential than he would have been had he stayed the course at Michigan State. Never aspiring to be a world-shaker, he sought to speak to just that remnant, and despite his protestations of failure, he succeeded. To the end of his career, Kirk held a consistent vision of the purpose of education and the principles upon which it ought to stand. His summary of the proper end of education is best quoted at length, for what he says is rich in content:

> To what truths, then, ought the Academy to be dedicated? To the proposition that the end of education is the elevation of the reason of the human person, for the human person's own sake. To the proposition that the higher imagination is better than the sensate triumph. To the proposition that the fear of God, and not the mastery over man and nature, is the object of learning. To the proposition that quality is worth more than quantity. To the proposition that justice takes precedence over power. To the proposition that order is more lovable than egoism. To the proposition that to believe all things, if the choice

must be made, is nobler than to doubt all things. To the proposition that honor outweighs success. To the proposition that tolerance is wiser than ideology. To the proposition, Socratic and Christian, that the unexamined life is not worth living. If the Academy holds by these propositions, not all the forces of Caesar can break down its walls; but if the Academy is bent upon sneering at everything in heaven and earth, or upon reforming itself after the model of the market-place, not all the eloquence of the prophets can save it.[30]

Such a vision is not the pie-in-the-sky moonshine of an educational moss-back; Kirk was deadly serious about the need for renewal in the higher learning. He believed that our time demands more than questionably educated young men and women eager for degrees in order to secure high-paying jobs. The failure of schools—primary, secondary, and college level—to quicken fallow minds accounts for many of our national difficulties, many of them formidable. He wrote, "Our public men tend to lack moral imagination and strength of will: our cities turn ugly and violent because vision and courage are lacking. Mediocrity in a pattern of education may not be ruinous in itself, and yet it may contribute gradually to private and public decadence. Mediocre appeals for excellence will not suffice, in the absence of sincere and vigorous educational reform."[31] This very concept made its way into Annette Kirk's contribution to *A Nation at Risk* (1983), a work strongly cautionary in tone and guardedly hopeful of prospects for humanistic renewal in American education. It remains to be seen whether American society, which so often views conservative thought as being content with the idea that things are fine just the way they are, will act prudently upon Russell and Annette Kirk's patient, insistent call for judicious reform. An Augustan Age in education may be much to ask for, but movement in its direction is preferable to the fanaticism, triviality, and mediocrity that serve as landmarks along the route to Avernus.

NOTES

1. *Decadence and Renewal in the Higher Learning*, p. 341.
2. *Decadence and Renewal*, p. 341.
3. Kirk to Person, October 31, 1987. Hannah's own few extant letters to Kirk, on file at the Russell Kirk Center for Cultural Renewal, were written after Kirk's departure from Michigan State and indicate by their tone and wording an administrator nervously trying to make peace with someone he recognizes as a formidable adversary.
4. Quoted in Chuck Moss, "Kirk: Godfather of Modern Conservatism," *The Detroit News*, March 1, 1989, 15A. For all these hard words, it is ironic and commendable that Michigan State is home to the Russell Kirk Society, an organization of students founded in 1997 and devoted to humane learning and the study of Kirk's writings.

5. Moss, "Kirk: Godfather of Modern Conservatism," 15A.

6. Stanlis, from *Your Family and Middlebury,* a journal mailed to students' parents and other friends of Middlebury College, quoted in Kirk, "Professor? What Professor?" *National Review* 20, May 21, 1968, 503.

7. "Professor? What Professor?," 503.

8. Stanlis, "Prophet of American Higher Education," *The Intercollegiate Review* 30, Fall, 1994, 77.

9. *Decadence and Renewal in the Higher Learning,* p. 341.

10. Panichas, "*Academic Freedom* Views Modern Educational Trends," *The Springfield Republican,* July 10, 1955, 5C.

11. *Academic Freedom: An Essay in Definition,* p. 3.

12. Nisbet, review of *Academic Freedom,* in *The Western Political Quarterly* 9, March, 1956, 216–17.

13. "The End of Learning: A Place to Stand," *Discipleship Journal,* no. 23, 1984, 27.

14. Panichas, "Academic Freedom Views Modern Education Trends," 5C.

15. "The End of Learning: A Place to Stand," 27.

16. *Academic Freedom,* p. 118.

17. Metzger, review of *Academic Freedom,* in *Political Science Quarterly* 70, December, 1955, 599. Metzger's own discourse on academic freedom, published in two parts as *Development of Academic Freedom in the United States* (with Richard Hofstadter) and *Academic Freedom in the Age of the University,* appeared a few months after Kirk's study, in 1955. Kirk reviewed the first-named volume in the November 20, 1955 issue of the *Chicago Sunday Tribune Magazine of Books,* and found it "full of valuable information." Kirk recognized the authors as endeavoring to impartiality; "Nevertheless, for the most part they are partisans of 'liberal' ideology, of the theory that the new and untried is better than the old and tried."

18. Wriston, "A Conservative View of Academic Freedom," *The Yale Review* n.s. 44, June, 1955, 608–9.

19. *Academic Freedom,* p. 121.

20. Buckley, "Essay in Confusion," *The Freeman* 5, July, 1955, 576.

21. See Suzanne Fields, "Death to Defectives," *The Washington Times,* April 19, 1999, http://www.washtimes.com/opinion/fields.html. Interestingly the president of Princeton University defends the retention of the professor in question, one Peter Singer, in the name of academic freedom.

22. "The Rarity of the God-Fearing Man," in *The Intemperate Professor and Other Cultural Splenetics,* p. 74.

23. Quoted in Philip Yancey, "Nietzsche Was Right," *Books & Culture* 4, no. 1 (January-February 1998): 17.

24. *Decadence and Renewal in the Higher Learning,* p. 341.

25. Evans, review of *Decadence and Renewal in the Higher Learning,* in *National Review* 31, April 27, 1979, 575.

26. *Decadence and Renewal,* p. 341.

27. "Imagination Against Ideology," *National Review* 32, December 31, 1980, 1576.

28. *Decadence and Renewal,* p. 343.

29. Hovey, "Academe—and the Abyss?" *Modern Age* 23, Fall, 1979, 420.

30. *Academic Freedom,* pp. 190–91.

31. *Decadence and Renewal in the Higher Learning,* p. 342.

5

Laws Written and Unwritten: Kirk on the Roots of American Justice

The champion of natural law knows that there is law for man, and law for thing, and that our moral order is not the creation of coffee house philosophers. Human nature is not vulpine nature, leonine nature, or serpentine nature. Natural law is bound up with the concept of the dignity of man, and with the experience of humankind ever since the beginning of social community.

—Russell Kirk

In a book-lined anteroom just off the largest guest room at Piety Hill, there is a writing desk, and on top of this is a small collection of books on natural law and legal theory. Among these books are Peter J. Stanlis's *Edmund Burke and the Natural Law*, Hadley Arkes's *Beyond the Constitution*, Russell Hittinger's *Critique of the New Natural Law Theory*, Leo Strauss's *Natural Right and History*, as well as some three dozen others works. These are the sources Kirk intended to consult in writing the book he planned but did not live to write: a full-length treatment of law and justice.

Kirk had a longtime interest in the law, the fruit of his reading in Edmund Burke and John Adams; and he published numerous essays on the subject. One of the last essays he published, "Natural Law and the Constitution of the United States," appeared in the *Notre Dame Law Review* shortly before his death. Having spent two consecutive terms as justice of the peace for Morton Township, of which Mecosta is a part, during the early 1960s, Kirk had some experience with the day-to-day routine of settling legal issues. Beyond this, he was widely read in the history of law and appeared as an expert witness in several trials related to church-state relations during the last two decades of his life.

From extensive reading and from firsthand experience in legal matters, Kirk understood that the idea of justice is one of three fundamental virtues that forms the bond that unites American society, the other two being order and freedom. Justice, according to his understanding, is something other than that law that can whip all comers in a court of law; it is that principle and process by which every man and woman in society are accorded the things that are rightfully their own: their lives, their dignity, their property, their station in life. To those who seek to deny others their rights, Justice puts her hand to the sword hilt, judiciously punishing the wrongdoer and making plain the consequences of fraud, violence, and other unlawful practices. As Kirk wrote in *The American Cause*, "The allegorical figure of Justice always holds a sword. Justice is the cornerstone of the world—divine justice and human justice. It is the first necessity of any decent society."[1]

Justice, according to Thomas Aquinas, is "a certain rectitude of mind, whereby a man does what he ought to do in the circumstance confronting him"; or, as Justinian phrased it, "a habit whereby a man renders to each one his due with constant and perpetual will." It is necessarily ethical in nature, and it lies in the heart of law. As Kirk made plain in his chapters on America's English inheritance in *The Roots of American Order*, *America's British Culture*, and *The Conservative Constitution* (a work later revised and republished as *Rights and Duties*), the law stands supreme, being no respecter of rank or station: this is the essence of British legal theory and legal practice, and it passed into America during the early colonial settlements, becoming enmeshed in American legal thought from that time forward. As Arthur R. Hogue put it, in his *Origins of the Common Law* (1985), "The supremacy of law implies that all agencies of government must act upon established principles; even the highest bodies and officials are not permitted to act upon arbitrary will or caprice. The supremacy of law means that all the acts of government agencies are subject to examination in the courts, which are compelled in their turn to follow established procedures, 'due process,' and to reach decisions guided not by whim but by generally accepted principles and sound reason."[2] Under precedent extending back to the Magna Carta and beyond, the law is superior to even the king—or the president, for that matter. In this precept of *lex rex*, a legal philosophy perhaps best articulated by Samuel Rutherford in his 1644 treatise by that title, lies the beginning of the principle of a government of laws, not of men. Law is not merely a handy construct cobbled together by rulers and legislators, but rather the very source of their authority. As Kirk wrote in *The Roots of American Order*, it is, in essence, the expression of natural justice and the ancient ways of a people.

Kirk recognized that America's justice system is rooted in England's common-law heritage, a heritage perhaps unfamiliar to the lay reader. Being noncodified, the common law is quite different from statutory law—that is, different from the written statutes issued by the sovereign political authority. Founded upon national, rather than local, customs and precedents, the common law is the outgrowth of centuries of judicial decisions upon the basis of what the people believe to be just. In this sense, it is organic in nature. Kirk also describes the common law as "prescriptive" law, and as "customary" or "traditional" law, derived from the experience of people living in community and settling their differences by legal means over a very long period of time. It is a fundamental part of America's British culture: the fundamental body of law in England and the Commonwealth nations, as well as the United States. In all these countries, statutory law was a later development, coming into being in part to address satisfactorily cases in which the common law was deemed inadequate.

Based upon numerous precedents rather than a systematic compilation of statutes, the common law is not a corpus of acts passed by a legislature or a parliament; it is, Kirk wrote, the "people's law," so to speak, for it has grown over the centuries, out of practical cases of actual contest at law, and is sanctioned by popular assent to its fairness. The common law has been called "unwritten law," notably by one of Kirk's most able commentators, Russell Hittinger. The implication is that the United States is blessed with really two constitutions, one written, the other unwritten. Hittinger has stated, "Without an unwritten constitution, the political order would only represent juxtapositions of power: first, the specific powers and absence of governmental powers spelled out by the Constitution; second, the powers exercised by the people to legislate, at their discretion, where they are not forbidden to do so by the Constitution; and third, the liberty of individuals to proceed at will in the absence of any positive law pertaining to the choice at hand. So put, this scheme captures fairly well how a written Constitution of enumerated and delegated powers delineates powers and liberties."[3]

Being the soul of political and legal continuity, opposed to innovation, the common law is viewed with suspicion if not contempt by those jurists and challengers of existing statutes who see their role not as interpreting law but crafting new laws to fit their own ideas of how society ought to be ordered. (This said, it is not surprising that on one occasion, while standing trial on charges related to assisted suicide, Dr. Jack Kevorkian appeared before the television cameras outside the courtroom dressed in an absurd costume reminiscent of an eighteenth-century English gentleman, complete with powdered wig and knee-breeches, the better to mock the very idea of common law.) It is America's common law heritage that keeps legal innovations, many not so extreme as the issue of assisted suicide, from taking root.

Several questions naturally arise: Can experience alone, no matter how deeply rooted in a people's history, be a sure guide to justice? Is experience, tradition, its own highest value? Must there not be a higher sanction, whether based in religion or philosophy, to undergird collective experience with meaning?

NATURAL LAW AND NATURAL RIGHTS

English courts of common law and courts of equity have for centuries claimed that they derive their sanction from the established customs or the ethical beliefs of the realm. Elements of natural law, concepts that the English (and, thus, the Americans) owe greatly to Cicero, became established, over time, as the guiding light for both forms of law, common law and equity. Cicero wrote that the natural law originated before "any written law existed or any state had been established." The unwritten law is antecedent to the written law and informs it, the unwritten law being

the highest reason, implanted in Nature, which commands what ought to be done and forbids the opposite. This reason, when firmly fixed and fully developed in the human mind, is Law. And so they believe that Law is intelligence, whose natural function it is to command right conduct and forbid wrongdoing. They think that this quality has derived its name in Greek from the idea of granting to every man his own, and in our language I believe it has been named from the idea of choosing [between justified and unjustified claims]. For as they have attributed the idea of fairness to the word law, so we have given it that of selection, though both ideas properly belong to Law. Now if this is correct, as I think it to be in general, then the origin of Justice is to be found in Law; for Law is a natural force; it is the mind and reason of the intelligent man, the standard by which Justice and Injustice are measured.[4]

"Law, then, at base is a knowledge of the ethical norms for the human being," growing as it does out of recognition of enduring natural laws, Kirk concluded. Natural law, in which much of common law has its being, has been defined by Kirk as "a loosely-knit body of rules of action prescribed by an authority superior to the state. These rules variously (according to several different schools of natural law and natural rights speculation) are derived from divine commandment, from right reason with which man is endowed by his Creator, from the nature of mankind empirically regarded, from the abstract Reason of the Enlightenment, or from the long experience of humankind in community."[5] In his book *The Abolition of Man*, C. S. Lewis demonstrated how elements of natural law, which he called the *tao*, is encountered across the spectrum of many religious and philosophical systems, and thus across a multitude of cultures of both the East and West. Being a body of norms governing the life of the soul and the life of the community, and from there to the life of the commonwealth, natural law pertains to a people's culture across the whole of life, not to matters of law merely.

Natural law figures much in Kirk's writings on justice. It was first expounded by Cicero, by whom the English were widely influenced, then by Seneca and Aristotle, eventually being "baptized" by the Church Fathers, the Schoolmen, and St. Thomas Aquinas. Kirk has written "From the Schoolmen that understanding of natural law enters into English common law, and in the sixteenth century obtains fresh expression in Hooker's *Laws of Ecclesiastical Policy* and the later writings of other Anglican divines. This apprehension of natural law passes into America during colonial times, and in some degree survives, if often submerged, in twentieth century America."[6]

Linked inseparably with natural law, with its attendant duties demanded of the individual to the small community to which he belongs— of family, guild, church, neighborhood, or other voluntary grouping—are the true rights of humanity, not the natural rights written of during the Enlightenment and the years of the American and French Revolutions. The "chartered rights of Englishmen" described by Burke, arising from custom, convention, and continuity and attached to corresponding duties, are far removed from the abstractions that sailed (and continue to sail) under the colors of natural rights. The latter are innumerable and the source of much legislative mischief, the "right" to "freedom from fear," being one, others being the "right" to work in a smoke-free environment, and the "right" to two weeks of paid vacation per year, to cite but three random examples. Contrary to this, English jurist William Blackstone described "the absolute rights of man" as consisting of three articles: "the right of personal security, the right of personal liberty, and the right of private property." Blackstone hastened to add that even these "absolute rights" are not absolute in practice, for "every man, when he enters into society, gives up a part of his natural liberty, as the price of so valuable a purchase; and, in consideration of receiving the advantages of mutual commerce, obliges himself to conform to these laws which the community has thought proper to establish." In these words, "more clearly expressed than by Locke," wrote Kirk, "is a fundamental doctrine of American politics."[7]

Kirk saw the common law, grounded in natural law, as one of America's most important inheritances from England, important because it provided the seedbed of stable, virtuous order in England and early America. Upon that seedbed there grew and flourished a free society. Common law was recognized and embraced willingly by a people who recognized it as a longtime outgrowth of their common experience rather than a despot's imposition. Thus it became the foundation of English and American order. And from order springs freedom.

As Kirk noted in *The Roots of American Order*, common-law principles worked upon public affairs in America more powerfully than any other influences except Protestant Christianity and the colonial social experience itself. The common law was introduced into every American colony by colonial charter. Leading American public men of the last quarter of the eighteenth century and their successors in the first quarter of the nineteenth century, from Republicans like Jefferson and Madison to Federalists like Fisher Ames and Joseph Story, were well read in the common-law exponent of medieval times and the Renaissance, especially through Blackstone's *Commentaries on the Laws of England*. A strong advocate of ancient usage and precedent, Blackstone acknowledged the significance of natural law in supplying an underpinning to common law, describing the former as follows: "This law of nature, being co-eval with mankind and dictated by God himself, is of course superior in obligation to any other. It is binding over all the globe, and all countries, and at all times; no human laws are of any validity if contrary to this; and such of them as are valid derive all their force, and all their authority, mediately or immediately from this original."[8]

But if natural law is indeed "dictated by God himself," and is thus a higher law than the written law, does this not open the door for civil disobedience on a wide scale, with each person potentially appealing to a "higher law," obeying only the laws he sees fit to obey according to his understanding of divine justice? No, said Kirk, answering this question in a lecture delivered at the University of Notre Dame Law School in late 1993. On that occasion, he cited the so-called "higher law" controversy of 1850, which arose after Senator William Henry Seward declared that there exists "a higher law than the Constitution," the senator speaking specifically about the right of Abolitionists and Free-Soilers to violate the law of the land in regard to issues related to slavery. Shortly after Seward uttered his much-publicized words, one of Kirk's heroes of conservative thought, Orestes Brownson, published a lengthy essay entitled *The Higher Law*, in which he refuted Seward and his supporters in their claim that the Constitution ought to be transcended by appeals to a moral law superior to written law.

Brownson agreed with Seward that there is indeed a higher law than the Constitution, even as Blackstone had claimed. "The law of God is supreme, and overrides all human enactments, and every human enactment incompatible with it is null and void from the beginning, and cannot be obeyed with a good conscience, for [with a nod to the words of the Apostles recorded in Acts 5:29] 'we must obey God rather than men.' This is the great truth statesmen and lawyers are extremely prone to overlook. . . ." As private citizens, Brownson said, we cannot be bound to obey a law that contravenes the law of God. But Seward, or any other public official sworn to uphold the laws of the land, "had no right, while holding his seat in the Senate under the Constitution, to appeal to the higher law against the Constitution, because that was to deny the array authority by which he held his seat. . . . After having taken his oath to support the Constitution, the Senator had, so far as he was concerned, settled the question, and it was no longer for him an open question. In calling God to witness his determination to support the Constitution, he had called God to witness his conviction of the comparability of the Constitution with the law of God, and therefore left himself no plea for appealing from it to a higher law." Brownson warned that if the individual places himself above the state, he assumes a station "wholly incompatible with the simplest conception of government. No civil government can exist, none is conceivable even, where every individual is free to disobey its orders whenever they do not happen to square with his private convictions of what is the law of God."[9] Kirk concluded of this issue, "Brownson's argument . . . in substance is this, in his own words: 'Mr. Seward and his friends asserted a great and glorious principle, but misapplied it.' It was not for them to utter commands in the name of God. Their claims, if carried far enough, would lead to anarchy. The arguments of some of their adversaries would lead to what Brownson called 'statolatory,' the worship of the state."

> The cry for liberty [wrote Brownson] abolishes all loyalty, and destroys the principle and the spirit of obedience, while the usurpations of the state leave to conscience no freedom, to religion no independence. The state tramples on the spiritual prerogatives of the Church, assumes to itself the functions of schoolmaster and director of consciences, and the multitude clap their hands, and call it liberty and progress![10]

Brownson concluded with words to which Kirk wholeheartedly assented, given his own strong belief that America's abortion laws, brought into being by the Court's majority decision in *Roe v. Wade* (1973), had struck a terrible blow at the American family, but his nonparticipation in acts of civil disobedience in defiance of those laws:

If men were less blind and headstrong, they would see that the higher law can be asserted without any attack upon legitimate civil authority, and legitimate civil authority and the majesty of the law can be vindicated without asserting the absolute supremacy of the civil power, and falling into statolatory,—as absurd a species of idolatry as the worship of sticks and stones.[11]

American society could scarcely have cohered at all, during its fledgling years as a republic, had not the common law been adapted to American circumstances. To Kirk's dismay, during the twentieth century the common law heritage of the United States has steadily faded from recognition in favor of statutory law, with some legislators succeeding in enacting statutes, driven by expediency and passion, and of dubious constitutionality, which deal with subjects already adequately covered by the common law, "hate-crime" laws being a prime example of such overreaching.

KIRK ON THE CONSTITUTION

In the United States, the Bill of Rights, the first ten amendments to the federal Constitution, incorporate many of the civil liberties originally guarded by Anglo-American common law, thus reaffirming its importance. Thus the personal liberty Americans enjoy owes perhaps more to the common law than to any other element of the nation's heritage.

Once, at a legal symposium at which Kirk was present, historian Clinton Rossiter claimed incautiously that a nation's constitution can be created overnight. Witness, he continued, the guiding instruments composed by several European countries shortly after each of the two world wars. Kirk answered Rossiter's statement with a simple question: "Where are those constitutions now?" Indeed, the framers of any enduring constitution must consider "the history, the moral order, the resources, the prospects of a country—and much else besides," wrote Kirk in one of his essays in *The Conservative Constitution*. Furthermore, wrote Kirk, those framers must have some understanding of what Edmund Burke called the contract of eternal society, all of which is related intimately with the truths of natural law.

This eternal contract, linking the living with preceding generations and with generations yet unborn, is bound up with custom, convention, prescription, and the moral imagination—the biblical view of humanity as fallen, driven by appetites that need to be checked, yet beloved of God and made for eternity. It is an organic contract, far removed from the various compacts of fear and expedience described by Hobbes, Locke, and Rousseau. This view of the body politic, as Kirk argued, also guided the deliberations of the Framers of the American Constitution. Far from being the heirs of Enlightenment thinkers and the innovative *philosophes*, given to natural rights theory, the Framers were instead the inheritors and guardians of what Burke termed "the chartered rights of Englishmen." Those rights, based on prescription and usage, extended back to the Glorious Revolution of 1688 and beyond, and found their most prominent spokesman in Burke.

Burke's thoughts, particularly as expressed in a publication he wrote and edited, the *Annual Register* (which was read avidly on both sides of the Atlantic during the late eighteenth century), were closely aligned to the Framers' outlook. Derived from such an inheritance and with its sober view of humanity's state, the Constitution was never intended as a license for utopians or a weapon for ideologues. It is not, as the English man of letters Thomas Babington Macaulay claimed, "all sail and no anchor." It is, as Kirk called it, a *conservative* constitution. In his foreword to *Rights and Duties*, Russell Hittinger explained, "For Kirk, to call the Constitution and its purposes 'conservative' means that the basic law preserves the pattern of political order through time and change. This conserving propensity is rooted chiefly in the 'unwritten constitution,' consisting of many different ideals, purposes, habits, and practices which are only partially expressed in the written artifact." He continued:

> The written Constitution, for example, prescribes the ways that changes are to be enacted; it does not prescribe any particular amendment, and it gives no advice on how deeply or how often amendments ought to be adopted. During the era of the New Deal, the Constitution was amended only twice (neither amendment concerned the agenda of the New Deal), even though the party of reform eventually controlled all three branches of the United States government and had ample opportunity to embed its political aims in the basic law. However important, constitutional texts, legal mechanics, and political power cannot themselves explain the fact that Americans have so rarely altered the frame of the basic law.[12]

The Conservative Constitution, written as "an attempt to understand the Constitution of the United States as a framework for a conservative political order in North America," elaborates upon key sections of *The Roots of American Order,* a work of wide scope and astonishing learning to which the earlier portion of this chapter is indebted. It consists of fifteen essays written during the late 1980s by Kirk on matters specifically related to the Constitution's origins and intents. Particularly noteworthy is his chapter entitled "The First Clause of the First Amendment: Politics and Religion," which considers American church-state relations. It is a most lucid, well-argued essay on that subject, interpreting those relations in a manner that runs counter to much legal thinking today. Kirk demonstrates that the First Amendment was never intended to quash religious expression in the public square, but rather to ensure religious toleration, so far as this issue concerned the federal government; and so that such expression be unhindered by the constraints that would necessarily prevail if America had, like Great Britain, a national church, intolerant of all others and supported, however grudgingly, by tax monies. Congress was thus prevented from interfering with the Congregational churches already established by 1787 in several New England states.

Perhaps the principle point of the book, articulated by Kirk and shared by his intellectual ancestor Burke, is found in the concluding chapter of this volume:

> Great states with good constitutions develop when most people think of their duties and restrain their appetites. Great states sink toward their dissolution when most people think of their privileges and indulge their appetites freely. . . . And no matter how admirable a constitution may look upon paper, it will be ineffectual unless the written constitution, the web of custom and convention, affirms an enduring moral order of obligation and personal responsibility.[13]

No constitution—for that matter, no civilization—can long endure, which oversees a people who recognize no such thing as duty or restraint, but countenance the indulging of every passion, every appetite. Kirk deemed such a society decadent wherein the Bill of Rights is invoked as if it were a suicide pact—"from those National Riflemen who would defend to the death the inalienable right of a mugger to buy a Saturday-night special, to those humanitarians who insist that even imminent peril to public health must not be permitted to impede exercise of the inalienable right to engage in sexual perversions."[14] Kirk was a strict constructionist in interpreting the Constitution, believing that it was intended by the Framers as a source of America's first principles, to be consulted in legal matters that such matters might be conformed to it. He and other constructionists were at swords' point with the numerous constitutional liberals who seek to make the Constitution a "living document," meaning that its meaning and intent ought to be constantly reinterpreted according to the needs of the hour so that it can be used as a tool for enlightened social change. In such instances wherein prudence is cast aside in favor of expediency and passion, the Constitution, in Joseph Sobran's words, becomes "liberated from history, logic and the dictionary," with words and legal concepts meaning whatever the justices want them to mean, *à la* Humpty Dumpty in *Alice*.[15] The meaning of laws *evolves*, rather than remaining constant, which to the liberal connotes stasis and death. (Liberal jurists ensure that the law never "evolves" in a rightward direction.) Conservative constructionists, who believe it is the responsibility of jurists to interpret law, not make law, have often found themselves fighting a (for the most part) losing war of ideas with legal innovators during the second half of the twentieth century, constantly outmaneuvered and defeated in matters of rhetoric by opponents who are not averse to demagoguery to achieve their ends. To cite one important example, the rule of *stare decisis*, "to stand by decided cases," whereby all judges are supposed to be bound by previous decisions, is the central distinction of the common law. The purpose of *stare decisis* is to ensure the evenhanded administration of justice from year to year, over the decades and centuries; which entails that jurists not be given a free hand to craft or bend laws or to decide cases according to personal whim, or to show partiality to particular persons or causes. According to the doctrine of *stare decisis*, judges must abide by the accumulated store of legal custom for the sake of order, with people understanding that the law is impartial and that the law does not change with the winds of the *zeitgeist*. For America's constitutional constructionists, it is a bitter pill to swallow when liberal attorneys and judges, having once overturned long-standing laws in order to accomplish a progressive change in any one area of legal contention, immediately and solemnly invoke the doctrine of *stare decisis* when their own innovations are challenged.

SHORING FRAGMENTS AGAINST IMPENDING RUIN

If we were to wake up tomorrow morning and discover that there were no longer any lawyers, civilization as we know it would come to an end—so stated one flamboyant attorney on his radio talk show during the final year of the American century.[16] (It might be added that, if we were to awaken tomorrow morning and discover that all the attorneys were still with us, but that there were no more plumbers, or doctors, or firefighters, or writers, or automobile mechanics, civilization as we know it would just as swiftly come to an end.) The words of this unctuous blowhard are true in an ironic sense; many Americans of a conservative bent behold a nation of increasingly litigious individuals seeking to become independently wealthy because of their own cupidity, malice, and clumsiness—for example, suing fast-food restaurants after spilling hot coffee in their own laps, countenancing lawsuits against state prison systems for not giving inmates taxpayer-funded access to pornography, bringing suit against a school district for expelling a boy whose World Wide Web site openly solicited a hit man to assassinate the little lad's school principal (this suit brought on the grounds that soliciting a hit man is protected speech), and other excesses—and consider the end of that particular aspect of "civilization as we know it" a consummation devoutly to be wished. The prospects for a reversal in this state of affairs seem remote.

"Let us not deceive ourselves; we are at the beginning of great troubles," wrote Burke in his *First Letter of the Regicide Peace*, believing Great Britain on the verge of a sea of troubles. "As it was with Britain in the closing years of the eighteenth century, so it is with America in the closing years of the twentieth," warned Kirk, concerning the decay of rule of law in the United States at the end of the twentieth century. His words, written near the end of his life, form a fitting summary of his ideas on the role of affirming right reason and natural law in making, interpreting, and defending law grounded in natural law.

> As did the British then, we confront an armed doctrine and are divided in our own counsels. And yet our own general complacency scarcely is shaken: most of us behave as if nothing very disagreeable ever could happen to the Constitution of the United States, and as if the political future of this nation would be a mere alternation of Republican and Democratic presidential victories, somewhat less interesting than professional baseball and football.
>
> The crash of empires and the collapse of constitutions have blinded and deafened most of the world since 1914. Only American territories and American laws have stood little touched amidst the general ruin. It is not accident that will preserve them for posterity. Of those Americans who dabble in politics at all, many think of such activities chiefly as a game, membership on a team, with minor prizes to be passed out after the latest victory. Yet a few men and women, like Burke, engage in politics not because they love the game, but because they know that the alternative to a politics of elevation is a politics of degradation. Let us try to be of their number.[17]

Because Kirk understood the just interpretation of law as the foundation of order in America, a foundation upon which arose the whole fabric of a free society, he indulged the prerogative of a master rhetorician, writing the above lines in tone faintly reminiscent of the prebattle harangue delivered by a commanding officer to his troops. A man not given to empty dramatics, Kirk firmly believed what he said in what is essentially a call for an act of recovery—the recovery of the sense of natural law in the individual, in the community, and (only then) in the governance of legal decision making. As attorney Gerald J. Russello has written, "Kirk remained convinced that natural law was important more for the person than for the society at large. He saw that natural law could be important to society only if each individual lived a life that was honest, harmed no one, and rendered to others their due. Kirk knew that political and social controversies are at root crises of faith. For society to recover from its troubles, men and women must rediscover that law written upon their hearts."[18]

NOTES

1. *The American Cause*, 51.
2. Hogue, quoted in Kirk, *America's British Culture*, p. 31.
3. Hittinger, foreword to *Rights and Duties: Reflections on Our Conservative*

Constitution, p. xxi. Hittinger's essay, incidentally, provides a detailed and intelligent discussion of the question of how the written law can continue to endure, in any form, if the unwritten law fades from the people's minds over time.

4. Quoted in Kirk, *The Roots of American Order*, p. 111.

5. "Natural Law and the Constitution," *Notre Dame Law Review* 69, 1994, 1036.

6. "Natural Law and the Constitution," 1036.

7. *The Roots of American Order*, p. 371.

8. Quoted in Kirk, *Roots of American Order*, p. 370.

9. Brownson, quoted in Kirk, "Natural Law and the Constitution," 1041–42.

10. "Natural Law and the Constitution," 1043.

11. "Natural Law and the Constitution," 1044.

12. Hittinger, Foreword to *Rights and Duties*, p. xv.

13. *The Conservative Constitution*, pp. 227–28.

14. *Conservative Constitution*, p. 227.

15. Sobran, "Blackmun's Odyssey," March 12, 1999, http://www.uexpress. com/cgi-bin/ups/prin . . . column/js/text/1999/03/js9903128650.html.

16. Geoffrey Fieger, on *Fieger Time*, WXYT AM, Detroit, Mich., January 15, 1999.

17. *Rights and Duties: Reflections on Our Conservative Constitution*, pp. 260–61.

18. Russello, "The Jurisprudence of Russell Kirk," *Modern Age* 38, Fall, 1996, 361. Russello's essay is essential reading for anyone wishing to grasp Kirk's thought on the law.

6

Horror and Redemption: Kirk's Short Stories and *Lord of the Hollow Dark*

The locale was to me . . . just the sort of mindless, mundane place where the horrors of a Hitchcock or a Polanski might have been inspired. There was horror in the very vegetation spreading under the hazy sun—an everyday buzz of nothing that bred the violent and bizarre. Those old woods, fields, shacks, sparse people—all ticking and withering in the sun—their stories clamped my heart in cold, calloused fingers.
　　　—from "Two Stories from Lenoir County," by Thomas N. Walters

　　　　　　　　　. . . for history is a pattern
　　　　Of timeless moments. . . .
　　　　　　　　　—from "Little Gidding," by T. S. Eliot

"How amazingly versatile and prolific you are. Now you have been writing what I should have least suspected of you—ghost stories!" wrote Eliot to Kirk in 1958.[1] Had he known Kirk better, the great poet would not have been surprised at Kirk's interest in stories of the supernatural, which stemmed from his boyhood reading and the lore attached to Piety Hill and environs.

For many years, Kirk and several visitors to his Mecosta home reported uncanny nocturnal sightings and sounds in and around the old place, which occurred periodically until it burned on Ash Wednesday, 1975. Kirk himself had his first encounter with the unexplained as a boy at Piety Hill when, awakening one winter night, he saw two men staring in a downstairs window at him. One was tall, bearded, and wore a tall hat, while the other was short, clean-shaven, and wore a small hat. Frightened, young Russell covered up his head and went back to sleep. In the morning, there were no footprints on the snow-covered lawn outside the window to indicate that anyone had been there the night before. Several years passed, and then one day Kirk's elderly Aunt Fay, who had often visited Piety Hill as a young girl, told him that during her childhood she had enjoyed the friendship of two men invisible to all other eyes. The men had names: a tall, bearded gentleman named Dr. Cady who wore a tall hat, and a short, beardless man named Patti who wore a turban. All of which made for an interesting story of coincidence, until one day, many years later, when Russell and Annette were startled to hear one of their daughters, then two years old, begin delightedly crying "Patti! Patti!" while pointing at an empty place in their empty yard.

These and apparitions of various sorts made themselves known over time, sometimes to even the most skeptical visitors. Such an atmosphere, combined with the occasionally bizarre natural occurrences of life in rural Mecosta County, went far toward shaping Kirk's self-styled "Gothic mind." (An example of the area's occasional instances of the bizarre and the grotesque found its way into Kirk's short piece "Lost Lake"—really a short memoir rather than a story. Here, Kirk relates the story of a local farming family who, having lost a newborn baby to pneumonia during a harsh Michigan winter, stored the baby's body in their woodshed until it could be buried in the spring, when the ground softened sufficiently. A week passed, springtime approached, and the parents seem to have forgotten about their dead child. Then, one day, neighbor children were invited over to play with a "new doll" the farmer's children had found in the woodshed. Stephen King could not have conceived a more ghastly incident than this real-life occurrence, especially since the children first asked the dead baby's mother for permission to play with the "doll"—and she agreed. Theodore Sturgeon aptly described "Lost Lake" as "a plotless sketch—more a portrait—of a locality . . . which leaves one with the uneasy belief that one has been there and will never be able quite to shake off its brooding innate enmity."[2]) "Do not let me hear / Of the wisdom of old men, but rather of their folly, / Their fear of fear and frenzy, their fear of possession, / Of belonging to another, or to others, or to God," Eliot had written in "East Coker," stating a sentiment with which Kirk would heartily concur. "A world without mystery," wrote M. E. Bradford, "would be of no interest to this disciple of Edmund Burke."[3] It is little wonder, then, that Kirk enjoyed telling and listening to ghost stories at Piety Hill when guests came to visit. In an autobiographical essay, Kirk wrote:

Mine was not an Enlightened mind . . . it was a Gothic mind, medieval in its temper and structure. I did not love cold harmony and perfect regularity of organization; what I sought was variety, mystery, tradition, the venerable, the awful. I despised sophisters and calculators; I was groping for faith, honor, and prescriptive loyalties. I would have given any number of neo-classical pediments for one poor battered gargoyle.[4]

Bradford has noted that the illative purpose of Kirk's horror fiction—his short stories and the novel *Lord of the Hollow Dark*—"is to encourage among his readers an awareness of the usually invisible things which brood just beyond the orbit of our consciousness and sometimes touch our lives in such a way as to remind us that there is more to our condition than we can account for by what Hamlet calls 'philosophy.'"[5]

Kirk began writing tales of the uncanny early in his career; by the time Eliot wrote of his surprise at this facet of the younger man's career, Kirk had already published nine ghost stories in various "little" magazines, as well as one nonsupernatural story that has never been reprinted. There followed a ten-year break, between 1957 and 1967, when Kirk wrote no short fiction; after that he wrote stories regularly until 1984. All the stories are informed by a Christian-humanist worldview, which Kirk had embraced even before his acceptance into the church in 1964. The stories were collected in three volumes, in which there is some overlap in content: *The Surly Sullen Bell* (1961), *The Princess of All Lands* (1979), and *Watchers at the Strait Gate* (1984).

How did Kirk approach the writing of these stories? C. S. Lewis once wrote that when he set out to compose his *Chronicles of Narnia*, and *Ransom Trilogy*, the process "began with seeing pictures in my head"[6]—not with a fully fleshed-out plot and structure in mind. As a writer of fiction, Kirk found his own approach similar to that of Lewis: it began with imagery married to the moral imagination. "It is imagery, rather than some narrowly deductive and inductive process, which gives us great poetry and scientific insights," he wrote in *Decadence and Renewal in the Higher Learning*. "When I write fiction, I do not commence with a well-concerted formal plot. Rather, there occur to my imagination certain images, little scenes, snatches of conversation, strong lines of prose. I patch together these fragments, retaining and embellishing the sound images, discarding the unsound, finding a continuity to join them. Presently I have a coherent narration, with some point to it." Kirk added, "Unless one has this sort of pictorial imagery—Walter Scott had it in a high degree—he never will become a writer of good fiction, whatever may be said of expository prose."[7]

"Henry James was a man with Swedenborgian forebears who didn't believe in ghosts; I am one with Swedenborgian forebears who *does* believe in ghosts; indeed, everybody who stays here in my ancestral house of Piety

Hill becomes a more fervent believer than even I am," he wrote in a letter to Eric Voegelin in 1971.[8] He acknowledged the influence of James upon his fiction writing, crafting the style of each story to fit its content, seeking a seamless melding of content with form. While this chapter is concerned primarily with thematic issues rather than matters of style, it is worth noting that Kirk proved himself adept at alternating easily between a Jamesian, limited-vision third-person narration and stream of consciousness within individual stories (as in, for example, "There's a Long, Long Trail a-Winding," "The Surly Sullen Bell," and "Behind the Stumps"), at omniscient third-person narrative ("Uncle Isaiah"), and even at pastiche (as in "The Reflex-Man of Whinnymuir Close," which is written in the form of a newly discovered eighteenth-century diary, and "The Cellar of Little Egypt," written in an unornamented, first-person style reminiscent, in its Midwestern gawkiness, of Ring Lardner or Sherwood Anderson).

Thematically and in terms of setting, Kirk's stories are of two basic sorts, often set in two recurrent locales. With several exceptions, the stories are set in either the "stump country" of north-central Michigan or in Britain. Among the others, one is set in a small Midwestern town similar to Kirk's hometown of Plymouth, one in the Balkan city of Split on the Adriatic, one in the African principality of Hamnegri, one in London, two in crumbling sections of St. Louis, and perhaps the author's most accomplished story, "The Invasion of the Church of the Holy Ghost," in a grimy inner-city neighborhood modeled after certain run-down sections of Cleveland and Los Angeles.[9] The stories feature one or the other of the following elements of supernatural experience—occasionally both. Certain of the stories, including "Behind the Stumps," "Uncle Isaiah," "What Shadows We Pursue," and "Sorworth Place," fit the model of the traditional fireside ghost story (such as that old childhood standby "The Golden Arm"), concerning individuals who "took to meddlin'" where they could have (or should have) let well enough alone. These stories tend to focus upon the reality of evil (particularly in the company of hubris, or the pride that goes before a fall) and the nature of justice through violent retribution. Dale J. Nelson has made the insightful point that in Kirk's stories, human evil manifests itself in the form of individuals who are destructive of community and the community of souls, citing the gangsters of "Uncle Isaiah" and "The Invasion of the Church of the Holy Ghost," the cold-blooded tax collector who serves the impersonal federal government in "Behind the Stumps," the rationalist and utilitarian planner of soulless housing projects in "Ex Tenebris," and the wicked husbands who abuse their wives in "Sorworth Place" and "The Surly Sullen Bell." Nelson notes that the wife abusers commit both "a violation of community, as well as a crime against a person, because every marriage creates a community."[10]

Dissenting from the generally positive appraisals of Kirk's accomplishment in his horror fiction, John A. Meixner charged Kirk with "fictional pamphleteering" in his portrayals, depicting evildoers "whose villainy arises directly from the fact that they are positivists, social scientists, progressives, and (it would seem) from non-British stock."[11] The issue of "non-British stock" is critically indefensible—an examination of the stories reveals no such pattern—and there is merit to the rest of Meixner's criticism only if the reader engages with a Kirk short story by focusing upon how the characters live up to one's own philosophical preconceptions, rather than reading the story as simply a story. Further, one might profitably ask: What, specifically, is false about depicting a wife abuser or a career criminal as an evildoer, regardless of his ethnicity?

Kirk's "nontraditional" stories, such as "Watchers at the Strait Gate," "An Encounter by Mortstone Pond," "Balgrummo's Hell," and "The Last God's Dream," focus upon the essential mystery of time and eternity. These tales feature a wraith or revenant that returns to the material world to appear upon special occasions, or that the mortal protagonist unexpectedly encounters. Kirk then artfully envelops this spectral sensibility and the other characters within metaphysical context present in Eliot's *Four Quartets*: what Eliot called "the point of intersection of the timeless / with time" in the poem "The Dry Salvages" and the "timeless moment" in "Little Gidding."

Whichever of these two techniques he employs, Kirk adheres to the famous dictum of another James—M. R. James—who wrote in the preface to his *More Ghost Stories of an Antiquary* (1911) that the setting of a ghostly tale must be "fairly familiar and the majority of the characters and their talk such as you may meet or hear any day." James continued:

> A ghost story of which the scene is laid in the twelfth or thirteenth century may succeed in being romantic or poetical: it will never put the reader into the position of saying to himself, "If I'm not very careful, something of this kind may happen to me!"[12]

Kirk openly acknowledged his literary kinship with M. R. James, in regard to setting and characterization. As M. E. Bradford suggested, he also bears the not-surprising influence of Edmund Burke in his Gothic and horror fiction, Kirk being intimately familiar with Burke's *Philosophical Enquiry into Our Ideas of the Sublime and Beautiful* (1757). This extended essay has long been considered a founding document of Gothicism and the body of supernatural literature that sprang from it. In fact, perhaps more than any other work of the eighteenth century, Burke's *Enquiry* has provided an aesthetical, psychological, and rhetorical vocabulary for writers who sought to build upon the great interest in Gothic literature founded on the eve of the nineteenth century by Horace Walpole and Anne Radcliffe. Burke believed that "terror is in all cases whatsoever . . . the ruling principle of the sublime," adding, "The passion caused by the great and sublime in nature . . . is Astonishment; and astonishment is the state of the soul, in which all its motions are suspended, with some degree of horror. In this case the mind is so entirely filled with its object, that it cannot entertain any other." This is brought home with special vividness in such stories by Kirk as "Behind the Stumps," in which the tax collector, having ranged over the Michigan countryside in pursuit of a delinquent taxpayer (locally rumored to be a witch), finds his mind "so entirely filled" with terror as he enters her seemingly abandoned farmhouse "that it cannot entertain any other" thought than those inspired by the brooding spirit of malice that permeates the old place. And in "Fate's Purse," based upon a true story from Kirk's tenure as a justice of the peace, the skinflint brother of a deceased miser inherits the dead man's stump-country farm and becomes consumed with fear of his brother's vengeance from beyond the grave, to the point of madness.

In most cases Kirk recreates scenes, characters, and speech styles vividly and believably; his recreations of lower-class speech, especially as spoken by the character discussed next, have the true ring of authenticity about them. It is only in Kirk's few ventures into characterizations based on character types with which he was unfamiliar (even through secondhand information), thereby straying from M. R. James's dictum about depicting "characters and their talk such as you may meet or hear any day," that inauthenticity creeps in; specifically, his characterizations of organized-crime gangsters (Bruno Costa in "Uncle Isaiah" and Franchetti in "The Invasion of the Church of the Holy Ghost"), who tend to act and speak as if they had just stepped out of a gangster movie of the 1930s, talking out of the side of their mouths and barking phrases like, "Cut the comedy!" (On this note, it also seems unlikely that an accomplished mob boss and shakedown artist like Costa would agree to meet a desperate man alone, on unfamiliar turf, late at night.) This aside, Kirk hewed faithfully to James's strategy. In one of the few lengthy and insightful articles on Kirk's short fiction, Don Herron expands upon the similarity between the fiction of each, noting that

> both authors use the classic form, but where the apparitions James invokes are hairy, thin, not-very human creations, the ghosts Kirk writes of are of recognizable human form—damned souls, for the most part. Also common to both authors, and beyond their intent to scare, are the background for the stories based upon their own specialties. The evoked atmosphere is similar, be it James the antiquarian writing of historied cathedrals and ancient curses or

Kirk the Conservative political thinker writing of the decay of tradition and the iron tread of progress. In James man is often in search of the old, deliberately associating himself with antiquity, and unprepared for what his delvings unearth. In Kirk man is usually attempting to further the state of modernity and to bury his history, uninteresting stuff!, under a pavement topped with shopping centers and tract housing. In both authors the Past creeps—or springs with claws rattling—into the Present. The result for man—Terror.[13]

And not terror only, but also—for the humble and the repentant—redemption. Among the recurring characters Kirk created, the following individual experiences both in abundance.

FRANK SARSFIELD

A solitary man is trudging along a highway during a snowstorm in rural upper Michigan. He has no home. He is cold and hungry, he has a weak heart that hurts him, and he doesn't know quite where he is. In the distance, off the main road, and within shouting distance of a prison's gates, looms a village and a snug-looking house, the first he has seen in a long time, but both appear abandoned. Still, the house might provide a night's shelter from the winter cold. The man lets himself in through the coal cellar, hoping nobody shoots him for a housebreaker. In the uppermost reaches of the strange house, he discovers several bedrooms, and on the door of one is a little brass plaque inscribed with the name "Frank," which is coincidentally his own name. In a nutshell, this is how Kirk introduces former convict and full-time hobo Frank Sarsfield and prepares the ground for "There's a Long, Long Trail a-Winding." This, his best-known story, won the 1977 World Fantasy Award as the best such story of the year.

While the reader may not be able to identify personally with the state of homelessness or wandering on the road, he can perhaps identify with walking a long distance in the snow, feet freezing, hoping to find a warm place soon. "If I'm not very careful. . . ." Even before the story takes a turn into the uncanny, the storyteller has come alongside the reader and is guiding him toward a place he may not wish to go. That destination is a place where the veil between the mortal and the immortal is thin, and where time sometimes folds back upon itself, making graphically plain the fact that "What might have been and what has been / Point to one end, which is always present."[14] At such times, things that are wrong can be made right—or the damned can reiterate their deserved condemnation.

Frank Sarsfield, a character based closely upon the Kirk family's "hobo-butler" Clinton Wallace, discovers this during the timeless moment he spends in the old house. Although Frank is a gentle man of the mid- to late twentieth century, he finds increasingly hard-to-deny evidence that he has stepped into a wrinkle in time, to an earlier period in American history. During the two days he spends in "Tamarack House," as the old dwelling is called, he sees in his dreams that the "abandoned" house is in fact inhabited by an old-fangled family, whose members accept him as if he had lived there all along. This family—a grandfather, a mother, a father, and three little girls—become very real to him as the story progresses. Their acceptance means much to Frank, who has a low opinion of himself as a ne'er-do-well, a petty thief, and a coward, beyond the reach of God's mercy. He is especially taken by the "middle" daughter, a charmer named Allegra. Frank is reminded that Tamarack House stands in the shadow of a maximum-security prison; and it is this place of punishment that provides the means of his ultimate deliverance from the prison-house of his own being. For in the end, peace-loving Frank must take decisive action after six murderous escaped convicts invade the house one dark morning and threaten Allegra, her mother, and her sisters—the grandfather having been felled by the desperate convicts, the girls' father being away on a business trip. Falling into a berserker rage, Frank makes terrible use of a double-bladed axe to rescue them. "Didn't Saint Paul say that the violent take heaven by storm?" he had wondered at one point in the story. No, Saint Matthew did in his Gospel, but no matter; by the story's end Frank, having run from responsibility for all his sixty years, has literally taken the kingdom of heaven through violence, saving the lives of Allegra and her family while losing his own, dying in the snowy front yard. There, before his eyes close for the last time, Frank reads the words inscribed on a memorial stone that he has fallen against in the yard:

IN LOVING MEMORY OF
FRANK
A SPIRIT IN PRISON, MADE FOR ETERNITY
WHO SAVED US AND DIED FOR US
January 14, 1915
"Why, if the Soul can fling the Dust aside,
And naked on the Air of Heaven ride,
Were't not a Shame—were't not a Shame for him
In this clay carcass crippled to abide?"[15]

Interestingly, the real "Frank Sarsfield," Clinton Wallace, was born in 1915 and died in the snow in Grand Rapids, Michigan while walking back to his small apartment after watching the prophetically titled motion picture *Across the Great Divide*—one year after Kirk wrote "There's a Long, Long Trail a-Winding." A further eerie coincidence occurred just two weeks before his death: On that day, Clinton's last day as a guest at Piety Hill, he arose after dinner to recite poetry for the assembled guests, and the final poem he declaimed was the quatrain from Omar Khayyam quoted on Frank Sarsfield's tombstone. Clinton had never quoted this passage before in his many recitations for the Kirks and had never read "Long, Long Trail"; nor, in his childlike humility, would he have believed that something of his own life story would appear among a collection considered by reviewer Thomas Fleming to be "as much moral fables as supernatural tales," written by "the godfather of American conservatism."[16]

A borrower of interesting and unusual names wherever he found them, Kirk borrowed the name "Tamarack House" for his story from the signboard of a craft shop that stands across Franklin Street from Piety Hill. And while he acknowledged Sarsfield as a portrayal of Wallace, he was more reticent about any correspondences between living people and other characters in the story. Such drawing of parallels is chancy, but two further correspondences seem likely.

At the time Kirk wrote "Long, Long Trail," he and Annette were the parents of three daughters, all with Latinate names. The youngest of these, Felicia, was a favorite of Clinton Wallace; in his eyes, she could do no wrong. Although the girl in the story is the middle daughter, the similarity between the names Allegra ("merry") and Felicia ("felicity") is so strong that it seems likely Kirk lightly based his young heroine upon his third daughter, if only in name and for her power to charm and captivate the lumbering hobo. But it may be that Kirk, who tended to blend the characteristics of several real-life models to form his literary characters, here blended aspects of his own middle daughter, Cecilia, with those of his youngest to form Allegra. Another possible conjunction of two persons is Father Justin O'Malley, who is mentioned almost in passing in "Long, Long Trail" (but is the central character in its sequel, "Watchers at the Strait Gate") and is conservative by temperament and conviction. His upper-Michigan parish will some day fall into the hands of a brisk, efficient, secularized episcopacy, which would prefer that O'Malley resign. He is a cigar smoker who has learned that the things will kill him if he doesn't cut back, and he occasionally takes a glass of strong drink. He likes solitude and reading, especially in the writings of John Henry Newman. He is based in large part upon Father John McDuffie, a priest from Grand Rapids, Michigan who instructed Kirk in the Catholic faith during the early 1960s; but he bears in respects a more than passing resemblance to Kirk himself. As with O'Malley and Sarsfield, Kirk was a friend and something of a confessor of Clinton Wallace, who told him of his petty crimes, spiritual beliefs, and sense of lifelong failure, all of which was transplanted with minor variation into "There's a Long, Long Trail a-Winding." (In "Watchers at the Strait Gate," perhaps the most emotionally moving story Kirk wrote, the pilgrim spirit of Frank Sarsfield returns from the purgatorial road late one winter's night to visit the ailing Father O'Malley, the only man who had "ever talked with me for hours as if I had a mind and was worth passing the time with." Frank comes to confess his few sins and to gently prepare his old friend for the same journey from this life to the next. Appropriately, the remains of the hobo Clinton Wallace and "the godfather of American conservatism" lie side by side today in the cemetery of St. Michael's Catholic Church in Remus, Michigan.)

In a review of *The Princess of All Lands,* Thomas Fleming described the characters in "Long, Long Trail" and the collection's other stories as "facing more than the terror of the unknown; they are confronted with their own selves and the consequences of their actions and moral choices."[17] Frank Sarsfield's purgation, coming about in a timeless moment that he can only understand in retrospect, illustrates this point—one articulated in Dante's *Divine Comedy* (with which Kirk was well familiar), intuited by the author early in life, and articulated to him by the distinguished Jesuit scholar Martin D'Arcy: The damned, the sainted, and those in the process of purgation, exist in the eternal present, the damned stuck like flies in amber within the sins that separated them from God and man, the pilgrims doing penance for sins that still prevent access to Heaven, and those who have been purged rejoicing forever within the stations in Heaven appropriate to their respective degrees of saintliness. "Heaven is a state," D'Arcy said to Kirk on one occasion, "in which all the good things of your life are present to you whenever you desire them—not in memory merely, not somehow re-enacted, but present, beyond the barriers of time, in all their fullness. Thus husband and wife would experience in eternity, when they should will it, what they had experienced within mundane time, linear time; and human creatures, resurrected, will have perfected bodies." D'Arcy further explained that Hell is a state of being in which all the evil that one has done is eternally present—and there is no escape from it. "So it is that human creatures make their own destiny, their own Heaven and their own Hell," commented Kirk on D'Arcy's remarks.[18]

In an essay published in *Modern Age,* R. Andrew Newman quotes a telling passage from *The Sword of Imagination:* "No doctrine is more comforting than the teaching of Purgatory. . . . For purgatorily, one may be granted opportunity to atone for having let some precious life run out like water from a neglected tap into sterile sands." In the case of Frank Sarsfield, writes Newman, "God has given Frank a chance to let his goodness and his fondness of children blossom into a self-sacrificing love which allows three young girls and their mother to live and which propels his own soul closer to the lasting Easter vision."[19] This "Easter vision," of eternal resurrection from death into the fullness of life, comes at the end of a long, long trail, which is a trail of suffering. The "trail" is the pilgrimage through life here below, in what C. S. Lewis called the "Shadowlands"; those who earnestly seek redemption and mercy while upon that road find it at the end, and find the journey worth their suffering.

Kirk considered "Long, Long Trail" a story that presents the Purgatorial vision, to form part of "a trilogy with theological or transcendental implications" along with the Infernal "Balgrummo's Hell" and "Saviourgate," which presents the Paradisiacal vision.[20] This was not lost on one reader, novelist Madeleine L'Engle, who wrote of the "enormous pleasure" and "most willing suspension of disbelief" with which she read the stories in *The Princess of All Lands,* adding: "It is also refreshing to find stories of heavenly and profane love which, also, are willing to deal with the grand theological themes."[21]

"Balgrummo's Hell," which forms the diabolical segment of Kirk's trilogy, explores what happens to an unfortunate burglar, Rafe Horgan, who invades the rotting estate of an Edinburgh noble, Alexander Killan Finchburn, tenth Baron Balgrummo. Horgan had entered the rambling old hulk of a mansion in search of valuable oil paintings to steal, having heard that the aged Balgrummo was bedridden and near death. Having asked around beforehand, he had also learned that, way back in 1913, Balgrummo had overstepped himself in a bloody way while dabbling in Satanism after the manner of A. E. Waite and other turn-of-the-century devotees of the black arts. He has been confined by the authorities to Balgrummo Lodging for over fifty years, ever since the night of what his sole living relative calls "the Trouble"; and, like Boo Radley in *To Kill a Mockingbird,* he hasn't been seen since by his neighbors. On that long-ago night, Balgrummo's experiments had culminated in a murderous black mass of sorts in the mansion's chapel, which (Horgan has heard) is still decorated with an enormous, blasphemous cartoon by Henry Fuseli. In search of priceless art, he gets more than he bargained for, learning firsthand that feeble old Balgrummo, though on his deathbed, pervades every room of Balgrummo Lodging, stuck eternally in the horrible acts of a night in 1913. "What's the time of day in Hell?" Balgrummo's solicitor had asked rhetorically to an inquiring Horgan earlier in the narrative. He answers his own question:

> Hell knows no future and no past, but only the everlasting moment of damnation. Also Hell is spaceless; or, conceivably, it's a locked box, damnably confining. Here we have Lord Balgrummo shut up perpetually in his box called Balgrummo Lodging, where the fire is not quenched and the worm never dieth. One bloody and atrocious act, committed in that very box, literally is his enduring reality. He's not recollecting; he's experiencing, here and (for him) now. All the frightful excitement of that Trouble, the very act of profanation and terror, lifts him out of what we call Time.[22]

This, again, is the vision of Hell articulated by Martin D'Arcy. Between Time and the Timeless a great gulf is fixed; but Rafe Horgan—an arrogant, violent, unrepentant thief—has placed himself in a place of extreme danger, at what Eliot called "the point of intersection of the timeless / with time." And here Hell, being forever hungry, envelops Horgan, whose final vision is Lord Balgrummo's face "or what Balgrummo's must have been fifty years before, but possessed: eager, eager, eager; all appetite, passion, yearning after the abyss."

RALPH BAIN

Kirk had given pride of place in the collection *The Princess of All Lands* to "Sorworth Place," a traditional ghost story that introduces Ralph Bain, who is visiting a small town on the Scottish coast. An aimless wanderer and something of a wastrel, though good-hearted, Bain risks his life protecting a beautiful young widow, Ann Lurlin, from the one-year-in-the-grave corpse of her brutal husband, come hideously to life to reclaim her for his own. In "Saviourgate," the final story in the collection, Kirk reintroduces Bain who, having crossed "the great divide," is now living comfortably within a wrinkle in time, standing drinks for a lost man in the Crosskeys, a cozy pub on Saviourgate Street in London. Having blundered into Saviourgate while hurrying through the city's unfamiliar streets, a certain Mark Findlay worries about a train he has to catch while Bain, who had scraped acquaintance with Findlay many years earlier, tries to get him to understand that he need not worry, saying that he can catch that train any time he so desires. He, Bain explains, has crossed "the Border" between time and the timeless—though by accident and before his time. Puzzled but comfortable within the warm pub, Findlay listens skeptically as one of Bain's friends, Canon Hoodman, explains that

> all the good moments or hours or days that you ever experienced are forever present to you, whenever you want them, after you've crossed the Border. We were told that we shall have bodies; we have them. You say that you've not yet crossed the Border, Findlay. Well, once you have crossed—and if really you're still in Time, that may be a long while yet for you—then, God willing, you'll understand as we two can't make you understand.[23]

Bidding Bain and the priest farewell, Findlay steps out into the night air and, having been given directions, hurries toward his train. He discovers that the hour is nowhere near as late as he had earlier thought and that the Crosskeys, upon his looking back at it, is a pile of rubble, having been destroyed in the London Blitz many years earlier and never restored.

For Ralph Bain, an act of selfless heroism on behalf of a woman he could never possess has carried him across "the Border" into the scene of his young manhood's fondest memories, not to be replayed recurrently like events captured on videotape, but real and present, to be enjoyed whenever he so chooses. To Findlay, the Saviour's "gate" has been opened for a few minutes, and he has been granted a glimpse of godly acceptance and love that he may yet enjoy, should he so choose. Russell Kirk, always reticent about directly stating the how-to's of entering into divine grace, nevertheless leaves a clear clue in the story; for to enter into the company of Bain and his friends Findlay must go by the sign of the cross, the key to everlasting bliss.

In *Paradise*, Piccarda dei Donati tells Dante that to spirits in Heaven it is "the essence of our blissful fate / To dwell in the divine will's radius, / Wherein our wills themselves are integrate," for there "His will is our peace." In response to this, Dante reports:

> Then I saw plain how Heav'n is everywhere
> Paradise, though the grace of the First Good
> Falls differently in different regions there.[24]

Not all of the blessed will be situated in the same proximity to the Divine Presence; in "Saviourgate," Ralph Bain explains that not all of the blessed will find themselves in the taproom of the Crosskeys in prewar London upon crossing "the Border." Each will experience the timeless moment (or timeless moments) particular to his own life and circumstances; as Bain notes, "In our Father's house are many mansions, but they're not all on the same floor."

The vision of *The Divine Comedy* is apparent in the trilogy discussed above and throughout much of Kirk's horror fiction. In one story, "The Peculiar Demesne of Archvicar Gerontion," Kirk even has his mortal protagonist pursued by a moaning "corpse-candle" straight out of the *Inferno*—about which more below.

MINISTER WITHOUT PORTFOLIO

Kirk considered his most intriguing and well developed characters to be Frank Sarsfield and the mysterious Manfred Arcane, who styled himself "Minister without Portfolio to the Hereditary President of the Commonwealth of Hamnegri, and de facto Field Commander of the Armies of That August Prince." Arcane appears in four of Kirk's works of fiction, being introduced in the satiric novel *A Creature of the Twilight*, continuing his adventures in the stories "The Last God's Dream" and "The Peculiar

Demesne of Archvicar Gerontion," and concluding his story in the horror novel *Lord of the Hollow Dark.*

In Manfred Arcane, Kirk let his imagination run more freely than in the creation of any of his other characters. Arcane is described in "The Last God's Dream" as a sharp-featured, eloquent man: "He was . . . swarthy, white-haired and white-bearded" and he "wore a beautiful light silk suit cut in a military fashion, and his English, his genuine English English, was exquisite." Arcane is a lively punster, as is evidenced from the following brief colloquy from "The Last God's Dream," in which he speaks with a companion about being overheard by the Yugoslav secret police in the midst of his telling a lengthy anecdote:

> "Ah, that's of no consequence, Don Pelayo," Arcane told him, in English. "Let the police agents listen! They'll not apprehend me, not even my moral. . . . Do you fancy, old friend, that I'm senile? Not yet, not yet, even though you find me in my anecdotage."

Elsewhere in the same story, Manfred Arcane is described as "curiously handsome, with a beak for a nose, looking considerably like an arctic owl. His skin, contrasting with hair and beard, seemed almost unwrinkled, rather as if he had undergone plastic surgery." He is the bastard son of a Viennese gypsy woman and an unknown nobleman—or at least he says he is. He was schooled in England, "idled about Vienna," served in the cavalry of a native prince of India, fought on the "illiberal side" in the Spanish Civil War, romanced an Italian countess, served as a double agent in Italy during World War II, and near the end of the war led a ragtag band of reprobates in liberating a Nazi concentration camp. In telling of his very active life, he is forever changing the details of his mysterious past, though one thing is sure about him: Arcane's life could never be called boring. A lively talker, he is at once charismatic, sardonic, and self-effacing. He is a good man, but he chooses to wear a mask of ribaldry with a hint of the scandalous; one moment he is speaking of his Catholic faith and a little later he credits his frequent hair-breadth escapes from violent death to the fact that "the devil protects his own." "All my days have I done evil," he begins his narration in *A Creature of the Twilight*; and his statement seems equal parts boast and lament. In Hamnegri he is held in awe by common people, who see him as something of an uncanny presence and call him "the Father of Shadows." He is accompanied through life by a small retinue of associates who, though fluctuating in number from story to story, are as unconventional as he: his beautiful, quick-tempered young Sicilian assistant (and eventually, his wife), Melchiora Caola, her illegitimate young son Guido, a wise old woman named Grizel Fergusson, two African assistants styled Cleon and Brasidas (whose names mean, respectively, the mortar and the pestle of war), and a genteel but menacing, one-eyed Spanish colonel named Jesus Pelayo Fuentes y Iturbide, commander of the "Interracial Peace Volunteers, a body of well-disciplined men-at-arms in the service of the hereditary President of the Commonwealth of Hamnegri."

"The devil protects his own," said Arcane, in "The Last God's Dream"; and in a later story, the devil almost claims his own, after years of "protection." In this story, "The Peculiar Demesne of Archvicar Gerontion," Arcane encounters a being from the Pit, arguably derived by Kirk from *The Divine Comedy*.

In Canto XXVI of the *Inferno*, Dante describes sinners in the Eighth Bowge of the Eighth Circle; these are the spirits of those who in their mortal state counseled others to practice fraud. As punishment for this sin, the damned are condemned to wander round the Eighth Bowge through eternity while wrapped entirely in a tall flame. When Dante's guide Virgil stops one such being and asks him to tell his story, the spirit within the flame speaks, but not before several moments of exertion and incomprehensible "muttering." According to Dorothy L. Sayers's translation, the flame itself "Began to mutter and move, as a wavering flame / Wrestles against the wind and is over-worn; And, like a speaking tongue vibrant to frame / Language, the tip of it flickering to and fro / Threw out a voice and answered. . . ."[25] Likewise, in "The Peculiar Demesne," Manfred Arcane finds himself in a dark place of torment where he is pursued by an "abominable corpse-candle" that seeks to take possession of his body. This, then, is a tale of old men and their frenzy, "Their fear of fear and frenzy, their fear of possession." The ancient archvicar of the story's title is a dangerous individual who has spent a long, dissolute life leading the "Church of the Divine Mystery," an heretical organization that served "as an instrument for deception and extortion, working principally upon silly old women." Yet the archvicar "did believe fervently in a supernatural realm," accessed through ingesting *kalanzi*, a powerful and dangerous narcotic developed by Gerontion himself. In his religion without God, Archvicar Gerontion has counseled his "flock" to practice the ultimate fraud: to believe that they can be as God and to gamble their lives on that hope. However, through overreaching—that great error of the prideful—Gerontion has been arrested, found guilty of trafficking in narcotics, and sentenced to death in the African city of Haggat in the nation of Hamnegri. During the days before his execution, Gerontion is placed, guarded, in the care and sumptuous domicile of Arcane, who talks easily with the old reprobate over coffee and raisins, extracting from him information about his past. It seems Gerontion has spent several lifetimes prowling the earth in search of those he can deceive, taking joy in the destruction of the unwary. His very name, taken after the doomed old man, the embodiment of emptiness in Eliot's poem of the same name, is an alias; he has had many others over the centuries. Like Eliot's Gerontion, the archvicar is no bringer of hope and life, but a provider of ultimate sterility and despair. In order to fulfill his demonic will over time, his spirit must take possession of a relatively healthy human body on the eve of his present body's demise, interpenetrating the new fleshly envelope while in a hellish netherworld—the archvicar's "demesne"—in which his mortal victims find themselves after taking a fatal dose of *kalanzi*. Arcane discovers this firsthand, after being tricked by his guest into eating a handful of raisins laced with an unseen sprinkle of the narcotic. Having accomplished this trickery and eating some of the tainted raisins himself, Gerontion gasps his dying words to Arcane, "I shall take your body."

Finding himself in an alternate world, a dark town of decay, graves, and ruins, Arcane flees from a pursuer who is described at first as a "light," then as "not a lantern of any sort, but rather a mass of glowing stuff, more phosphorescent than incandescent, and it seemed to be about the height of a man." As he narrates his story, Arcane relates:

> And out of this abominable corpse-candle, if I may call it that, came a voice. I suppose it may have been no more than a low murmur, but in that utter silence of the empty town it was tremendous. At first it gabbled and moaned, but then I made out words, and those words paralyzed me. They were these: "I must have your body."[26]

Elsewhere Arcane speaks of "that corpse-candle form, gabbling and moaning as if in extremity." As he and his pursuer reach the climax of their ghastly endgame, Arcane takes refuge in a ruined church and finds himself cornered. Terrified, he looks toward the doorway by which he had entered the church: "The tall glow of corruption had got so far as that doorway, and now lingered upon the threshold. For a moment, as if by a final frantic effort, it shone brightly." In the end, it is by faith Arcane is saved, not by his own ingenuity: he clasps an icon of Christ the King above the ruined altar, embracing it for dear life—and the corpse-candle "went out as if an extinguisher had been clapped over it." Arcane comes out of a drug-induced swoon to discover Gerontion dead on the floor, having failed in his mission of bodily possession.

Here and in other stories, Kirk is careful to note the correspondences, the similarities in temperament and susceptibility to sin, between the damned and the redeemed. In the case of "The Peculiar Demesne," Arcane shows himself guilty of a degree of pridefulness that almost costs him his life and his immortal soul; his devil-may-carelessness and momentary inattention give Gerontion just the narrow opportunity the latter needs to sprinkle *kalanzi* on the raisins and deliver Arcane into his twilight realm. In "The

Invasion of the Church of the Holy Ghost," Father Thomas Montrose allows himself to succumb to the same lust of the eye that had earlier led the depraved pimp and drug lord "Sherm the Screamer" into a hinted-at lust for his own sister and a scheme to sell her into a life of prostitution. "You're jest like me, buster!" exclaims the murderous housebreaker "Butte" to the reforming convict Eddie Cain in "Lex Talionis," to which Eddie can only reply, "Too true." "Hell!" screeches the degenerate "Daddy" to his kidnapped captive, Yolande, in "The Princess of all Lands," "You're jest like me!" Thus the world of Kirk's horror fiction is not one in which the morally stainless withstand the inherently depraved; rather, with a nod to George MacDonald's famous aphorism, it is a world of crucial choices, divided between people who have chosen to say to God, "Thy will be done," and people to whom God says, "*Thy* will be done." "Like the dragon that lies beside the road, Satan and his minions remain a continuous threat," wrote Andrew Lytle of Kirk's ghostly fiction. "But it is nothing, no thing, unless the unwary, tempted, accept it for the truth. The intended victim is almost always seized through the sensibility. This precipitates the drama of the soul—salvation or damnation." Writing of "The Peculiar Demesne of Archvicar Gerontion," Lytle added:

> This is almost allegory, but there is too much of life's concrete detail for such an abstraction. The struggle, perhaps, could be the basic allegory underlying all great actions, in literature and out. The soul occupies perilously the body. It is by the flesh that it is saved or lost.[27]

A GATHERING OF PILGRIMS

In *Lord of the Hollow Dark*, Kirk's third and final work of long fiction, Arcane presides over a lengthy tale in which the diabolical, the purgatorial, and the divine visions are worked out in the lives of several people, including the spectral presence of Ralph Bain, summoned to what Kirk's readers will find a familiar setting, Balgrummo Lodging.

To the mists and reek of the Lodging are summoned a small band of society's misfits who become unlikely comrades in arms, but with no weapons but faith and reason: a young single mother named Deborah Fitzgerald and her baby, both betrayed by the baby's father; a libidinous lout and ne'er-do-well named Sweeney; and the eloquent, cheroot-smoking Manfred Arcane and his retinue: wise, garrulous old Lady Grizel Ferguson; the beautiful, hot-tempered woman Melchiora; and Arcane's good-at-need African attendant, Brasidas. For this particular occasion, which has almost the air of a grim costume party, all in attendance at Balgrummo Lodging have been assigned names from Eliot's poetry for the duration:

Arcane, is styled after his old nemesis Archvicar Gerontion, and in time he, Lady Ferguson ("Madame Sesostris"), Melchiora ("Fresca"), Brasidas ("Phlebas"), Deborah ("Marina"), and Sweeney ("Apeneck Sweeney") are joined by the energetic presence of Ralph Bain, who is called Coriolan. They have been called to Balgrummo Lodging at the behest of a certain Mr. Apollinax who, like his counterpart in Eliot's poem, is a spiritually empty intellectual with a "tinkling" laugh. It may be remembered that Eliot modeled his Apollinax after Bertrand Russell, who (to the poet) represented man devoid of the moral imagination, a being who trusts entirely to defecated rationality.

It is written in the Christian Scriptures that demons seek to inhabit empty vessels of humanity; for in the spiritual world, as in the material, a vacuum cannot exist for long. So it is with Apollinax. Fascinated by Lord Balgrummo's long-ago experiments in necromancy and Satanism, Apollinax (whose true name is never revealed) has deliberately sought out a number of persons whose absence would not be noticed in the world at large, to entice them into participating in a celebration of spiritual dissolution. Considering himself a lord over time itself, he calls this event a "Timeless Moment," and it will involve certain forbidden rites, aided by liberal doses of *kalanzi*, which will result in the destruction of all the participants except Apollinax—though most of the intended victims are unaware of their impending doom. Waif-like Deborah Fitzgerald and her baby, Michael, have been singled out by the mysterious Apollinax for special torment, he taking his cue from the now-uncovered Fuseli painting first described in the story "Balgrummo's Hell," depicting an obscene tormenting of the Virgin and Child.

In addition to the individuals named above, there are numerous other participants in Apollinax's ugly charade, fools who have entirely given over their allegiance to their "Master." During their few days in Balgrummo Lodging, the aspirants to the "Timeless Moment" discover that they are in fact prisoners within the crumbling mansion, under armed guard by a motley collection of bepimpled, *kalanzi*-addled "acolytes" of Apollinax. Only the Father of Shadows understands and anticipates Apollinax's plan and seeks to inform, protect, and rescue his companions from a horrid death-in-life in Balgrummo's Hell. Thanks to Arcane's initiative, what is hell for many proves a place of purgation for others.

The way of purgatory is necessarily a way of pain; the possibility of purgation necessarily entails pain chosen, even embraced, for a greater good. Ralph Bain, in an act that echoes his self-sacrificial act on behalf of lovely Ann Lurlin in "Sorworth Place," loses his life again and gladly—this time on behalf of Deborah and her child. For his part, Arcane nearly dies. Sweeney chooses to throw in with Arcane and is battered from pillar to post, learning a hard, cleansing object lesson in humility and respect for others, as well as awe for the reality of the world beyond this world. But for Apollinax and his other acolytes and disciples, Balgrummo's Hell proves a hell indeed.

As the action unfolds in *Lord of the Hollow Dark*, Arcane reveals his identity and objective to Deborah and Sweeney. Before the demise of the original "Archvicar Gerontion," as recorded in "The Peculiar Demesne," Apollinax had been one of the old reprobate's key contacts for the import and sale of *kalanzi* in Europe. Having ferreted out this information from Gerontion before his death, Arcane has determined to track down Apollinax and end the latter's career as a drug lord. The ingestion of drugs having been recognized as an intrinsic part of necromancy since biblical times, it is not surprising that Apollinax has chosen empty, ill-fated Balgrummo Lodging to conduct the ceremony of the Timeless Moment. With Arcane preferring final settlements with his enemies, an exciting endgame is promised.

The unholy sacrament is to be held in the upper layers of an ancient, underground system of passages underneath the Lodging dating from medieval times. At a crucial moment in the ceremony, "Archvicar Gerontion," whose true identity is unknown to Apollinax, is compelled to conjure the shade of Lord Balgrummo, the dead but still-feared "Minataur" of the underground maze; failing (apparently) in this, Arcane flees further into the depths of the weem with his colleagues, leaving the disciples and acolytes to continue their depraved sacrament on their own.

Arcane figures that the underground tunnel system will eventually lead to an exit on the outer bounderies of the estate, away from the house itself. He and the others are vindicated in this belief, though the outcome is far from hopeful until the last moments before emerging. Like a giant drain-trap, the path to freedom leads through a deep, deathly cold underground stream. In literature, a river traditionally represents both death and birth, or rebirth, reminiscent of baptism. Sweeney, having suffered one terrifying moment after another during his stay at the Lodging, dreams three times about stepping or falling into the river; and the third time he emerges a new man, this after having witnessed the tortuous death of one of Apollinax's disciples. Sweeney will never again attempt to force himself upon women; from now on he will honor them through his words and deeds.

As the party proceeds through the darkness, it becomes apparent that somebody has gone before them and prepared a way for their escape, carving handholds and footholds. Near the end of the novel, this same somebody borrows vitality, or virtue, from Arcane in order to assume solidity and confront Apollinax. The latter, having murdered or consented to the deaths of all his other disciples except the rebel Arcane and his fellow escapees, prepares to burn Balgrummo Lodging before departing the scene of his Satanic triumph. As he stands surveying the mansion's chapel, he is astonished to be joined by the commanding presence of the Minataur, come to destroy Apollinax, a being so given over to evil that there is no longer much of a human soul left within the husk of his body. Balgrummo's shade has indeed answered the earlier call of his beloved if illegitimate son, Manfred Arcane, and he has come to deal vengeance upon Apollinax with a sharp, double-bitted hatchet. Having believed he could assume the guise of Time the Devourer, the horrified Apollinax is swept into the abyss of time for which he had claimed to yearn for so long.

In the end, Arcane and his followers win through to light and fresh air. Sweeney has become a new man. Deborah Fitzgerald has grasped a new vision of life, one of mystery, thankfulness, and hope. And Lord Balgrummo, it is strongly implied, has been redeemed. Although considered a damned soul while he lived, Balgrummo had spent his final years repenting of his past misdeeds and, in the words of Christian Scripture, "working out his own salvation," delving through the weem in an act of prolonged purgatorial contrition, saving those who would be saved and leaving the rest to their self-willed destruction.

Lord of the Hollow Dark is one of Kirk's darker works of fiction and certainly his most ambitious. There is imagery of gloom, dampness, and rot throughout it. But there is also hope, especially in the promise of baby Michael's life, the redemption of Sweeney, the spiritual rebirth of Deborah, the good humor of Arcane, and the salvation of Alexander Fillan Inchburn, tenth Baron Balgrummo. Here, for the first time, writes Don Herron, "Kirk unleashes his ghosts from the story and novelette form; they spirit through this virtuoso literary performance, which is at once a Gothic novel in the tradition of Mrs. Radcliffe and a mystical Romance that conjures up the likes of Machen. . . . A book of diabolism, disguises, banishing, bogles, the works."[28]

OTHER STORIES

In an appraisal of *Watchers at the Strait Gate* that could apply to *Lord of the Hollow Dark* and all of Kirk's short fiction, T. John Jamieson wrote, "I believe these stories are to be taken as fables which show the reality of evil, in all its horror, as well as the power of the justice which will ultimately triumph over it. They are also myths which play upon our sense of the lingering presence of human personalities, in order to reveal to us the Eternal Social Contract. Wherever we are, we are there by the grace of previous human and divine effort; by maintaining our consciousness of it, we may preserve the accomplishments of the past and add something of our own to bequeath to posterity."[29] This concept is nowhere more apparent than in the most keenly personal of Kirk's stories, "An Encounter by Mort-stone Pond." The outline of this tale seems to have been inspired by a reading of Ray Bradbury's story "A Touch of Petulance," which Kirk admired. In an undated letter to Bradbury concerning "A Touch of Petulance," Kirk wrote:

> Did you ever have yourself that kind of experience: I mean the young self encountering the old self, literally or almost literally, and the old self (at another time) encountering the young self? I never did; but a friend of mind in Alabama (no credulous or superstitious man) had precisely that experience. As a boy, in deep sorrow, he became aware of a presence that comforted him stoically; and forty years later, walking the same street after decades of absence, he was aware of a sorrowful small boy walking invisibly beside him—his youthful self, from across the gulf of time. My friend himself had been his own comforter. The man recognized the boy he had been once, although the boy had not recognized in his invisible comforter the man whom he would become.[30]

In his own short story, placed in a setting based on the author's boyhood home in the old millhouse in Plymouth, Kirk tenderly examines a lonely young boy's encounter with a ghostly presence on the eve of the lad's departure from home. The boy, Gerard Peirce, has lost his parents to death, and is taking a final walk near the millpond in his Midwestern hometown before leaving to live with relatives out West. To his initial bewilderment and terror, Gerard senses an unseen presence at his side and hears reassuring words from outside time, concerning himself and his parents, which graphically sum up the implications of the moral imagination: "This too shall pass. You will grow to be a man. They will love you always, being made for eternity." Many years pass, and a day comes when elderly Gerard Peirce walks once again by the same millpond, having come home at long last to visit his parents' graves at the nearby cemetery. He is in poor health, having spent his life as a soldier and taken some painful wounds that will never heal. General Peirce limps to his father's monument. Then he senses an unseen presence; it is that of a small, frightened boy, to whom he offers special words of comfort that seem to come from outside time.

The paragraphs that then follow summarize much of Kirk's metaphysic:

> The marvels of time, of consciousness, of personality, nearly undid him. He sank down before his father's granite shaft.
> We are essences, the General thought, essences that flow like mercury. Each of us is a myriad of particles of energy, held temporarily in combination by purposes or forces we understand no better than did Lucretius.
> We are essences—but insubstantial really, such stuff as dreams are made of, not understanding death because we do not know what life is. Across the gulf

of years, had the boy who was to be a man and the man who had been a boy
met in some fashion? Had a conscience spoken briefly to a conscience?
   Personality is a mask: the soul seems indefinable. What gives coherence to
our essences? In erring reason's spite, the General wondered, am I part of that
once-venerated Mystical Body? . . .
   Did those few words of assurance my older self gave to my younger self really issue from me? Or were they put into my consciousness by a tender
Other?[31]

"I think, therefore I am," runs René Descartes's famous dictum, which
Kirk considered and rejected at an early age. The truth, he believed is, "I
am, therefore I think." To the man or woman who believes this, God and
the transcendent—if they exist—are not the creations of human imagination; rather humanity is God's creation, or possibly even His dream.
(Kirk's story "The Last God's Dream," narrated in large part by the eloquent Manfred Arcane, treats the latter possibility.) Holding to orthodox
Christian belief, Kirk believed we are not creators of life's moral norms; we
are at best vessels of obedience, indifference, or active disobedience,
granted free will and assigned works to undertake in mortal life.
   Sometimes these works, which include ministering to "spirits in
prison," are far from pleasant, and sometimes the cost of obedience is high.
Ralph Bain loses his life protecting a woman from assault in "Sorworth
Place"; in agony of spirit, ex-convict Eddie Cain must conduct a rapist,
thief, and murderer to the point of the latter's disembodiment and damnation (in "Lex Talionis"); and in "The Princess of All Lands," beautiful
Yolande, driving alone through a small Michigan town, picks up a literal
hitchhiker-from-hell and then must endure an unwanted confrontation
with three demon-filled beings filled with lust and murderous intent, herself armed only with intelligence and faith. (In *The Sword of Imagination*,
Kirk relates in rich detail the extent to which this story was based upon two
real-life episodes: the first, in which the Kirks endured unexpected peri-
odic visits from a man they came to call "the Death Indian"; the other, in
which his wife Annette was kidnapped late one autumn afternoon by an
armed hitchhiker.) In these stories and others, race is not to the swift, nor
the battle to the strong, in the stoic words of Ecclesiastes. At best, the pro-
tagonists are saved from spiritual destruction by the agency of "a tender
Other," whose ways can be at times rough, with (in some cases) no sure
"sign" given that the horror they have endured is gone forever.
   This brings us to what this writer considers Kirk's most accomplished
story, "The Invasion of the Church of the Holy Ghost." Originally published in *The Magazine of Fantasy and Science Fiction,* this story introduces
Father Thomas Montrose, a black, Jamaican-born Episcopalian rector of an
inner-city parish in Hawkhill, a crumbling area given over to seedy bars,

Russell Kirk and his younger sister, Carolyn, outside their grandfather's house on Mill Street in Plymouth, sometime during the mid 1920s.

Street scene in the north end of Plymouth, not far from Russell Kirk's birthplace, sometime near the time of his birth.

The young scholar, in a portrait probably taken at Duke University in 1940.

Russell and "the beauteous Annette" Kirk on their wedding day, September 19, 1964.

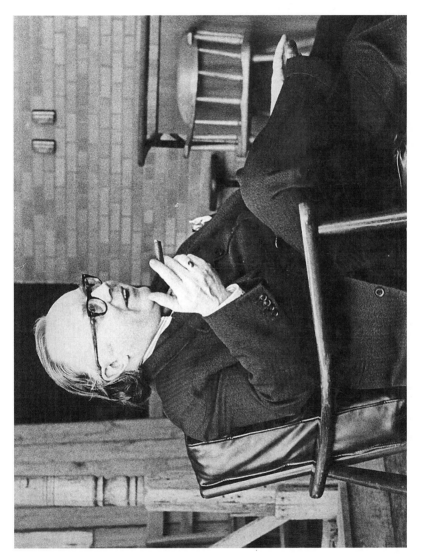

Kirk gets straight to the point, in an appearance sometime during the 1970s.

Cigar in hand, Kirk stands before the Old House of Piety Hill, built by his great-grandfather, Amos Johnson, in 1878.

The Old House burns to the ground, Ash Wednesday, 1975. Only a metal fire-door prevented the brick annex, at right, from being gutted by flames.

The Kirk family stands before the newly revamped Piety Hill, during the spring or summer of 1976. Annette holds Andrea, as Russell stands with (from left) Felicia, Monica, and Cecilia.

The Kirk Library, a former toy factory bought and refurnished by Russell Kirk to house his 10,000-volume personal library and papers.

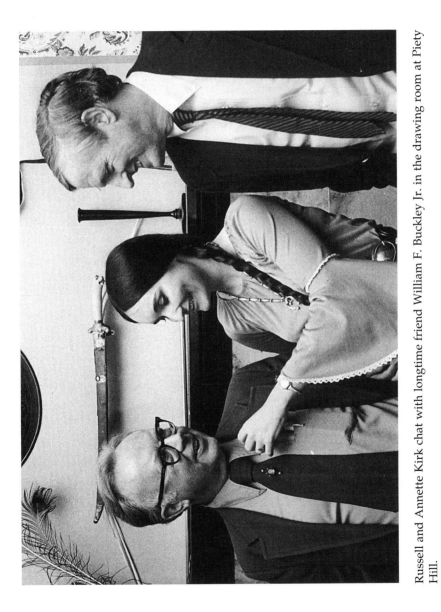

Russell and Annette Kirk chat with longtime friend William F. Buckley Jr. in the drawing room at Piety Hill.

Russell and Annette Kirk with Henry and Eleanor Regnery. It was publisher Regnery who recognized the merits of *The Conservative Mind*, publishing Kirk's seminal work to wide acclaim in 1953.

Guest speaker Malcolm Muggeridge makes a point while Russell Kirk looks on, during the seminar "Pilgrims in the Dark Wood of Our Time," held at Piety Hill in 1978.

Friends and mutual admirers Ray Bradbury and Russell Kirk, in Los Angeles (1981).

Honored by conservative leaders and colleagues for his achievement, Kirk addresses his audience at the Mayflower Hotel in Washington, D.C., October 1, 1981.

Russell and Annette Kirk confer for a moment at the Kirk Library.

Annette Kirk clarifies the intent and findings of the President's Commission on Excellence in Education and its final report, *A Nation at Risk*, at a conference in Washington, D.C. in 1983. At her side, Russell Kirk listens intently.

The Kirks pose with President Ronald Reagan in January 1989, when Reagan awarded Russell Kirk the Presidential Medal of Freedom.

Michigan governor John Engler, a longtime admirer of Russell Kirk, congratulates his friend upon the occasion of Kirk's seventy-fifth birthday and the fortieth anniversary of the initial publication of *The Conservative Mind*. Joining Russell Kirk and Engler are (from left) Gleaves Whitney, Annette Kirk, and Michelle Engler. This celebration, which included several hundred other well-wishers, took place at the Dearborn Inn in Dearborn, Michigan in early October, 1993.

In the final summer of his life, Kirk stands for a portrait on the lawn of the library.

Kirk's gravesite, at the back of the cemetery at St. Michael's Catholic Church, Remus, Michigan. At the bottom of the stone is Kirk's chosen epitaph, one of his favorite passages from Eliot:

"The communication of the dead
is tongued with fire
Beyond the language of the living."

prostitution, numbers games, and overall decay. A believing Christian, Montrose acknowledges the apostle Paul's admonition that he is battling against the wicked hosts of this present darkness. To extend the metaphor, Montrose is fighting what seems to be a losing rear-guard action in the crumbling neighborhood of Hawkhill with its saloons lining the ironically named Pentecost Road, though he can claim small victories now and again: here, a prostitute taken off the street and given sanctuary in his church before giving up her vocation and going home; there, a tiny number of faithful convinced to attend worship services on a somewhat regular basis. Mostly, though, Hawkhill is a lost cause, a once-respectable neighborhood slowly falling to ruin amid an atmosphere of alternating fear, boredom, and aimless indifference. "You have only to spend a year in the neighborhood of Pentecost Road to understand that Satan is a person and a conscious force, no figure of myth merely. He takes possession of empty vessels," writes Montrose, whose "memoir" of the events that follow serves as the framework for "The Invasion." These few words summarize greatly the theme of this story, stating a truth that Montrose discovers to his own horror and would have cost him dearly had he not met an unlikely friend during his years in Hawkhill. For into the life of Father Montrose had come a blind man of preternatural abilities, Homer ("Fork") Causland, piano player in the Mustang Bar on Pentecost Road in Hawkhill. To the priest, Causland comes to be an irritant, a seer, an ally, and, ultimately, a deliverer.

Blind Homer had earned his curious nickname at a time before the action of this story begins. Living alone on the top floor of a shabby rooming house, he had incurred the wrath of a local pimp-cum-drug dealer-cum-local religious figure named Sherm ("the Screamer") Tilton. The Screamer and a band of his toughest gang members had swooped down on Causland's rooming house in the wee hours of the morning, prepared to torture and murder their victim. Unfortunately for them, they found Causland awake and prepared, and in the brief exchange that ensued, the blind man dispatched his attackers with the aid of a pitchfork and a pump-action shotgun dropped by one of his would-be killers. The scene of the bloody aftermath, reminiscent of Frank Sarsfield's rampage among the brutal convicts in "Long, Long Trail," reveals a handful of Causland's attackers dead or dying, and the Screamer lying dead with Causland's pitchfork buried in his upper ribs. To the fearful residents of Hawkhill, this feat of vengeful survival earned Homer Causland the nickname "Fork."

Not long after Montrose and Causland meet, Kirk grafts in a scene straight out of Flannery O'Connor. Just outside the Mustang, the two comrades pause to witness an impromptu presentation by a sidewalk evangelist who preaches on the danger of being spiritually empty, using a ventriloquist's dummy as a prop. "'Cept you take the Lord Jesus for your personal saviour, you're no better 'n this here dummy!" he shouts, adding:

> Where you goin' to spend eternity? You want to spend it with the Whore o' Babylon and the Beast, whose number is six six six? The wages of sin is death. You want to be like this here dummy, no brains in your head? You want to be cast into the fire eternal? Brothers and sisters, death is all around us. Old Mister Death, he comes here, he comes there. Old Mister Death, he grabs you when you're on a high, when you're drinkin' and fornicatin', and he takes the breath out o' your body, leavin' you no better than this here dummy! He takes you where the worm never dieth and the fire is not quenched. 'Cept you follow the Lord Jesus, Ol' Man Death put his bony hands on you, and you curl up like a worm. . . .[32]

In a short time, something worse than death reaches for Montrose from beyond the grave, offering a lure the celibate priest finds hard to resist. Julie Tilton, the Screamer's sister, as tall and beautiful as she is innocent, arrives at the Mustang one evening looking for her brother. She has not heard of Sherm's criminal history, nor of his death. Being an innocent she turns heads in the Mustang, some of them on the shoulders of evil men, who menace her. In a short time, having given Julie shelter in the church, Montrose finds himself infatuated with his young guest, dwelling on her smooth, inviting sexual presence, and soon becoming consumed with lust for her. "Doc, exert your will, as you're given to saying in your sermons: don't let anything occupy you," warns Fork. Montrose knows that Fork has intuited his passion for Julie, and he hates the blind man for it. He first suspects that something is terribly wrong with him when a local mob tough, Franchetti, pays a call at the church, demanding that the priest release Julie into the tender care of Sherm's old gang, or the surviving remnant of it. Like a man possessed, Montrose beats and tramples Franchetti to a bloody pulp, dumps the unconscious hoodlum into an alley dumpster, and takes his wallet. Something has indeed begun to occupy Montrose, something evil. He is about to learn the truth voiced by the narrator to Oliver Onions's classic ghost story "The Beckoning Fair One": "We are not gods. We cannot drive out devils. We must see selfishly to it that devils do not enter into ourselves."

For his part in the death of Sherm the Screamer, Causland has been marked for death by the mob in Hawkhill. For his part in attempting to shelter the Screamer's sister from the mean streets of Hawkhill, Montrose has been marked for damnation by the spirit of murder and lust that has already set its hooks in him. That spirit reveals its identity near the story's end, and it is only by the timely intervention of Fork Causland, or a semblance of him, that Julie Tilton isn't ravished and Thomas Montrose isn't fully possessed and destroyed. Experience, that hard teacher of fools and the unwary, brings home to Montrose that the war in the heavenly realm spoken of by the apostle Paul is as real as warfare in the material world, and that in the same way nature abhors a vacuum, an unwary vessel of honor can be filled with evil and overwhelmed if it will not be filled with the wisdom of the Holy Spirit.

I have called this, Kirk's final short story, the author's greatest. It fully develops two converging stories while skillfully sketching in a small army of secondary figures. It features two parallel climaxes, the first foreshadowing the second: the bloody encounter at Causland's rooming house and the successful throwing back of the invasion of Holy Ghost Church by the unquiet dead, emissaries from hell. It closes on a note of existential gloom in which faith, the faith that saves Montrose, is truly the substance of things hoped for, the evidence of things not seen. In terms of story alone, it entertains and thrills in the best tradition of the Gothic tale; at a deeper level, it draws the attentive reader into a realm of thought beyond the reaches of understanding. Like the Christian Scripture, as described in an old saying, this story is like the ocean: the uninitiated can play in the shallows all day, while the more skillful can swim in the depths with their feet never touching bottom. It is Kirk's most vivid and thoughtful exploration of the realm in which ghosts live: the so-called "Interval" between a human spirit leaving its body and its departure to its eternal destination. "I don't know anyone since [Charles] Williams who has so powerfully looked onto, or into, that region that lies on the far side of the scrim so thinly shielding us from the Unconditioned," wrote Thomas Howard to Kirk, who makes it clear in this particular story that a man who has served as an instrument for demonic forces in life may well be used for malign purposes in death.[33]

It is Death incarnate who proves to be a tool in the hands of God to rescue Montrose at the moment of his near-possession by a procession of ghastly demons. Death, here, is at once a friend, an enemy, a life-giver(!), and a deliverer, not simply a robed and cowled bugbear to be shunned; and in this Kirk's thought runs exactly parallel with those of Peter Kreeft, whose ruminative book-length essay *Love Is Stronger Than Death* (1979) Kirk much admired and recommended for a National Book Award four years before writing "The Invasion."[34] The nature of death and the inscrutability of grace received are at the heart of this story. In the end, Montrose is left alive and unharmed in body but profoundly shaken in spirit. He knows he neither deserves nor even understands the deliverance that has been visited upon him, seeing that he is entirely undeserving of his deliverance from the demons who sought to unite fully with him. He can only sit safely behind the church's locked bronze door, think distractedly about the charms of Julie Tilton, write about what he has experienced, and pray that the suffering and fear that overtook him on the night of the invasion of his church by infernal forces will not be visited upon him again. "Winter is coming on, this is a night of sleet," he writes at the story's conclusion. "What is tapping now, so faintly, at the great knocker on the bronze door? It never can be she. Has the order of release been sent? 'Watch ye, stand fast in the faith, quit you like men, be strong.' I'll unbar the little door. Pray for us sinners now and at the hour of our death."

"I did not love cold harmony and perfect regularity of organization; what I sought was variety, mystery, tradition, the venerable, the awful," Kirk wrote at the midpoint of his life's journey. Pat endings and reductionist reasoning reminiscent of the faculty lounge were far from his way of thinking. Life begins and ends in mystery, Kirk believed, and this is reflected throughout his canon of work, with special effectiveness in his ghostly fiction.[35]

NOTES

1. Eliot to Kirk, March 15, 1958. Russell Kirk Center for Cultural Renewal, Mecosta, Mich.

2. Sturgeon, "A Viewpoint, A Dewpoint," *National Review* 14 (February 12, 1963), 120.

3. Bradford, "The Wizard of Mecosta," *National Review* 32 (December 12, 1980), 1514.

4. "The Reflections of a Gothic Mind," in *Confessions of a Bohemian Tory*, p. 23. Kirk liked this self-defining phrase, going so far as to integrate it intact into his memoir, *The Sword of Imagination*.

5. Bradford, "The Wizard of Mecosta," p. 1514.

6. Lewis, "It All Began with a Picture . . . ," in Walter Hooper, ed., *On Stories, and Other Essays on Literature*, p. 53.

7. "Progressive Decadence," in *Decadence and Renewal in the Higher Learning: An Episodic History of American University and College since 1953*, p. 231.

8. Kirk to Eric Voegelin, July 19, 1971. Russell Kirk Center for Cultural Renewal, Mecosta, Mich.

9. Conversation with the author, October 16, 1988.

10. Nelson, "Russell Kirk and Basil Smith," *Ghosts and Scholars*, no. 20 (1995): 46–48. The "little" magazine in which this essay appears focuses upon the literary accomplishment and influence of M. R. James.

11. Meixner, "Morrison, Kirk, Malamud," *The Sewanee Review* 72, no. 3. Summer, 1964, 541.

12. James, preface to *More Ghost Stories of an Antiquary*, p. vii.

13. Herron, "The Crepuscular Romantic: An Appreciation of the Fiction of Russell Kirk," *The Romantist*, no. 3, 1979, 9.

14. Eliot, "Burnt Norton," in *Four Quartets*, p. 13.

15. "There's a Long, Long Trail a-Winding," in *The Princess of All Lands*, p. 218. All other quotations from "Long, Long Trail" are from this edition.

16. Fleming, "Kirk's Tales of Supernatural Are Well-Written, Masterful," *The Post and Courier*, Charleston, S.C., n.d., n.p.

17. Fleming, "Kirk's Tales of the Supernatural," n.p.

18. "The Last Homely House," *The Sword of Imagination* (Grand Rapids, Mich., 1995), p. 341.

19. Newman, "Pilgrimages and Easter Destinations in the Ghostly Tales of Russell Kirk," *Modern Age* 40, no. 2, summer, 1998, 315.

20. "Prologue," *The Princess of All Lands*, p. viii.

21. From a letter Madeleine L'Engle wrote to Arkham House Publishers, May 9, 1979. Russell Kirk Center for Cultural Renewal, Mecosta, Mich.

22. "Balgrummo's Hell," in *The Princess of All Lands*, p. 176. All other quotations from "Balgrummo's Hell" are from this edition.

23. "Saviourgate," in *The Princess of All Lands*, pp. 231–32. All other quotations from "Saviourgate" are from this edition.

24. Dante, "Canto III," in *Paradise*, trans. Dorothy L. Sayers and Barbara Reynolds, p. 75.

25. Dante, "Canto XXVI," in *Hell*, trans. Dorothy L. Sayers, p. 235.

26. "The Peculiar Demesne of Archvicar Gerontion," in *Watchers at the Strait Gate*, p. 96. All other quotations from "The Peculiar Demesne" are from this edition.

27. Lytle, "The Terrors of the Soul," in James E. Person Jr., ed., *The Unbought Grace of Life: Essays in Honor of Russell Kirk*, p. 88. This appraisal was originally published in a slightly different form as a review of Kirk's *Watchers at the Strait Gate* in 1985.

28. Herron, "The Crepuscular Romantic," p. 9.

29. Jamieson, review of *Watchers at the Strait Gate*, in *The American Spectator* 18, no. 2, February, 1985, 43.

30. Undated letter to Ray Bradbury, written sometime during the years 1979–81.

31. "An Encounter by Mortstone Pond," in *Watchers at the Strait Gate*, p. 233.

32. "The Invasion of the Church of the Holy Ghost," in *Watchers at the Strait Gate*, p. 27.

33. Howard to Kirk, "St. Laurence 1984." Russell Kirk Center for Cultural Renewal, Mecosta, Mich.

34. See Kirk, "Criminal Character and Mercy," in George Panichas, ed., *Modern Age: The First Twenty-Five Years, A Selection*, p. 400.

35. An especially insightful, short assessment of Kirk's themes and intent is Robert Champ's essay "Russell Kirk's Fiction of Enchantment," which appears in *The Intercollegiate Review* 30, no. 1, Fall, 1994, 39–42. Having written of the Christian themes that permeate Kirk's later short fiction (as well as *Lord of the Hollow Dark*), Champ concludes with words with which I heartily agree: "None of this, I hasten to add, detracts one whit from the pure fun of the stories. To put it in the vernacular, Kirk is a 'great read.' He builds tension with a master's hand, he creates three dimensional characters the reader comes quickly to care about or distrust, he knows where to twist a plot in such a way as to cause a catch in the reader's breath. And he writes very scary stories."

7

Novels Gothic to Baroque:
Old House of Fear and
A Creature of the Twilight

And as the sun rose, he took her in his arms. Rash, proud, and
strange the girl was, perhaps a little mad; but in that moment he
loved her more than all the kingdoms of the earth.

> —from *Old House of Fear*

Were there no owls . . . rats would inherit the earth.

> —from *A Creature of the Twilight*

Just across and a little down the main road from my grandmother's farm
in Deep Creek, Virginia, there was for many years a path leading back into
the fields and woodlands. At a spot about one hundred yards along that
path, there was the discernible foundation of a small wooden house, which
was known since time out of mind as "the house George Washington slept
in." A house had indeed once stood on this site, and legend had it that
Washington had spent one night in it while surveying the nearby Dismal
Swamp, during the years before the American War for Independence. Several generations of children who lived on the nearby farms knew this spot
as the site of the Washington house; my mother and grandmother both
knew the site well.

Today several of the farms along the main road have been sold to developers who have built single-family houses and put in paved streets. The farm lane that led back to the site has been paved over, and the foundation of the vanished house has itself disappeared. Today, almost nobody remembers "the house George Washington slept in," and the few who hear of it dismiss it as a figment of the locals' imagination. Surely, they say, there are many such sites in the states along the East Coast, each claimed by gullible, if well-meaning, people who want to believe that their little corner of the world is more significant than it might appear to outsiders.

But are all such legendary sites hoaxes? Are the words "legend" and "myth" necessarily synonymous with "tall tales" and "noble lies"? Is there something more than a nugget of truth in the claims of the locals—and if so, does it matter? If a story is old but undocumented by written records, is its veracity entirely suspect?

In *Old House of Fear* and *A Creature of the Twilight*, Kirk spins lively and (especially in the case of *Old House*) thought-provoking tales about the nature and role of myth. In each novel, as Faulkner once stated, the past is not dead; it isn't even past.

GOTHICISM *REDIVIVUS*

It was a source of quiet pride to Kirk that he played a signal role in bringing the Gothic tale back into popularity with his novel *Old House of Fear*, which appeared in 1961. The Gothic tale, characterized by its setting and atmosphere—the former tending toward ill-storied mansions located in remote, rustic areas, the latter toward gloom and impending disaster—flourished for many years: from the age of Horace Walpole and Anne Radcliffe into the early twentieth century, when it died with Edith Wharton. The genre also typically featured an unlikely, melancholy hero who confronts a half-remembered legend concerning a dark presence who once terrorized the region in life and is still rumored to haunt the land in death, or an innocent who was tortured to death sometime in the distant past and who is said to still walk the land after nightfall. With this, Kirk's first novel, the Gothic genre was reanimated—to the surprise of some readers, who knew Kirk only as a writer on conservative culture, to the sardonic delight of other readers, and to the unfeigned satisfaction of still others. "We follow him with dazed and delighted attention from the first muffled cry to the final midnight scream," wrote *The New Yorker*, true to form.[1] Many other readers delighted in this tale, finding it a welcome throwback to the well-told Gothic novels of their parents' age.

Describing his novel as lying "in unblushing line of direct descent" from Walpole's *The Castle of Otranto*, Kirk "transports the Gothic conventions into our century, rattling ghostly chains in a rattling good yarn," according to Don Herron.[2] The novel concerns a Scottish-born American attorney and confirmed bachelor, Hugh Logan, who is assigned by a wealthy Michigan industrialist named Duncan MacAskival to make all the necessary arrangements and then purchase a piece of property for him: the Scottish island of Carnglass. This, the MacAskival's ancestral home, is located on the hard horn of the world in the westernmost Hebrides. Logan is informed by his employer that, once on the island, he must seek out his family's "Old House of Fear," wherein lives the aged Lady MacAskival, owner of the island, and her retainers. Logan further learns that the "Fear" of the old house is a Gaelic word, not English: it is sometimes spelled "fir" or "fhir," and it means "man."

Logan's first stop is Glasgow, and there, having made his intentions known, he finds that this will be an assignment more complicated than he is accustomed to. He meets with the Carnglass factor, a furtive individual who gives him little encouragement for success in buying the island. After leaving this meeting, Logan is attacked by a small band of roughnecks who clearly intend to send him a strong warning. Rescued by police constables, Logan sets his face toward Carnglass. While on the way to the coast, he discovers he is being followed and has a bizarre encounter with a certain Captain Gare, who speaks and acts like a broken, middle-aged version of one of P. G. Wodehouse's Drones. Herron has written that this encounter with Captain Gare, incidentally

> is taken from a chance meeting Kirk once had with a man calling himself "Captain Gair" on a lonely street in medieval St. Andrews. As he recalls in his *Confessions [of a Bohemian Tory]*, this man asked for cigarettes; Kirk had none. "No, no," went on my Captain, nervously, "I don't require cigarettes. I don't smoke—nor drink, either. It's petrol—yes, that's it, petrol, petrol."[3]

A few days later, Logan manages to have himself put ashore at Carnglass. There he finds that he is on an island beset by frightening legends from the past and a band of present-day murderers and ex-convicts seeking to separate the failing Lady MacAskival from her vast fortune by first oiling their way into her confidence and then pocketing the inheritance upon her death. During the course of his adventures on the island, cut off from all contact with the civilized world, Logan encounters a rough-edged veteran of the Irish Republican Army, Seamas Donley, a man skilled at laying and setting off explosives; Dr. Edmund Jackman, a communist operative seeking to return to the good graces of his Kremlin masters by spying out Western missile defenses in the Hebrides and appropriating much-needed currency from ailing Lady MacAskival; beautiful, red-haired Mary MacAskival, the older woman's niece and true heir; and several bit players. In the background of the story, unseen and feared, is a mythical creature

long believed to inhabit Carnglass: the Firgower, a savage being who is re-
putedly half-man, half-goat, with a third eye in the middle of its forehead.

Undergirding the entire plotline of Logan's adventures on Carnglass is
the long, occasionally violent, but altogether homely and unique history of
the island. The MacAskivals have inhabited Carnglass for centuries, with
their family descended from Viking sea-raiders who swept over the island
in centuries past. Family legends of times past have been gilded or con-
fused with the centuries' passing. The oldest such legend concerns a beautiful young woman named Merin or Mary, herself the Pictish heiress of
Carnglass, who was taken captive by the violent Firgower and then rescued by Sigurd Askival, a Viking. From this couple sprang the entire
MacAskival clan, who, as of 1914, have been banished from Carnglass by
the degenerate, delusional laird to the nearby island of Daldour. At the
time the action in this novel begins, only the laird's widow and her niece
inhabit the Old House.

The burden of *Old House of Fear* tells of desperate pursuit, hairbreadth
escapes, dashes through secret underground passages, romance, and rescue. In the tradition of the Gothic novel, the uncanny creature rumored to
roam Carnglass is revealed to have natural origins, though he is real
nonetheless. Also according to Gothic convention, the stubborn bachelor
Logan and the untamable Lady Mary fall in love. And in the same tradition, the endgame between Logan and Jackman culminates in an encounter at the edge of a rocky cliff overlooking the sea, where there can be
only one victor.

Summarized in this way, *Old House of Fear* sounds like a potboiler, to be
read indoors on a rainy day at the beach: a book filled with muffled cries
and midnight screams, as the glib *New Yorker* reviewer would have it. But
this novel is far superior to such fare. For here, Kirk creates in his characters, especially Hugh Logan and Edmund Jackman, three-dimensional beings who possess the depth, quirks, and growth reminiscent of the characters crafted in the best of modern literature. As a reviewer for the
long-vanished *Los Angeles Herald & Express* put it, "Russell Kirk, in this
'Gothic romance,' as he calls it, has gone beyond the mere surface delin-
eation of his characters, particularly of the villain, and has created vivid,
three-dimensional characters who act and react as they do because their
personalities demand it, not because of the conventions of a mystery story."

Logan is introduced as a fairly staid individual, a World War II veteran
who has tasted horror firsthand on Okinawa and who now seeks nothing
more than the routine, pursuing (as much as any attorney can manage) the
path of least resistance. As told through Kirk's third-person narrator, he is
also a man who tends to rationalize that which ought not to be rational-
ized, seeking, as the story progresses, to convince himself that his steadily

worsening circumstances are not really as bad as they seem, and that the evidence of his own eyes is altogether too sinister to be true. Fairly early in the novel, as has been mentioned, Logan is attacked by four razor-wielding thugs in a Glasgow slum. In the midst of struggling with them, he realizes, "This was no simple robbery: they meant to slash or cripple him, or something worse."[4] Yet a mere day or two later, after the excitement of the scuffle has worn off, Logan is ready to snap his fingers at "the impromptu and ineffectual measures" employed by his "ill-organized and eccentric" adversaries.

Later, on the isle of Carnglass, Logan listens with horror as Seamas Donley, before taking his perilous leave of the island, speaks of the murderous activities of Dr. Jackman and his armed thugs. Donley had hired on as one of Jackman's crew, but he draws the line at cold-blooded murder, and he takes Logan into his confidence. Donley describes the torment and death of one man who had earlier crossed Jackman, as well as Jackman's anaconda smile and smooth, ice-water-for-blood mannerisms. As for Logan, he has spoken with nobody on the island but Donley, though he has seen Jackman's boys hunting for the Irishman like boys hunting a rabbit. For his part, to this point, Logan has prudently kept himself hidden. But after helping Donley leave the island in the only craft afloat, a rowboat, and then getting a night's sleep, he is ready to speak with Jackman as man among men. Why, the thing to do, he reasons, is to "go straight up to the door" of the Old House of Fear and try to see old Lady MacAskival. And even if Jackman's trusties wouldn't let him see her, "at least they could not mistake him for Donley; and he could lay his cards before this Dr. Jackman— or as many of his cards as might seem prudent. In Jackman, at least, as Logan took it, he would confront a rational being."[5] Rational, yes, he is to discover. Rational and depraved.

Prudence leads Logan to approach the Old House by a roundabout way, for something tells him that the handful of riflemen he has seen roaming the island are not to be trusted. As he looks upon the facade of the house, he is startled to see a young, red-haired woman standing in an upper window. This is Mary MacAskival, and she unbars the door for Logan to enter the house. Once inside, the story's action hastens toward its conclusion; Kirk has taken half the book to get to this point, spending much time performing the preliminary spadework of letting the reader inside Logan's sharp if increasingly troubled mind, painting the bleak, windswept landscape of Carnglass, and creating an atmosphere of tension and impending catastrophe.

Mary persuades Hugh that he is in danger from Jackman and that for now he ought to pretend to be her fiancé from the mainland, who proposed to her during her last trip off the island—not that she has a fiancé, but for that matter Jackman has never asked her about one. In a short time, Jackman discovers the "happily engaged couple"; shocked to find Logan in the house, he takes the attorney into another room, where the two men converse together in Mary's absence while playing a game of chess, at Jackman's suggestion. Here Jackman reveals himself to be a smooth liar, telling Logan a chilling, utterly false story of Mary's upbringing. Mary is a minor, only fifteen years old. Mary is not an heiress; she is penniless. Mary is not even a MacAskival. Mary is sexually promiscuous. Mary is in fact insane. Mary will bring only unhappiness into his life if they marry. It is the hallmark of a smooth liar that he is utterly believable, and after a few minutes of conversation with Jackman, Logan is convinced that Mary MacAskival is everything Jackman has said of her. Altogether well-spoken and every inch the "rational man" Logan had earlier expected, Jackman puts on a stellar performance. He is aided by a peculiar physical deformity, a pulsing "third eye" (really a scarred-over indentation in his skull from a bullet wound taken in the Spanish Civil War). The effect he has upon Logan is similar to that achieved near the climax of C. S. Lewis's *The Silver Chair;* in the scene lit by a small fire, the evil Green Witch traps Lucy, Eustace, the Prince, and Puddleglum in her underground lair. There, she fills the air with the mind-numbing aroma of a drug she had tossed into a fire and proceeds to speak in gentle, reasonable tones in an attempt to convince her captives that there is in truth no sun in the sky, no upper world, no Aslan the King, no hope, only the underground world and darkness. In Lewis's story, the children and the prince nearly succumb, until Puddleglum breaks the witch's spell by loudly denouncing her and stamping out the tainted fire with his bare feet. In Kirk's story, there is no Puddleglum on hand to thwart Jackman, who successfully convinces Logan that beautiful Mary is, in Kirk's gentle term, a "hussy."

But as Logan soon discovers, "Jackman was plausible, but Mary MacAskival was all candor." In a conversation with Mary, Logan not only grows to trust her but to fall in love with her; and for her part, Mary finds that she wants only one man for her husband (assuming she can escape the toils of Jackman and his thugs): Hugh Logan. He at last puts away all doubt as to Jackman's nature and intentions and determines to help Mary somehow rid the island of Jackman and his interlopers.

Interestingly, immediately after this decision, Logan's ruse is uncovered and he is taken prisoner by Jackman and his men. While they know Logan is no slightly simple-minded swain from the mainland, they are otherwise unsure just who he is or what he intends, and they intend to find out. It is during a session of interrogation that Logan discovers that Jackman is a man haunted by demons who have arisen at his bidding. The mystery of Logan's true identity rattles him badly, and he suspects nearly anything of his captive. To intensify his crisis, Jackman, for a man ostensibly given to the dialectical materialism of Marxism, has dabbled too long and too deeply in the black arts to escape the influence of very real dark forces. He has enticed the elderly Lady MacAskival to place him in charge of her affairs by convincing her that it is by his mystical powers that he prevents the unsettled spirit of her long-dead husband from entering the house and tormenting her. In doing this, or perhaps even before this, he senses that he is dealing in matters that would best be left alone, but that he is in too deeply. Contrary to what at least one reviewer has written of *Old House of Fear*, Jackman is not an evil man because he is a Marxist; he is an evil man because he has slowly but surely embraced the diabolical imagination and set himself at murderous odds with the community of souls on Carnglass and elsewhere. In a set speech, Jackman articulates the timeless-moment metaphysic written of by Eliot and articulated by Father Martin D'Arcy. Speaking with his captive, he falls into a horror-induced reverie, confessing the living hell of his own existence:

> Jackman's eyes were vacant now; he seemed to have forgotten to whom he spoke. "Hell endures," he went on. "I have been in Hell always. This Carnglass is Hell. Don't you know you were here in Carnglass before, infinitely long ago? We fought here then—and I lost. In Carnglass there is no time. Eternity is real here, and change is the delusion. I know this in the nights, when I walk the corridors. It is only in the day I can pretend that I am alive, or that what things I do can possibly save me from the torment. In the nights it is Hell that is real, and the [Communist] Party is a sham. Do you understand that? And I know that you came here to send me to the torment, as you did before."[6]

Jackman, like Apollinax at the end of *Lord of the Hollow Dark,* is stuck like a fly in amber within a timeless moment of damnation. As we have seen in the chapter on Kirk's short stories, Kirk embraced Eliot's timeless-moment metaphysic, where at the still point of the turning world, where time and the timeless intersect, the damned, the sainted, and those in the midst of purgation, exist in the eternal present, the damned stuck forever within the sins that separate them from God and man, the pilgrims doing penance for sins that prevent their access to Heaven, and the cleansed rejoicing forever in the presence of God. On one occasion, D'Arcy explained to Kirk that Hell is a state of being in which all the evil that one has done is eternally present—and there is no escape from it. "So it is," wrote Kirk of D'Arcy's remarks, "that human creatures make their own destiny, their own Heaven and their own Hell."[7]

With this said, it seems inevitable that in the end Jackman plunges in roiling darkness to his death after Mary and Hugh have been rescued from his clutches by several of Mary's relatives from Daldour, who secretly arrive in Carnglass in their lobster boats after the besieged couple lit a signal fire that could be seen across the water. It might be argued that by having Hugh and Mary rescued in the nick of time by "the cavalry," Kirk sailed precariously close to the wind, what with his bringing a *deus ex machina* into a twentieth-century novel. Yet, the tactic works. (If there is a weakness in the storyline, it is that Kirk never develops the elder Lady MacAskival, who is seen only once midway through the novel and then disappears from the plot completely.) Throughout the novel, Kirk has stated plainly that the MacAskivals of Daldour have visited Carnglass often for purposes of game-poaching, and that the clan is hardheaded and loyal to its own. In fact, on the novel's first page, he portrays a puzzling scene of several rough-hewn boatmen approaching Carnglass by night but then turning back to their home port after being fired upon by unseen riflemen ashore. In the end of *Old House of Fear*, the rustic MacAskivals arrive and save Hugh from one gun-toting captor; but Mary's fate is far from certain at that point. It is all rather a near thing, with everything capable of being lost with one false turn, until the final page, where Logan and two of his new comrades peer over the cliff face to the surging ocean, which has swallowed up Edmund Jackman without a trace.

It is interesting but not surprising that Kirk, a bachelor at the time he wrote *Old House of Fear*, ended his novel with this scene. Reserved and bashful by nature, he ended it with a moment of awed contemplation instead of one with the hero and heroine clutching each other in a passionate embrace, kissing each other ecstatically in the knowledge that they have all their lives before them, all the lonely, beautiful island to themselves, and nothing standing between themselves and a happy marriage that will last a lifetime. It is left unsaid that in the future the Old House will not be a place of *fear* but of *man* (or *humanity*) and the linking of generations past with generations yet unborn. By putting an end to his false rationalizing and taking decisive action, Logan has restored the contract of human society on a small, almost forgotten island in the Hebrides.

Symbolically there is a distinct parallel between the ancient story of Merin's rescue from the Firgower by Sigurd Askival and the present-day rescue of Mary MacAskival from Jackman by Logan. Throughout the novel, Jackman, with his "third eye," is closely identified with the goatish Firgower. Goats and goat heads have long been considered symbols of evil and male sexual abandon; however, Edmund Jackman, though bearing the "third eye" of the Firgower, does not burn with lust for Mary; rather he is in thrall to a more powerful aphrodisiac: the lust for power over others. Logan discerns as much during his conversations with Jackman, during which he also notes that his captor has supped long on horrors, having served as a most willing torturer of men in Eastern Europe as a tool of the communists. Looking upon Jackman and his cadaverous henchman, Royall,

> Logan almost felt a touch of pity for them. Both must have been reared and educated well enough—very well, indeed. What flaws of character or intellectual false turnings had brought them into this ruthless business, he could not tell. They might have commenced, like others, full of humanitarian sentimentality. And then, perhaps, demon ideology, with its imperatives and its inexorable dogmas, its sobersided caricature of religion, had swept them on to horrors. Ideological fanaticism had made of Jackman the goat-man, mastered by lust: but not the lust for women's bodies. Jackman's was the *libido dominandi*, the tormented seeking after power that ceases not until death. And in the flame of that lust for power, Jackman and Royall would be burnt up, today or next week or next month: they were at the end of their devil's bargain, and the fiend would claim his own.[8]

Having looked into the abyss and having embraced the diabolical imagination, Jackman knows that evil is real, that he has gone past the point of turning back, and that he is likely among the damned. As a result, his mind totters on the brink of insanity. The grim vision of the materialist leads to something wicked he in no wise expected; and in the end, as Chesterton once wrote of Satan, he falls by gravity.

INTRODUCING MANFRED ARCANE

Arriving in Mecosta, Michigan two years before her husband's second novel appeared, newlywed Annette Kirk surveyed this back-country village by night and remarked to Russell, "It's so dark!" "Yes," he replied, "but the dark belongs to us."

The dark, the mysterious, the varied, the interesting had a lifelong special fascination for Kirk, who had enjoyed the fiction of Nathaniel Hawthorne and Robert Louis Stevenson in his boyhood. In *A Creature of the Twilight: His Memorials*, he crafted an adventure novel set in postcolonial North Africa, a land he had visited and greatly admired. In such a setting, Kirk could tell a strong adventure yarn while poking fun at Western designs for meddling in and attempting to manage the culture of other lands.

In his intelligent essay "The Crepuscular Romantic: An Appreciation of the Fiction of Russell Kirk," Don Herron focuses primarily upon Kirk's supernatural fiction, but takes the time to provide a brief description of *A Creature of the Twilight* as "an adventure, a tale of revolution in the Third World, with attendant battles and political machinations." And this it surely is, and a black comedy as well—a lengthy send-up of all the transparently opportunistic, unctuously invoked and acted-upon policies by which the world's major powers seek to gain political influence in the less-industrialized portions of the globe.

In narrative form, Kirk's second novel is a tour de force, written in numerous voices. As Herron notes, it is a tale about a bloody revolution in the North African nation of Hamnegri, told through various diary entries, diplomatic cables, personal letters, and other forms of record, all conveyed through the narration of a suave, Machiavellian loyalist, a slightly ditsy female Peace Corps volunteer, an alcoholic American man, an opportunistic American politician, a Scottish soldier of fortune, a hard-boiled American journalist, a tabloid writer, a French journalist, a strong woman who was left for dead by the Mau-Mau during an earlier stay in Africa, and numerous other sources. In each form, Kirk moves skillfully and, with allowances made for changes in the tone of some of the above-named media, quite convincingly. It is a novel unlike anything Kirk wrote before or since; he described it in a letter to Edmund Fuller as "a baroque romance" he had written "principally for the fun of it."[9]

A Creature of the Twilight introduces to the world stage the Father of Shadows, Manfred Arcane. He is at the center of the novel, which is baroque only in his ornate, even courtly dialogue and writings. Dubbed a "creature of the twilight" by a fevered writer for the Soviet newspaper *Pravda*, Arcane confides to the reader his willing identification as a creature of the twilight, the time of deepening shadows, and he keeps a caged pet owl near at hand. (In Kirk's short story "The Last God's Dream," published after *A Creature of the Twilight*, the white-haired Arcane is described as "curiously handsome, with a beak for a nose, looking considerably like an arctic owl.") The bastard son of a Viennese gypsy woman and a disgraced nobleman, he has a colorful past—so colorful that he has prudently chosen to mask his identity, hiding in the shadows (as it were) by using the name Manfred Arcane, which is not his real name. The owl, a nocturnal creature, is known traditionally as a symbol of wisdom. Its solemn expressions and cartoonish reputation belie the fact that it is also a silent stalker and deft killer. Throughout Hamnegri's port city of Haggat, Arcane is respected and feared, not for threatening and bullying; he does none of this, but he does maintain civil order by exercising prudential wisdom and by dealing swiftly and decisively with lawbreakers.

"All my days have I done evil," he begins his "Memorials." This is in part a wry boast, but it is more a sad confession. Arcane is a devout Catholic who sees his earthly life as a pilgrimage to atone for the sins of his youth, chief among them his failure to rescue the beautiful love of his life from death in the Nazi concentration camp of Oberhalden. Aside from this grim portion of his history, Arcane is a trickster supreme, and he knows it and is at once amused and repelled by his machinations. At one point, he wryly describes the harbor at Haggat:

> We could see the half-built docks that the Soviets were paying for; near them, the half-built petrol refinery that the Americans were paying for; and trailing toward the refinery, from the desert infinity, the snake of the half-built pipeline that the French were paying for. A tidy portion of all these funds had gone into the pockets of Postmaster-General M'Rundu and other Hamnegrian statesmen. As for me, I had my two per cent royalty, skillfully negotiated, upon the crude oil already gushing from the Hamnegrian wells; and so I rose superior to base corruption.[10]

As a source of further needed atonement, several individuals meet horrible deaths before this tale is through, and Arcane plays a key role in the demise of each. But several of the more evil-doing of Arcane's enemies richly deserve release from this life; and a period of armed revolution is no time for needless guilt and handwringing, especially when one is set up for betrayal and murder by a trio of blackmailers and former Nazis.

For a fairly thick book, the plot of *A Creature of the Twilight* is fairly simple and straightforward. In the North African nation of Hamnegri, a bloody *coup d'etat* deposes the rightful Sultan and sets the stage for a Marxist takeover. Arcane, Minister without Portfolio and the man responsible for much of the oil-produced prosperity Hamnegri enjoys, quickly crowns a new Sultan, the son of the deposed ruler. He then shrewdly takes the steps necessary to ensure that the heavily armed "Progressivist" forces, headquartered far to the south of Haggat in the nation's capital city of Awala, do not overwhelm the ragtag remnants of the "Legitimist" forces under his personal command and take over the important port city of Haggat.

Arcane is assisted by his small core group of friends, allies, and hangerson. These include his beautiful young Sicilian assistant (and expert codebreaker) Melchiora Caola, a wise old woman named Lady Grizel Fergusson, two African assistants styled Cleon and Brasidas, an on-the-wagon American journalist and stand-in press spokesman named Augustus Randolph, a hulking, terribly mutilated concentration camp survivor called Arpad Nemo, and a one-eyed Spanish colonel named Jesus Pelayo Fuentes y Iturbide, commander of the Interracial Peace Volunteers, a body of well-disciplined soldiers of fortune in the service of the Sultan of Hamnegri.

Arrayed against the Legitimists are a host of foes great and negligible. There is the opportunist T. William Tallstall, special U.S. envoy to Hamnegri and a probable presidential candidate, who is primarily a "trimmer," who makes brave noises on behalf of whichever side happens to be winning at the moment, but who happens to like the sound of the word "progressive." There are the well-supplied Progressive forces themselves, sweeping inexorably northward from their desert fastness. The most serious threat to Arcane and his forces comes in the form of three East German Maoists, former Nazis and torturers in a concentration camp. These rough beasts have come to Hamnegri to blackmail Arcane into ensuring that the Progressives prevail—and to liquidate the Father of Shadows. (They firmly believe, and they convince certain others in the story to believe, that Arcane's true identity is that of a sadistic Macedonian colonel formerly of the foreign S.S. named Spanos who had turned traitor to the Nazis during the final days of World War II. The spokesman among the trio of Nazis-*cum*-Maoists, Major Klopke, informs "Spanos" that his son is under guard back in Eastern Europe and will undergo exquisite torture and death if the Minister without Portfolio fails to follow his, Klopke's, orders to the letter.) To illustrate the urgency of his mission and what he will do to fulfill it, Klopke gloatingly tells of how, during his days at the head of the Oberhalden concentration camp, he had supervised the systematic mutilation and castration of a portly Hungarian man of law, reducing this gentle, cultured man, mockingly nicknamed "the Judge," to a self-loathing, living horror. Hearing this story, Arcane lets on that he will comply, though not meekly. Taking offense at a mild remonstrance to comport himself lawfully while in Haggat, Klopke takes to blustering:

> "Do you think you're Napoleon?" Klopke demanded. But he sidled toward the door.
>
> "Sometimes," Arcane answered, all silky again, "sometimes. And on occasion I believe I am a god. But more often I'm a beast among lesser beasts. Look: here's one beast I fancy."
>
> Reaching under the table, Manfred Arcane lifted up a cage. In it was the owl he had bought, a few days before, in the Square of the Stakes.
>
> "Rightly, for once, *Pravda* describes me as a creature of the twilight," Arcane resumed. "The owl is myself, and I am the owl. Mark the claws." In the twilight room, the Kalidu owl dilated his pupils and flexed his talons, as if he understood Arcane.
>
> "I don't follow you," Klopke grumbled, no longer smirking, and feeling behind him for the door.
>
> "As the Americans say, 'You don't get me?' . . . No, dear Major Klopke, I fear you don't get me. But never despair: some day you may—or *vice versa*."[11]

Klopke is now placed in the background of the story, still present and a threat, but of secondary importance to the impending winner-take-all battle between the Legitimists and the Progressives. Perhaps the high point of Kirk's sardonic humor comes as the loyalist military forces gather to depart for the front and are treated to a hortatory harangue by Arcane. He exhorts the Sultan's troops in an outrageous hodgepodge of snatches from the speeches and prose of Shakespeare, Winston Churchill, Jesus of Nazareth, John McRae, Rudyard Kipling, John F. Kennedy, Edmund Burke, Stonewall Jackson, and several other historic figures. One example will suffice, this from Arcane's address to the Muslim element among Haggat's troops, as transcribed from a radio broadcast, by "Our Sultan's Voice of Justice":

> "Would you live forever?" he inquired, rhetorically, of them. "Great Achmet [the new Sultan] expects every man to do his duty. If the loathsome enemy demand, 'Have you struck your colors?' you will reply, 'We have not yet begun to fight!' When the hurly-burly's done, then you may cross the river and lie in the shade of the trees; but until that hour, blow rope, come wrack, at least we'll die with harness on our back. Fire not until you see the whites of their eyes. A coward dies a thousand times before his death; the brave man tastes of death but once."[12]

Kirk tacks precariously close to the wind in the passages that comprise Arcane's prebattle harangue. However, it works—and the chapter that includes Arcane's remonstrances gets a bit funnier with each rereading.

Humor now recedes as Arcane and his forces disappear into the wilderness and join with the enemy. Arpad Nemo and the minister's other colleagues remain in Haggat to maintain order. For a time the outcome of the battle is in question, but within a short time, because of stratagems devised by Arcane that anticipated *hubris* at every turn by both the enemy forces and a handful of backstabbers within his own ranks, the day is won for the loyalists. Arcane is carried back to Haggat badly wounded, shot in the back by a man in the hire of Klopke. The Progressives have been destroyed in almost biblical fashion; only a small number survive to return to Awala and tell of the terror that lives in the north of Hamnegri. By defeating the Progressives, with their close ties to nations driven by ideology, Arcane has accomplished much: As essayist Robert Champ has written, Arcane has restored the proper relation between past and present in Hamnegri, a relation of historical continuity, specifically "the grounding of government in the experience of the governed and the sanctioning of values found in a people's inherited traditions and religion."[13]

By winning the battle, Arcane has also failed Klopke, and now a final account must be settled, for the Minister without Portfolio learns to his satisfaction that it was indeed by order of Klopke that he was shot. Lying on a cushioned matress, in great pain and apparently near death, Arcane summons a priest and the three Germans to the flat, cool roof of his villa by night. The priest has been asked to come because someone is about to die. All who climb to the rooftop to join Cleon, Brasidas, and the reclining Arcane assume that the dying man is Arcane. Their assumption is wrong.

Having first dropped the mask of Spanos, revealing that he himself did away with Spanos and then stole the brutal Macedonian's identity papers during World War II, Arcane has the three former Nazis abruptly seized and disarmed by Loyalist guards who have silently ascended to the roof during this climactic meeting. Addressing the astonished Klopke and his two associates, Arcane briefly tells of the entire charade that has led to this moment, and then he plays his ace:

> "Now I must give you to someone."
> A man, enormous, strode out from the shadows to confront the Germans. In his gown and hood, he might have been a decent subject of the Sultan; but when he flung back his cowl, everyone saw the mutilated and seared head of Arpad Nemo.
> Klopke sucked in his breath audibly, and spoke two heavy words: "The Judge!"
> "Yes, the Judge," Arcane told him, "and your judge. If he will pity you, so will I."
> In that silent, devastated face of Arpad's shone no spark of mercy.[14]

Those who embrace the diabolical imagination, setting themselves against the community of souls by embracing (in this case) genocidal ideology, find that the gods of the copybook headings return with fire and slaughter. In the antagonist world, the ideologue of this stripe finds himself subjected to the primitive law of the claw, *lex talionis*. Nothing is left for Klopke and his two colleagues but to submit to a primitive hunt to the death in a short, closed-off street in Haggat, the three Germans finding themselves the quarry for the first time in their lives, pursued by the merciless, knife-wielding Arpad Nemo, who has lived for this moment.

"All told," concludes Don Herron, "this baroque Romance, this black comedy, this fast adventure, makes an excellent advent for Manfred Arcane; his darkling presence is more than enough reason for reading the book."[15] At one period of his existence, Arcane reminisces with self-mockery, he was Dionysius; at another, Dis; at still another, Ares. "All this divinity, you are to understand, found lodging in the little person of Manfred Arcane—to employ the name by which I have chosen, for some years, to be known." Dionysius is, of course, the Greek god symbolic of heedless self-abandon. Dis is the lord of death and the underworld. Ares is the god of war. Arcane has in some sense been all of these during his unusual life; and with order restored to Hamnegri, he can resume his life of travel, rest, storytelling, and civil administration. Like the owl, though, he will remain vigilant. "Were there no owls, my darling and delight," Arcane writes to Melchiora, with whom he falls in love and marries at the last, "rats would inherit the earth. Buss me, sybil! Strolling in forgotten ways with your mirabilary lover, remember always that the owl-light belongs to us."

I leave it to other critics, those of an extra-literary bent, to assess the extent to which Arcane is a projection of his creator. In Manfred Arcane are combined the man of contemplation, which Kirk certainly was, and the flamboyant man of action, which the bashful Kirk could mostly dream of—though he was by no means a library-bound scholar merely, but a man who took action on various issues and for various causes throughout his life. To be sure, though: In Manfred Arcane, the central figure of two novels and two short stories, Kirk created one of the most memorable, though critically neglected, heroes in modern literature.

NOTES

1. Review of *Old House of Fear* in *The New Yorker* 37, August 12, 1961, 92. The anonymous reviewer sniffs that the novel's plot, "it need hardly be said, is absurd," but goes on to praise Kirk's "majestically archaic" style, rich atmosphere, and "intimations of impending doom."

2. Herron, "The Crepuscular Romantic: An Appreciation of the Fiction of Russell Kirk," *The Romantist*, no. 3, 1979, 4.

3. Herron, "The Crepuscular Romantic," 4.

4. *Old House of Fear*, p. 26. All quotations from this novel are taken from the Avon paperbound edition.

5. *Old House of Fear*, p. 71.

6. *Old House of Fear*, p. 138.

7. *The Sword of Imagination* (Grand Rapids, Mich., 1995), p. 341.

8. *Old House of Fear*, p. 141.

9. Kirk to Edmund Fuller, May 10, 1966. This letter is on file at the Russell Kirk Center for Cultural Renewal, Mecosta, Michigan.

10. *A Creature of the Twilight: His Memorials*, p. 29.

11. *Creature of the Twilight*, p. 155.

12. *Creature of the Twilight*, p. 190.

13. Champ, "Russell Kirk's Fiction of Enchantment," *The Intercollegiate Review* 30, Fall, 1994, 41.

14. *Creature of the Twilight*, p. 312.

15. Herron, "The Crepuscular Romantic," 8.

8

To Rouse and Fortify the Living: Kirk as a Critic of Literature

My own conception of the image of man, and of the writer's great theme, is well expressed in some words of Stephen F. Bayne, to whom the great sense of writing and reading alike is "that we may see man as he is, single and whole, reasoning and choosing and believing, half of this world and half of some other, the only animal who must decide what kind of animal he will be, the only beast it is shameful to call a beast, whose soul, as Boethius said, "albeit in a cloudy memory, yet seeks back his own good, but like a drunken man knows not the way home."
—from *Man in Modern Fiction*, by Edmund Fuller

It is the everlasting battle in which there are no truces, the battle between the smile and the leer, between innocence and sophistication, beauty and lust, truth and cynicism, love and pornography; it is the conflict between Dickens and Mailer, Michelangelo and Picasso, Augustine and Updike, Thomas Mann and *Garp*. It is the battle between substance and display, integrity and materialism, good cheer and quiet desperation, duty and hedonism; between earnestness and flippancy, the absolute and the expedient, the eternal and the ephemeral, the moral imperative and the

passing whim. It is the ancient fight between the gentleman and
the mob, the mother and the barbarian, the immaculate child and
the old roué, the monk and the thug, the spirit and the brute: it is
the war between the human and the anti-human.

—from *Panic among the Philistines*, by Bryan F. Griffin

Describing the moral imagination, though without using that term, G. K.
Chesterton once wrote that for Catholics "it is a fundamental dogma of the
faith that all human beings, without any exception whatever, were spe-
cially made, were shaped and pointed like shining arrows, for the end of
hitting the mark of Beatitude. It is true that the shafts are feathered with
free will, and therefore throw the shadow of all the tragic possibilities of
free will; and that the Church . . . does also draw attention to the darkness
of that potential tragedy. But that does not make any difference to the glo-
riousness of the potential glory. In one aspect it is even a part of it; since
the freedom is itself a glory."[1]

From a similar vision sprang the theory Kirk brought to literary criticism
and education, one that viewed humanity as flawed, bent on error, yet
beloved by its Creator and made for eternity. Whether reviewing books or
illuminating literature within lengthier works of literary criticism proper,
Kirk viewed the works at hand through the lens of the moral imagination.

As a critic, Kirk owed much to the New Humanist critics of the early
twentieth century, notably Irving Babbitt and Paul Elmer More, whose
work flourished from the 1900s through the early 1930s. These men and
others among the school of the New Humanism caught Kirk's attention
early in life, as they frequently contributed to the now-vanished *Bookman*
and other middlebrow literary periodicals that his grandfather received
regularly at his home in Plymouth where Kirk's family lived during much
of the boy's early life. (It was in part a tribute to the old *Bookman* that Kirk
named the second quarterly periodical he founded *The University Bookman.*)

Much was written of the New Humanists during their heyday, much of
it hostile. The most common critical attacks came in the form of caricature;
that is, it became commonly understood that as critics, the New Humanists
focused upon works of literature as expressions of moral uplift, holding
each book they assessed to a puritanical litmus test to see if sweetness and
light emerge triumphant while evil is thwarted. But no matter how skillfully such influential advocates of realism as H. L. Mencken denounced
them for their attempts to make "Puritanism" a literary force, the fact remains that there was much more to Babbitt and More than their detractors
cared to admit, though humanism was not without its weaknesses as a philosophy. (To his credit, Mencken eventually came to admit that More was
the most intelligent of the New Humanists, and well worth reading.)[2]

The critical philosophy that influenced Russell Kirk grew out of a larger movement, which sought to draw from life and knowledge to develop the mature man and woman, whose chief virtues are prudence and humility, and whose primary moral characteristics are self-control and the willingness to curb personal desires for the benefit of greater cultural needs. The source of this curving influence is what Babbitt called the "inner check" and what More identified on occasion as the *frein vital* ("will to restrain") and other occasions as the Holy Spirit, "the indwelling and grace-giving spirit of God."[3] To the chief proponents of the New Humanism, this restraining influence could be effective only in a culture devoted to tradition: to Babbitt, a tradition of Classicism; to More, a tradition grounded in America's Protestant heritage. The humanists thus appealed to first principles and developed their thoughts and arguments from that source. As Babbitt explained, the humanist as opposed to the humanitarian, "is interested in the perfecting of the individual rather than in schemes for the elevation of mankind as a whole; and although he allows largely for sympathy, he insists that it be disciplined and tempered by judgment."[4] The teacher of humane literature does not labor under the illusion that it is his duty to hew to a party line, serving up literature as agitprop and encouraging his charges to "conform to the group," or jibe at most of the literature written before the mid-twentieth century as having arisen from the imaginations of sexists, racists, homophobes, Anglophiles, and (perhaps worst of all) mere males.

Further, recognizing that culture springs from the cult—that religion or faith gives shape to culture through commonly held truths and ritual—religion in some form, More and Babbitt held, is necessary. As adherents to the New Humanism were fond of noting, life must have something more to it than science, for humanity, as Babbitt wrote, will never be satisfied with reason divorced from all principle. It is by faith—what the New Humanists called the "higher will"—by reverence for myth and tradition, and by the attendant illative sense of apprehending truth and virtue, man is (and indeed must) be capable of interests and truths that are over and above refined rationality. "For purpose that will not end in bitter defeat; for values that will not mock us like empty masks, must we not look for a happiness based on something beyond the swaying tides of mortal success and failure?" More wrote. "Will not the humanist, unless he adds to his creed the faith and the hope of religion, find himself at the last, despite his protests, dragged back into the camp of the naturalist?"[5]

Chesterton, a contemporary of More and a critic of the New Humanism, understood that More's philosophy is quite different from humanitarianism: that modern humanism begins with "a very right realization that modern science and organization are in a sense only too natural. They herd us like the beasts along lines of heredity or tribal doom; they melt us into the mud of materialism or sink us in the sea of subconsciousness." It was precisely this eventual outcome of modern tendencies of thought that the humanist sought to avoid. "We need," continued Chesterton, "a rally of the really human thing; will which is morals, memory which is tradition, culture which is the mental thrift of our fathers."[6]

As Chesterton pointed out (and as Kirk came to discover), humanism in the best sense, though including many truths known to pagan antiquity, was essentially a product of Catholic faith and tradition, and for some would-be adherents to divorce it from that tradition was to sever it from solid foundations and thus weaken it, delivering it to the service of mere good intentions. And that way lies ideology and modern gnosticism: the belief that human nature, being essentially good, can be enlisted to join in a program or political effort that will bring about not merely a tolerable social order, but a social order free from all the foibles and errors to which humanity is prone. John Cardinal Newman expressed a thought similar to that of Chesterton on humanism when he said that there can be no middle ground ultimately between Catholicism and agnosticism.

Humanistic criticism had two guiding laws, which More went so far as to call "the charter of humanism": distinctions and mediation. Without going into great detail, it might be said that the "charter of humanism" required that the critic view the past as a resource from which to draw examples of that which is in conformity to nature and what departs from those norms. Sifting the literature at hand through the grid of normative thought, such critics prudently "balance and weigh and measure"; wrote More, "they are by intellect hesitators, but at heart very much in earnest." More and Kirk thus stand in a long tradition of critical thinking that began with one of Kirk's heroes, Cicero, and extends through Desiderius Erasmus, Nicolas Boileau, the third earl of Shaftesbury, Charles-Augustin Sainte-Beuve, T. S. Eliot, and C. S. Lewis. More wrote that these critics, specifically the first four in the preceding list,

> are the exemplars . . . of what may be called the critical spirit: discriminators between the false and the true, the deformed and the normal; preachers of harmony and proportion and order, prophets of the religion of taste. If they deal much with the criticism of literature, this is because in literature more manifestly than anywhere else life displays its infinitely varied motives and results; and their practice is always to render literature itself more consciously a criticism of life.[7]

As this relates to Kirk in particular, Frederick D. Wilhelmsen has stated, "Russell Kirk sized up his topic, walked around it, probed it peculiarities, smelled the wind, and then enveloped the whole in his Christian vision of

Good and Evil. That vision invariably ended in a judgment suffused with that wisdom which our ancestors called prudence."[8]

The role of literary critic related to Kirk's chosen vocation as a man of letters and the responsibilities that inhere in that role. The man of letters is no mere scribbler or literary prostitute, shaping and selling his wares according to whatever is selling this season. Rather, he is a custodian of the *Logos*, and it is his responsibility to use and interpret the Word according to the vested wisdom of his literary forebears. "We need to remind ourselves that men of letters and teachers of literature are entrusted with a social responsibility; they have no right to be nihilists or fantastic or neoterists, because the terms on which they hold their trust are conservative," he once wrote, adding,

> Whatever the immediate political opinions of the guardian of the Word, his first duty is conservative in the larger sense of that adjective: his work, his end, is to shelter and promulgate an inherited body of learning and myth. The man of letters and the teacher of literature have no right to be irresponsible dilettantes or reckless iconoclasts; they are placed in their high dignity so that they may preserve the ideas which make all men one, not so that they may indulge an appetite for denigration and a taste for anarchic cleverness. In a time like ours, when the political and religious institutions which kept some continuity in civilization are weakened or broken, the responsibility of the teacher or writer is greater than ever; it is possible that the only tie with the past that will survive our century may be a literary continuity, just as in the ages which followed the collapse of the Roman state.[9]

Kirk did not write these words lightly, for in 1969, when he wrote this passage, he firmly believed that the United States was well along in a period of decadence. In these words he echoed a man he deeply admired, Christopher Dawson, a cultural historian who exercised a profound influence upon Eliot. Near the end of his life, Dawson wrote, "We are living in a world that is far less stable than that of the early Roman Empire. There is no doubt that the world is on the move again as never before and that the pace is faster and more furious than anything that man has known before." But as with Kirk, so with Dawson; hope springs eternal: "But there is nothing in this situation which should cause Christians to despair. On the contrary, it is the kind of situation for which their faith has always prepared them and which provides the opportunity for the fulfillment of their mission." Given this, it is small wonder that Kirk did not view book reviewing as mere finger-work, to be gotten through quickly so that he could move on to more important projects. (Indeed, the last piece of writing Kirk commenced—but never finished—before his death was an appraisal of Conor Cruise O'Brien's thematic biography of Burke, *The Great Melody*, for *The Sewanee Review*.) Reviewing and, to a greater extent, criticism, were to him both part and parcel of being a writer; and the aim of critiquing literature, as with the aim of writing, is ethical: to teach what it is to be a mature man, to teach what it is to be a mature woman. Until fairly early in the twentieth century, it was widely assumed, even taken for granted, that the purpose of literature is to help form or reinforce the normative consciousness: to teach and affirm the true nature of man, his responsibilities to his neighbors and his nation, his dignity (and shame) as a creature, and his significance within the greater scheme of things. With the inauspicious advent and then the tidal spread of pornography, literary naturalism, and a host of other "isms" from the eighteenth century until today, this assumption of literature's end is no longer common. For Kirk, this path away from humanistic literature leads to folly and confusion. As Kirk wrote in *Enemies of the Permanent Things*, "Literature is meant to rouse and fortify the living, to renew the contract of eternal society. And the scholar who treats literature as a mound of ashes—mildly profitable ashes—is false to his discipline and his age."[10] In practical terms, this entailed one of the most invigorating of activities: Putting one's literary talent at the service of a noble but beleaguered cause—in this case, the restoration of normative letters, refusing to succumb to pressure to believe that because an idea or a way of life is no longer popular or "in season" it is therefore discredited, knowing that one is communicating with a remnant as part of a literary rearguard action against falsehood and despair.

In a letter written in 1967, Kirk spoke of the discouragements and triumphs of seeking to restore the normative consciousness through literature and criticism, specifically as it relates to his writing *Enemies of the Permanent Things:* "You are difficult to write about," he told Ray Bradbury, "in the sense that though the rising generation understands you, those 'whose hearts are dry as summer dust' don't; and they form the dominant serious literary public. They are at once the victims and the predators of what, in my books, I have called 'defecated rationality.' What dessicated minds, as you know! A conscience may speak to a conscience only if the auditor-conscience still is alive. But it is most heartening (cheerfulness *will* keep breaking in!) that the hungry imagination of the rising generation senses what you mean. I find that my three nephews, who have spent much of their lives in Persia, swear by practically all your books."[11]

Few scholars have commented upon Kirk's work with greater penetration than the Mecostan's longtime friend Peter J. Stanlis, perhaps the nation's foremost authority on Edmund Burke, and George A. Panichas, literary scholar and longtime editor of *Modern Age*. It is to the latter we turn here, for he has written tellingly on Kirk's role as a man of letters, in terms pertinent to this discussion. In a particularly insightful essay, worth quoting at some length, Panichas has said:

In Kirk we view the man of letters allegiant, above all, to his moral obligations and to his belief that "humane letters give to the imagination and the reason a moral bent." To be sure, a man of letters has a generalist orientation, is concerned with the human condition, with human destiny, with the totality of problems that relate to the process of civilization. But that orientation, and that concern, have a higher focus, ethical and moral in nature, mirrored in what Kirk terms "normative truths": John Henry Newman pinpoints its essential impulse when he speaks of the constant need to push things up to their first principles. Hence the man of letters has the task of teaching others that there are abiding standards by which we measure our ambitions and attainments but from which we also too often fall away. Kirk never failed to alert us to this falling away from the center, and for him as a man of letters this was a fundamental requirement, a "sacred function." What finally distinguished the man of letters from "the eager little knot of intellectuals hot after novelties" is precisely a willingness to judge matters in terms of authority, tradition, and the illative sense. In this triad resides the "moral bent" that Kirk affirms and that he sees as missing in modern consciousness. Above all, the man of letters is guardian of the Word, and his "normative duty" is to maintain the law of continuity and save the permanent things from totalist ideology. How to give heart, then, to the forces of "the Great Tradition" in human life and morality, is a question that Kirk sought to answer in his long career as a man of letters. . . .[12]

A reviewer of books throughout much of his career, Kirk wrote only one full-length work of literary criticism, *Eliot and His Age,* a book he spent much of his career planning to write, even mentioning to Eliot himself that he hoped to embark upon just such a work someday. This study and *Enemies of the Permanent Things,* an artful compilation, are the top favorites of Kirk's works among many of his readers—even more so than *The Conservative Mind.* Panichas has written, "For me *Enemies of the Permanent Things* remains the keystone of his books of essays insofar as it contains the central principles of his critical exposition and thought."[13]

Organizing this work into two parts, on the norms of literature and the norms of politics, Kirk seeks to examine the problems of modern literature as it reflects and relates to other aspects of culture, especially in the political realm. Briefly put, the "enemies" of the permanent things are those writers and teachers of literature who view the literary imagination as the handmaid of ideology or mere salacious titillation. If the purpose of humane literature is indeed to help form or reinforce the normative consciousness—to teach and affirm the true nature of the mature man and his significance—then the enemy of the permanent things is he who begins with the assumption that there is no such thing as "the normative consciousness" and moves from there to his logical postulates: that the true nature of man is pliable, meant to be governed by passive nonreference to cultural norms or active rebellion against such norms; or to be harnessed to a "higher" calling, dictated by self-styled elites and controllers. For a work called *Enemies of the Permanent Things,* Kirk does not merely name and lambast a host of transgressors against the permanent things, though he does name and take to book a representative sampling amid discussions of those he believes fulfill the role of champions of humane letters. Such figures as H. G. Wells, B. F. Skinner, C. P. Snow, Harvey Cox, and Robert C. W. Ettinger are subjected to Kirk's scorn—the last-named gentleman in particular. The chief prophet of cryogenics (freezing the recently deceased that they may be reanimated at a future date, when technology allows), Ettinger looked forward to a future of dubious wonders; he is quoted by Kirk as having once written:

> I am convinced that in a few hundred years the words of Shakespeare ... will interest us no more than the grunting of swine in a wallow. (Shakespeare scholars, along with censors, snuff grinders, and wig makers, will have to find new, perhaps unimaginable occupations.) Not only will his work be far too weak in intellect, and written in too vague and puny a language, but the problems which concerned him will be, in the main, no more than historical curiosities. Neither greed, nor lust, nor ambitious will in that society have any recognizable similarity to the qualities we know. With the virtually unlimited resources of that era, all ordinary wants will be readily satisfied, either by supplying them or removing them in the mind of the individual. .... Competitive drives, in their inter-personal sense, may or may not persist; but if they do, it will be in radically modified form.[14]

A world in which greed, lust, and ambition simply do not exist, thanks to human ingenuity: this is the gnostic vision. Kirk greets this description of Ettinger's brave new world with sarcasm, "What a charming prospect!" He goes on to blast Ettinger and his followers as grim ideologues willing and eager to sacrifice normal humanity for the sake of an intolerable earthly "immortality." Why intolerable? Because with all challenges removed, with science at the ready to alter each man to resemble Charles Atlas (if he so desires, assures Ettinger) and each woman to resemble Miss Universe (if *she* so desires, incessant smile and all), "life would be too unutterly boring to be worth living; but death from 'natural causes' having been abolished by compulsory cryogenic interment, the final escape-hatch would be sealed. Christian doctrine has a word for that condition: Hell."[15]

In *Enemies of the Permanent Things,* Kirk makes it deadly plain that he loathes ideology, but also has little patience with the sort of literature that is morally upright but otherwise dull and boring. Humanity can endure nearly anything but boredom, and Kirk was no exception to the rule. He shared with his New Humanist forebears a withering contempt for highflown idealism, sentimentality, baseless optimism, and overt moralism.

The insipid, endlessly dull adventures of Dick and Jane, stories of earnest student nurses and upright high school athletes appealed not at all to him, he having read Hawthorne, Scott, Kipling, Stevenson, and other major writers as a young boy, and having talked of literature with his grandfather, Frank Pierce. Little wonder, then, that he urged just such readings upon young readers of the present day, recommending especially the works of the above-named writers as well as C. S. Lewis's *Chronicles of Narnia* and (for young adult readers) J. R. R. Tolkien's *Lord of the Rings* trilogy and its prequel, *The Hobbit*, among many other works.

In these works, as in the writings of other authors he admired and praised in *Enemies of the Permanent Things*—Eliot, Bradbury, Jacquetta Hawkes, George Orwell, Camilo Cela, Eric Voegelin, Ralph Ellison, Max Picard, George MacDonald, and Charles Williams, among others—he found literature flush with imagination and given wholly to the *tao* and to the permanent things. The works of these authors, however far afield they may run in regard to future settings or to fantasy, draw deeply from life and the inherited wisdom of the race to show what it is to grow toward and become mature men and women, prudent and humble in the knowledge of humanity's flawed state. First principles are an understated given, and the truths of tradition and religion are held in honor, not ignored or sneered at. Wrongdoers in these fictions are often men who seek to overthrow established ways through some form of ideology or radical innovation, the natural fruit of hubris, the pride that goes before a fall. Such individuals are sometimes presented as thoughtless despoilers of the natural environment. There is in these tales a reverence for myth and tradition, and for the attendant illative sense of apprehending truth and virtue. Characters who demonstrate to the reader characteristics of moralistic idealism or sentimental nostalgia are in general headed for humiliation or ruin. Evil sometimes triumphs in the short term, but it is never glorified or presented as preferable to good, though it sometimes comes in an appealing manner, presented with pleasing words, or portrayed as the wave of all future-thinking persons.

Through the reading and study of humane letters, Kirk believed, the normative consciousness develops and thrives. The order of the soul is improved and thus, though indirectly, that of the commonwealth is maintained. Kirk identified four levels or genres of literature by which this consciousness is developed, being quick to state that among these four, the upper levels do not supplant the earlier, "but instead supplement and blend with them; and the process of becoming familiar with these four levels or bodies of normative knowledge extends from the age of three or four to the studies of college and university." He called these levels fantasy, narrative history and biography, reflective prose and poetic fiction, and philosophy and theology.

Literature of the fantastic and the fey, though pooh-poohed by many experts today for its violence and horror, is precisely what the healthy child needs, Kirk believed. As he stated on many occasions, all things begin and end in mystery; and it is in fantasy, in tales of wonder, that a sense of awe at life's mysteries begins, and with it the beginning of philosophy and the arousal of the normative consciousness. Intelligent children want answers to the ultimate questions. They also love mysteries; and with a curious quickness, they apprehend allegories. In one of his "To the Point" columns, "The Moral Imagination of Children," Kirk praised Lewis's seven-volume *Chronicles of Narnia* by writing:

> Too many twentieth-century books for children actually starve the moral imagination, or bore the child with goody-goody, platitudinous "real-life situation" didacticism. In one of his admirable books for children, the late C. S Lewis described one child-character, Eustace, as miseducated by books with pictures of grain elevators and fat foreign children doing exercises.
>
> It is equally bad to offer only an arid rationalism. Elsewhere, Lewis tells of the little girl whose parents told her that God was Perfect Substance. This reminded their offspring of tapioca pudding; and she detested tapioca pudding; so she grew up with a marked prejudice against God. . . .
>
> Later in life, children who read the *Narnia Chronicles* will encounter many people who, like the witch [a deceiver who appears in the fourth volume, *The Silver Chair*], insist that nothing exists but what is immediately perceived by our five senses. Yet the witch lied; and one of the very practical functions of allegories for children is this: by waking the moral imagination, to teach children that many false spirits are gone forth into the world.[16]

Kirk knew, with child psychologist Bruno Bettelheim, that the minds of children, far from being innocent, are filled with anxious, angry, and destructive imaginings. Both men believed it remarkable that parents, worried about the possibility of traumatizing their children through fairy stories and tales of fantasy, should remain oblivious to the reassuring messages to be found in fairy tales. Aside from *Narnia*, Kirk had high regard for such stories and poems as Tolkien's *Farmer Giles of Ham*, Stevenson's *A Child's Garden of Verses*, John Ruskin's *The King of the Golden River*, Walter de la Mare's *Peacock Pie*, Hilaire Belloc's *Cautionary Tales*, *The Arabian Nights*, Kenneth Grahame's *The Wind in the Willows*, E. B. White's *Charlotte's Web*, nearly everything from among Ray Bradbury's fiction (especially *The Martian Chronicles* and *Fahrenheit 451*), and James Thurber's *The Thirteen Clocks*, to name but a few.[17] There exists no guarantee that such books will bring the reader material success or earthly power, Kirk said. "Yet such reading will teach us about what it is to be a real man or a real woman. Of this we may be certain, that when the wisdom derived from high imaginative literature is ignored, order in the soul and order in the commonwealth are crumbling."[18]

Chesterton once wrote that he considered George MacDonald's children's story *The Princess and the Goblin*, of all the stories he had ever read, "the most real, the most realistic, in the exact sense of the phrase the most like life." *The most like life?* Twenty years before he made that startling claim, Chesterton had stated its explanation in his weekly column in *The Illustrated London News*, saying,

> Most realistic fiction deals with modern towns—that is, with one short transition period in the smallest corner of the smallest of the four continents. Fairytales deal with that life of field and hut and palace, those simple relations with the ox and with the king which actually are the experience of the greatest number of men for the greatest number of centuries. The real farmer in most real places really does send out his three sons to seek their fortune; he knows uncommonly well that they will not get it from him. The real king of the majority of earthly royal houses is really ready to offer to some wild adventurer "the half of his kingdom." His kingdom is so uncommonly small to begin with that the division does not seem unnatural. Even in these physical matters the fairytale only seems incredible because we are in a somewhat exceptional position. It seems incredible to us because the big civilisation we have built is a specialist and singular and somewhat morbid thing. In short, it only seems incredible to us because we ourselves shall very soon be incredible.[19]

Like Kirk (himself an admirer of this story), Chesterton held by MacDonald's belief that the fantasy story "cannot help having some meaning; if it have proportion and harmony it has vitality, and vitality is truth. The beauty may be plainer in it than the truth, but without the truth the beauty could not be, and the fairy tale would give no delight." MacDonald adds significantly: "Everyone, however, who feels the story, will read its meaning after his own nature and development: one man will read one meaning in it, another will read another."[20] To MacDonald as to Kirk, there is no lockstep party line to be pushed in fairy stories, for as MacDonald's literary disciple C. S. Lewis once wrote, "Myth is thus like manna; it is to each man a different dish and to each the dish he needs. It does not grow old nor stick at frontiers racial, sexual, or philosophic; and even from the same man at the same moment it can elicit different responses at different levels."[21]

During his boyhood, Kirk took long walks with his grandfather around the north end of Plymouth and along the railroad tracks, discussing everything from the trivial to the character of Richard III, aspects of Puritan domestic life, and the ferocity of the ancient Assyrians. From these talks, Kirk developed an interest in reading narrative histories and biographies, including Herodotus, Thucydides, James Boswell's *Life of Johnson*, H. G. Wells's *Outline of History*, and many other such works. (In time he came to mistrust the mechanistic view of humanity portrayed in Wells's *Outline*.) As a young man, he specialized in history at Michigan State, Duke, and St.

Andrews. He advocated the reading of honest biographies and histories, believing, "Reading of grand lives does something to form decent lives." On this matter, it may be instructive to mention, as an example, Kirk's review of Edward E. Ericson Jr.'s *Solzhenitsyn and the Modern World* (1993). Here, as in all his reviews, Kirk immediately engages with the text at hand; there is no sense that because Kirk admires Solzhenitsyn and is on friendly terms with Ericson, his review is on "automatic pilot," unwinding predictably and in such a manner that he need not have even read the book. Plainly Kirk has read and ruminated over every page of Ericson's work, weighing the truth, significance, style, outlook, organization, and learnedness of Solzhenitsyn and the modern world. A skillful use of apt allusions, typical of Kirk, is at play when he writes:

> Ericson finds it necessary to reply at some length to the sort of intellectuals whom Solzhenitsyn calls "the smatterers"—the folk puffed by that little knowledge which is a dangerous thing: people who talk about the West and democracy and nationalism almost incessantly, but whose knowledge of such abstractions is sufficiently shallow. These smatterers' primary complaint against Solzhenitsyn is this, even if they do not or cannot express coherently their basic difference with him: Solzhenitsyn rejects the Enlightenment of the eighteenth century. The stalwart Russian, whether or not he has read Coleridge's prose, agrees with Samuel Taylor Coleridge that the alleged Enlightenment was full of Enlighteners but singularly deficient in Light.[22]

Likewise, Kirk describes Wendell Berry's book *The Unsettling of America: Culture and Agriculture* (1978) in terms that succinctly summarized the author's stature as a humanist and high skill as a writer, reflecting an area of great interest to Kirk, the decline of agriculture in America, while alluding to a contemporary episode in the news that uncharacteristically dates the review for a moment, before a judicious turn of phrase ties the section together thematically:

> Berry is possessed of an intellect at once philosophic and poetic, and he writes most movingly. Humane culture has no better friend today than he. If, on taking up this book the reader fancies that agriculture is all a matter of economics—why, he will have his eyes opened for him. Yet while the ground literally is disappearing beneath our feet, the American public is told it ought to worry about such phenomena as the overdrafts of Bert Lance. It is the terrible national overdraft upon our soil and our culture, so burningly described by Berry, which ought to be every thinking American's urgent concern.[23]

"I began to read Sir Walter Scott when I was twelve or thirteen; and I think I learnt from the Waverley novels, and from Shakespeare, more of the varieties of character than ever I have got since from the manuals of psychology," wrote Kirk in *Enemies of the Permanent Things*.[24] He highly valued reflective prose and poetic fiction not for entertainment only, though he greatly enjoyed the pleasure of reading fiction. He considered humane fiction truer than fact, believing that in accomplished fiction the reader obtains the distilled wisdom of men and women of genius. Through such reading, he believed, we acquire understanding of human nature that could otherwise only be attained, without literature, at the end of a long life, after many needless, painful experiences. A little-remarked though major influence upon Kirk's outlook, derived from his experiences in reading poetry and fiction, was Dante, whose *Divine Comedy* provides a thematic undercurrent to several of his short stories and to his final novel, *Lord of the Hollow Dark*. Kirk picked up Dante after first reading Mark Twain's *The Mysterious Stranger*—"an atheist tract delightfully disguised as a romance of medieval Austria. It did not turn me into a juvenile atheist; but it set me to inquiring after first causes—and in time, paradoxically, it led me to Dante, my mainstay ever since."[25] (Interestingly, during the final week of his life, a physically weak Kirk reread *The Mysterious Stranger*, "defying the Foul Fiend" one last time by wrestling with Twain's statement of rejection of God. Although this may seem an odd choice in reading for a dying Catholic, it seemed to Annette Kirk that her husband wanted to face once more that last challenge to his own faith—the mysteries of suffering, both by the dying and the living who were left behind— and to triumph.)

"For the crown of normative literary studies, we turn, about the age of nineteen or twenty, to abstraction and generalization, chastened by logic," Kirk wrote, indicating his fourth level of literature by which humane consciousness is developed, philosophy and theology.[26] Although he had little use for Ralph Waldo Emerson's transcendentalist philosophy, he agreed with and frequently quoted a short poem of Emerson's that he initially discovered as the epigraph that opens Babbitt's *Literature and the American College*:

> There are two laws discrete
> Not reconciled—
> Law for man, and law for thing;
> The last builds town and fleet,
> But it runs wild,
> And doth the man unking.

There is a law for humanity and there is a law for beasts and inanimate objects: a truth that sounds oddly simplistic, though the great tyrannies of the past two centuries, along with the petty systems and bureaucracies which have to some extent aped the tyrannies—viewing people not by the light of the moral imagination, but as things to be used and then done away with—have brought much misery upon mankind by ignoring it. One learns of the "law for man" by reading Plato, Cicero, Marcus Aurelius, Epictetus, the Bible, Augustine, the Schoolmen, Sir Thomas More, John Henry Newman, Miguel de Unamuno, Eliot, Eric Voegelin, and others recognized as possessing a sound, rooted understanding of the nature of man, his purpose, and his place in the order of things. Of such as these, and of the other writers and works represented in the preceding three levels of literature, Kirk concludes " 'Scientific' truth, or what is popularly taken to be scientific truth, alters from year to year—with accelerating speed, indeed, in our day. But poetic and moral truth changes little with the elapse of the centuries; and the norms of politics are fairly constant. Although virtue and wisdom are not identical, humane letters give to the imagination and the reason a moral bent."[27]

As in his myriad writings on American education, Kirk reserves his sharpest arrows for the many college and university professors who possess no true philosophy ("love of wisdom") but are instead philodoxers ("lovers of opinion"). A philodoxer, he writes, "is a purveyor of *doxa*, illusory opinions and vain wishes. Out of the *doxa* comes disorder, in the soul and in the body politic. But *eunomia*, righteousness, the disciplined harmony of a man's soul, Solon said, makes 'all things proper and sensible in the affairs of men.' Eric Voegelin is a philosopher, as well as an historian and a professor of the *nomos*—that is, of institutions and traditions."[28] Commenting upon this particular section of *Enemies of the Permanent Things*, Frederick Wilhelmsen, in a largely favorable review, notes that "Value-free" behavioral science, "instead of contenting itself with the modest role of an auxiliary instrument in the service of wisdom, has carved out an empire for itself within the academy which starves norms and impoverishes students bent upon vision rather than statistics." As an antidote to such pretensions, Wilhelmsen writes, Kirk advances the works of Voegelin, specifically *The New Science of Politics* and *Order and History*, acknowledging a distinct debt to Voegelin. In his essay-chapter "Eric Voegelin's Normative Labor," Kirk succinctly elucidates his subject's theses, these being the discovery of a divine order and the very constitution of history as a mode of being in ancient Israel; the leap into being through the discovery of philosophical truth in Plato and Aristotle; and gnosticism—the impulse to institute life-changing political ideology to create a terrestrial paradise—as the immanentizing of Christian hope.

But Wilhelmsen suggests that in this essay Kirk takes Voegelin too uncritically, Wilhelmsen finding Voegelin's philosophy too much given to empiricism, and adding:

The split between immanence and transcendence makes the Incarnation not only theoretically difficult to justify apologetically, but it also makes the Incarnation terribly messy and unaristocratic for a man so enamored of Plato. Kirk does not ask Voegelin whether the Resurrection was an historical event: if it was not, "our faith is in vain" says St. Paul. Nor does Kirk ask Voegelin how his increasing distaste for doctrinal definitions of the *depositum fidei* distinguished his position from that of the modernists condemned by the encyclical *Pascendi*. Voegelinian experience may be an interesting luxury but most of us Christians live by the creeds.[29]

Kirk was not one to give even his friends or conservative allies a free pass when it came to assessing their books. He judged works by Buckley, Willmoore Kendall, and Frank Meyer with the same discernment with which he approached the new publications of anyone else. (His own *Academic Freedom* is, in part, a firm but gentlemanly rebuttal to the philosophy of education elucidated in Buckley's *God and Man at Yale* [1951].) In one instance, this not from a review proper, he spoke of Meyer's *In Defense of Freedom* (1962) as "mostly John Stuart Mill *redivivus*—though forced into the Procrustean bed of ideology, as often is the way with ex-Marxist writers.[30] This brief phrase prompted a personal letter to Kirk from a young conservative writer for *National Review*, Garry Wills, who respectfully urged Kirk to refrain from using such terms as "ex-Marxist," as they carried much weight upon being published by a prominent conservative such as Russell Kirk, and thus carried also the potential for causing needless division within the growing conservative movement, especially when published in a nonmovement periodical such as *The Commonweal*.[31] Kirk's reply to Wills is lost; though it is instructive that as a reviewer and social critic the older man continued to engage forthrightly and, when the occasion arose, pointedly, when it came to writing of conservative figures and literature. He tended to be polite but firm in disagreements with compatriots and friends; but a writer of gelded prose: Never.

In regard to literary censorship, Kirk found it grimly amusing that despite the common depiction of conservatives and humanist writers as witch-hunters and would-be censors of literary tastes, America's most prominent (and successful) forces for censoring free expression often lay on the left: the sensitive individuals who succeed in banning *The Adventures of Huckleberry Finn* from local libraries because of its racial language, the craven university administrators who withhold funding from conservative campus newspapers or countenance their being quietly appropriated and disposed of by correct-thinking students, the shoutings-down of conservative speakers on campus by free-speech advocates, the earnest Midwestern librarian who found, nestled among a newly arrived consignment of textbooks, a single copy of Bradbury's *Fahrenheit 451*, which caused great consternation to her upon opening it and reading it. Firing off a furious letter to Bradbury's publisher, this guardian of refined thinking declared of the offensive novel on censorship, "I took it right out in back and burned it."[32] Is there a need for humanistic literature? As Kirk wryly concludes his telling of this episode regarding *Fahrenheit 451*, "Tomorrow is already here."

Kirk wrote of this episode first in a *National Review* column in 1967, first alerting Bradbury that it would appear in "a piece called 'Librarians and Fahrenheit 451,' touching upon the censorial matters I raised in my previous letter to you. More important, you will make some appearance in the great fat book I am to commence writing, *The Age of Eliot: English and American Letters in the Twentieth Century*. Holt, Rinehart, and Winston want to publish it; I won't be finished for two years, if then."[33]

Indeed, Kirk's promised book on Eliot did not appear for over four years. It was published not by Holt but by Random House, Bradbury is mentioned not at all within its covers, and it appeared under the title *Eliot and His Age: T. S. Eliot's Moral Imagination in the Twentieth Century*. It was, though, "a great fat book," rich in insight into Eliot's life, thought, and literature. Sometime after the appearance of the second edition in 1984, Peter Kreeft went so far as to write a letter to Kirk about *Eliot and His Age*, claiming "It helps to dispel an illusion I have had for a long time: that the more interesting the original writer, the duller the books about him. Most of the books about Plato, Augustine, Pascal, . . . Dostoyevski, and C. S. Lewis are depressingly dull; and the commentaries on the Bible are often the worst offenders of all. But here is a great readable, and it seems to me on-target book about a great, readable and on-target writer."[34]

Drawing upon his recollections of personal conversations with the great man, his readings in the body of secondary literature about Eliot, personal letters, and his own readings in Eliot's works—including the complete, bound set of *The Criterion* he kept and periodically read in his library—Kirk crafted a ruminative survey of Eliot's canon of poetry and prose, inserting just enough biographical information to provide timely and interesting finger-posts along the way. The result is a work of extended literary criticism as well as a critical study of Eliot's moral and social thought (as the work's subtitle sufficiently suggests), which reviewer John Chamberlain called "a most distinguished work."[35]

Of all the scholars who have written about Eliot to date, none has quite gone so far as Kirk in engaging with the journalism the American exile published in the magazine he edited from 1922 to 1939, *The Criterion*. Kirk wrote that Eliot, after that publication's demise, "found none of his Commentaries and few of his reviews from his own quarterly enduring enough to include in his several volumes of collected essays. Yet anyone who can afford to acquire the eighteen reprinted bound volumes of *The Criterion* will encounter there some of the best writing and some of the more seminal thought of the twentieth century."[36] From the insights quarried from that famous periodical, and from a close reading of Eliot's essays and reviews, Kirk portrays a man who was a prophet without honor in the English-speaking world before World War II, whose reputation advanced with major strides after the war, becoming recognized (and in some quarters, held in contempt) as an influential voice for Burkean conservatism. As Both Burke and Kirk believed, order in the soul and the order of the commonwealth are linked; and if the inner order holds to cultural and religious custom, convention, and continuity, the outer order will be healthy, not given to social upheaval, boredom, and lawlessness.

As in Eliot's poetry, Kirk discerns a pattern reminiscent of *The Divine Comedy* in the rise, ebb, and flow of its progress. Both Kirk and Eliot were fascinated by Dante, and the latter's career showed forth a distinct pattern: the early poetry, from "The Love Song of J. Alfred Prufrock" through *The Waste Land*, were Eliot's Inferno, a period of death-in-life during which he grappled with agnosticism and cosmic despair while enduring the onset and initial stages of his first wife's descent into insanity. He emerged from his terrestrial hell to a place of purgation, the foothills of a coming ascent, made plain in "Ash Wednesday" and the "Ariel Poems." In time, Eliot mounted up to Paradiso, when he discovered he could embrace a faith grounded in revelation and authority, becoming the author of not only the *Four Quartets*, but two of Kirk's favorite prose works, *The Idea of a Christian Society* and *Notes towards the Definition of Culture*.

On the topic of Eliot's alleged anti-Semitism, which is today one of the more widely discussed aspects of the poet's life largely on the strength of Anthony Julius's study *T. S. Eliot, Anti-Semitism and Literary Form* (1995), Kirk finds little worth pursuing at length. He does, though, face up to the controversial, widely quoted remark in Eliot's *After Strange Gods* (1934), which runs to the effect that "reasons of race and religion combine to make any large number of free-thinking Jews undesirable" in a stable, traditional local culture within the largely Protestant United States. Kirk quotes from several contemporaries of Eliot, some of them intimate, who defended the poet against charges of anti-Semitism and, in effect, said that Eliot's remarks reflected more on the assumptions of the class within which he moved than upon any actual contempt for the Jews as a people. Kirk notes that Eliot himself denied any anti-Semitic intent and was repentant that he had caused offense, going so far as to never bring *After Strange Gods* back into print after its first edition and to forbid permission to any writer or publisher seeking to quote from this book at length. On this issue he quotes George Orwell, who wrote, "In the early 'twenties, Eliot's antisemitic remarks were about on par with the automatic sneer one casts at Anglo-Indian colonels in boarding houses. On the other hand if they had been written after the [Nazi] persecutions began they would have meant something quite different. . . . Some people go round smelling after antisemitism all the time."[37] Still, Kirk had to admit of his friend, "What with the anti-Jewish virulence of Hitler and his supporters in the early thirties, nevertheless, Eliot was strangely insensitive to the drift of affairs when he referred slightingly to 'free-thinking Jews' in *After Strange Gods.*"[38] He notes that Eliot's sorrow at "the shame of motives late revealed, and the awareness of things ill done and done to others' harm," in the poem "Little Gidding," probably reflects—as some critics have suggested—remorse at having set down, in *After Strange Gods,* and perhaps in the poem "Burbank with a Baedeker: Bleistein with a Cigar," phrases of unwise prejudice.

On the whole, Kirk's *Eliot and His Age* was well received by critics. The Scottish man of letters George Scott-Moncrieff wrote, "Dr. Kirk puts us all in his debt for assembling in a book at once detailed and immensely readable the creed of a man whose thought becomes only more relevant as the years pass."[39] The few negative reviews it received tended to poke at small matters of detail or tone. Novelist and travel writer Paul Theroux praised Kirk for his "careful scholarship and . . . close reading of Eliot and his sources," but was bothered by "the off-putting tone of his apocalyptic Tory mode: 'So it came to pass that Bloomsbury—where dwelt a good many Gerontions—puffed and patronized Eliot'. . . ."[40] Reviewing Kirk in the influential *New York Times Book Review,* literary scholar Frank Kermode depicted the book as a lengthy exercise in toadying to the high reputation of Eliot.[41] Kermode missed a larger issue at work in *Eliot and His Age:* that Kirk perceived in Eliot not simply a friend but a kindred spirit—and that the feeling was mutual. Long before the writing of this book, Eliot himself had been impressed by Kirk's depth of understanding of his work; this degree of insight must be taken into account when assessing *Eliot and His Age,* and this Kermode failed to do amid executing tongue-in-cheek jibes at Kirk's awful conservatism and "smugness."

Another critic noted that Kirk speaks of *The Waste Land* as being a four-part poem. (It is, in fact, in five parts.) Kirk had taken pains to critically examine and interpret each section of *The Waste Land;* he knew perfectly well it was a five-part poem; but, strangely, he chose not to change his phrasing in subsequent editions of *Eliot and His Age* to reflect this. Likewise, T. S. Matthews, himself at work on a major biography of Eliot at the time Kirk's book appeared, wrote a collegial letter to Kirk about *Eliot and His Age,* stating that he found it "a pleasure to read, and more informative than I like to admit."[42] He then went on to list "a few very small points" that he noted as he had read, these points being a typo here, a slightly inaccurately worded quotation there, a small matter in need of rechecking still there—some 19 queries in all. Matthews added that he included this checklist so that Kirk might consider making these minor changes in other editions of an otherwise fine work. A week after receiving this letter, Kirk wrote to thank Matthews for his letter and suggestions, adding, "I mean to incorporate in revised, paperback, London, and other editions of my fat Eliot book your several suggestions and corrections. Some slips I had caught earlier, to my horror: but though even the index and all such things were corrected and sent back to Random House a year ago, and they didn't publish the book until this February, they would allow no changes! It's no wonder that in these United States the dog-food business does twice the volume of the trade-book business."[43] For reasons unknown, perhaps because Kirk had so many other projects ready to hand during the 1970s, none of the changes suggested by Matthews was made to subsequent editions of *Eliot and His Age* during Kirk's lifetime.

These matters aside, Kirk was pleased with *Eliot and His Age*, believing it a fitting study to an important figure in twentieth-century literature and culture. "In fifty years of writing, what had Eliot accomplished?" Kirk concluded. "He had endeavored consciously to redeem the time; at the end, he was under no illusion that he had succeeded." Yet his accomplishment was great, and Kirk praised him fulsomely:

> As a poet, he had confronted hard reality with the armed vision: he had at once restored to poetry the nerve of sensibility and the matter of metaphysics. He had taken the measure of his age in verse, and he had renewed that age's moral imagination. . . .
>
> As a dramatist, he had reinvigorated the verse-play, and it may be that his influence upon the stage has not yet come to its height. What mattered more to Eliot, he had done something to revive the ethical and religious character of the drama, waking religious feelings as no prose apologist could.
>
> As a critic of literature, he had rescued the critic's art from personal impressionism, and had upheld the great continuity of humane letters, defending simultaneously the permanent things and the claims of the renewing innovator. He had taught the rising generation how to open their eyes to the deeper meanings in a work of literary art. . . .
>
> As a critic of society, he had stripped the follies of the time. He had not spared the morals of his age, or its politics, or its economics, or its notions of education, or its strange gods. He had striven to renew modern man's understanding of the norms of order and justice and freedom, in the person and in the commonwealth. He had not offered the opiate of ideology: he had pleaded for a return to enduring principle, and for recognition of the tensions which are necessary to a tolerable civil social order.[44]

Still, the time remains unredeemed, wrote Kirk, for "prophets and saints fail in their generation at that labor, and no poet can prevail solitary against the pride and passion of man. Yet Eliot, more than anyone else in his age, exposed smugness and illusion; he reminded many a conscience that, as Audrey Fawcett Cahill writes, 'human existence is a challenging and perplexing and often painful experience; that it is fraught with contradictions and tensions; and that to live with any degree of consciousness is to be aware of unreconciled conflicts clamoring to be resolved.' He did not hold out false hopes of a terrestrial paradise, but he affirmed that a man's life, and the life of society, can be endurable only if matter is moved by spirit"—words that effectively answer Kermode's remark that Kirk "will not allow that to those holding different beliefs Tory Anglo-Catholicism is an ideology, too."[45] The Christian humanist is concerned with the life of the individual and the community, not with cobbling together a political system designed to create a gnostic, worry-free existence.

"The personal is political," some will rejoin, using a block-phrase that almost invariably issues from the mouths and writings of people to whom all of life is political (and miserably so). One writer Kirk deeply admired, though a man of the left, offered a somewhat different statement on the relation of politics and literature, pertinent to Eliot. "There is no such thing as genuinely non-political literature," wrote George Orwell at the end of World War II, "and least of all in an age like our own, when fears, hatred, and loyalties of a directly political kind are near to the surface of everyone's consciousness."[46] Kirk agreed with this statement, quoting it near the end of *Enemies of the Permanent Things*, but hastening to add the clarification that between literature that is incidentally political and literature that is blatantly, purposely propagandistic there is a great gulf fixed. It was to help prevent the death of literature by its being subjugated to the demands of ideologues that the storyteller and bookman Russell Kirk critiqued the books of even writers with whom he shared much sympathy with a penetrating and demanding eye.

NOTES

1. Chesterton, "Is Humanism a Religion?" *The Bookman* 69, May, 1929, 238.
2. For a fuller understanding of Mencken's view of Kirk's critical forebears, see his essay "The New Humanism," in *The American Mercury* 18, September, 1929, 123–24, and "Quod Est Veritas?" in *The American Mercury* 25, April, 1932, 506–10.
3. More to Paul R. Coleman-Norton, December 9, 1924, quoted in Arthur Hazard Dakin, *Paul Elmer More*, p. 211n.
4. Babbitt, *Literature and the American College* (Boston, 1908), p. 8. Plainly, then, by "humanism" I do not mean here the irritable, cocksure ideology popularly styled "secular humanism," with its "God is *really* dead—and a good thing, too!" credo, embraced by the people associated with the American Society of Humanists and *The Humanist* magazine.

5. More, from his *On Being Human,* quoted in Dakin, p. 281.

6. Chesterton, "Is Humanism a Religion?," p. 236.

7. More, *Shelburne Essays,* seventh series, p. 218.

8. Wilhelmsen, "The Wandering Sage of Mecosta," *The Intercollegiate Review* 30, Fall, 1994, 84.

9. *Enemies of the Permanent Things,* p. 68. All quotations from *Enemies of the Permanent Things* are taken from this edition.

10. *Enemies of the Permanent Things,* p. 72.

11. Kirk to Bradbury, September 12, 1967. This letter is on file at the Russell Kirk Center for Cultural Renewal, Mecosta, Michigan.

12. Panichas, "Russell Kirk as a Man of Letters," *The Intercollegiate Review* 30, Fall, 1994, 10.

13. Panichas, "Russell Kirk as a Man of Letters," 17n.

14. Ettinger, quoted in *Enemies of the Permanent Things* (La Salle, 1988), pp. 149–50.

15. *Enemies of the Permanent Things,* p. 151.

16. "The Moral Imagination of Children," *The New Orleans Times-Picayune,* October 5, 1966 (I)13.

17. These and many others among Kirk's favorite children's stories are listed and commented upon in the essay " 'The Box of Delights': A Literary Patrimony," by his daughter Cecilia A. Kirk Nelson, which appears in *Festschrift, The Unbought Grace of Life: Essays in Honor of Russell Kirk* (Peru, 1994), pp. 59–67. Of all the essays that appeared in that volume, this particular piece has been brought to my attention most often as the favorite among the *Festschrift*'s readers. In addition, two fairly hard to obtain essays by Russell Kirk, "Books for Small Children" and "Humane Literature for Young Readers," both published by the Textbook Evaluation Committee of America's Future, Inc., New Rochelle, N.Y. (n.d.) are also instructive.

18. "Humane Literature for Young Readers," *Textbook Evaluation Report,* no. 768 (New Rochelle, n.d.), pp. 8–9.

19. Chesterton, "Our Note Book," *The Illustrated London News* 127, November 18, 1905, 714.

20. MacDonald, *A Dish of Orts: Chiefly Papers on the Imagination and on Shakespeare,* p. 316.

21. Lewis, *Rehabilitations, and Other Essays,* pp. 29–30.

22. "What Solzhenitsyn Tells Us," *Crisis: A Journal of Lay Catholic Opinion* 11, October, 1993, 59.

23. Review of *The Unsettling of America,* by Wendell Berry, *The Birmingham News,* June 4, 1978, 6-E.

24. *Enemies of the Permanent Things,* p. 50.

25. *Enemies of the Permanent Things,* p. 50.

26. *Enemies of the Permanent Things,* p. 51.

27. *Enemies of the Permanent Things,* p. 51.

28. *Enemies of the Permanent Things,* p. 268.

29. Wilhelmsen, "A Standard for Public Virtue," *National Review* 21, August 26, 1969, 863.

30. "The Mood of Conservatism," *The Commonweal* 78, June 7, 1963, 298.

31. Wills to Kirk, n.d., though probably written in June 1963. In the years since

writing this letter, which is on file at the Kirk Center, Wills has grown much less solicitous about conservative unity, breaking ranks with the movement during the Nixon era and using his nationally syndicated column to become one of President Bill Clinton's most articulate defenders against conservative critics.

32. Quoted in *Enemies of the Permanent Things*, p. 117.

33. Kirk to Bradbury, September 12, 1967.

34. Kreeft to Kirk, July 16, 1985. This letter is on file at the Russell Kirk Center for Cultural Renewal, Mecosta, Michigan.

35. Chamberlain, review of *Eliot and His Age*, in *The Freeman*, 22, November, 1972, 703.

36. *Eliot and His Age*, p. 261. All quotations from *Eliot and His Age* are taken from this late edition of the work which—but for a few final remarks added by Kirk—follows the pagination of the first edition.

37. Orwell, *The Collected Essays, Journalism and Letters of George Orwell*, vol. IV, *In Front of Your Nose, 1945–1950*, p. 450.

38. *Eliot and His Age*, p. 211n.

39. Scott-Moncrieff, "Eliot Remembered," *The Sewanee Review*, 80, Autumn, 1972, 638.

40. Theroux, "The Way to East Coker," *Book World—The Washington Post*, March 12, 1972, 5.

41. See "There Was Time for Visions and Revision," *The New York Times Book Review*, March 26, 1972, 6–7, 20, 22.

42. Matthews to Kirk, August 1, 1972. This letter, along with Kirk's response, is on file at the Russell Kirk Center for Cultural Renewal, Mecosta, Michigan.

43. Kirk to Matthews, August 9, 1972.

44. *Eliot and His Age*, pp. 415–17.

45. Kermode, "There Was a Time for Visions and Revision," 20.

46. Orwell, *The Collected Essays, Journalism and Letters of George Orwell*, vol. IV, *In Front of Your Nose, 1945–1950*, p. 65.

9

Toward a Tolerable Social Order: Kirk's Social Criticism

What do you mean by "culture"? That's a word they used in Nazi Germany.

—Mario Cuomo, 1992

> What is a man,
> If his chief good and market of his time
> Be but to sleep and feed? a beast, no more.
> Sure he that made us with such large discourse,
> Looking before and after, gave us not
> That capability and godlike reason
> To fust in us unus'd.

—*Hamlet*, Act IV, Sc. 4, ll. 32–9

In the opening section of one of his books, *The Shaping of America* (1976), John Warwick Montgomery recounts the time he encountered a man selling anarchist newspapers in the Latin Quarter of Paris in the riot-filled year 1968. Montgomery asked to see one of the newspapers, looked at it briefly, and then started to saunter away with it—without paying. The outraged vendor pursued his "customer" and demanded to know what he was trying to do, walking off without paying. To which Montgomery replied that he was simply giving the man his first lesson in anarchy.

173

If there is no recognition of a transcendent order and normative conduct, then anything is allowed, a truth that has been repeatedly borne out during the twentieth century, the first century in recorded history in which rejection of traditional sources of moral invigoration has prevailed on a worldwide scale. The sophomoric taunt that "religion" has killed more people than any other force on earth was no longer operative by the dawn of the twentieth century's final decade. Ideologues the world over, with their belief in bringing about changes of the heart at the point of the bayonet, had in a single century systematically slaughtered untold millions. Ideology, the secular religion of bringing about a terrestrial paradise by human effort, had made its mark upon human history. Little wonder, then, that Russell Kirk frequently referred to it as "Demon Ideology." By century's end, the words of Aleksandr Solzhenitsyn rang eerily true: "If I were called upon to identify the principal trait of the entire twentieth century, I would be unable to find anything more precise and pithy than this statement: Men have forgotten God."

Ideology, "the science of Idiocy," as the elder John Adams called it, has at its heart the belief that every ill to which human nature is prone—selfishness, greed, the bent to violence, fear, intolerance—can be systematically eliminated by just the right combination of education, legal action, legislation, and (in some cases) armed coercion. The ideologue trusts that the troubles recognized by people of an earlier age as properly belonging to the realm of cognitive choice and matters of the spirit are, after all, really soluble in the life here below, through systems that can be cobbled together out of abstract reason, reason not grounded in experience. Further, the ideologue views with rigid and inflexible suspicion the belief that there are set norms of belief and action, disdaining norms as rigid and inflexible things and insisting that in opposition to this "dogma" an open mind be kept in regard to the validity of every revealed truth. (However, open-mindedness concerning the essential rightness of dogmatic open-mindedness toward every revealed truth is out of the question.) G. K. Chesterton lamented this very aspect of the thought of his friend H. G. Wells, writing, "I think he thought that the object of opening the mind is simply opening the mind. Whereas I am incurably convinced that the object of opening the mind, as of opening the mouth, is to shut it again on something solid."[1]

In opposition to the ideologue, the conservative is chastened by something solid, the principle of human imperfectability. Kirk wrote, "Man being imperfect, no perfect social order ever can be created. Because of human restlessness, mankind would grow rebellious under any utopian domination, and would break out once more in violent discontent—or else expire of boredom. To aim for Utopia is to end in disaster, the conservative says: We are not made for perfect things. All that we reasonably can expect is a tolerably ordered, just, and free society, in which some evils, maladjustments, and suffering continue to lurk. By proper attention to prudent reform, we may preserve and improve this tolerable order. But if the old institutional and moral safeguards of a nation are forgotten, then the anarchic impulses in man break loose: 'The ceremony of innocence is drowned.'"[2] The conservative is therefore at odds with the ideologue, whether of the left or right: those who, in the words of T. S. Eliot, would

> constantly try to escape
> From the darkness outside and within
> By dreaming of systems so perfect that no one will need
>   to be good.[3]

To the ideologue, this is stuff and nonsense: an excuse for doing nothing, quietism. "I have been disappointed in Kirk's disregard for modern thought," wrote reviewer Harry Cargas in *America*. "He refuses to come to grips with evolution, the military-industrial complex, racial discord, ecumenism. The contemporary forward moving world does not seem to make an impression on Dr. Kirk."[4] Another concerned reader, himself no ideologue, seemed to think that Kirk the social critic could not see the forest for the trees, writing:

Dear Mr. Kirk:
    You seem to be alarmed about the increasing amount of dishonesty and corruption that exist in our country, but the ones you mention are small timers.
    If you will read a book by Philip M. Stern called "The Great Treasury Raid," you will see what some of those boys in timber, oil, etc. are getting away with.
Sincerely,
Groucho Marx[5]

It may give the reader pause that Cargas was bothered that Kirk refused "to come to grips with evolution, the military-industrial complex, racial discord, ecumenism" in a volume of *literary* criticism, *Enemies of the Permanent Things;* and unfortunately Kirk's reply to the immortal Groucho regarding Stern's well-received book on tax evaders is lost. Of far greater moment is the issue of how Kirk approached the particulars of solutions to modern problems, the question of how to get from here to there in matters where reform of some sort is needed. For example, in defense of the principles of conservative philosophy over ideology in respect to society's ills, Kirk was fond of quoting Jesus of Nazareth as having said that the poor we will have with us always. The plain but unspoken implication, according to the ideologue, is that Kirk, and conservatives in general, would prefer to lift not a finger to help the impoverished—in fact, let them starve—rather than support positive legislation that would alleviate their lot. But Kirk never believed the unfortunate should be cast adrift in the world to root, pick, or die. If he is to be faulted for anything in regard to his criticisms of ideology, it is not that he attacked it, but that he so seldom spelled out plainly how, in practical terms, the conservative ought to address the plight of the destitute, the refugee, the friendless outcast.

But perhaps the reason for this failure, if failure it be, is that the example of Kirk's own life at Piety Hill during the final quarter-century of his life vividly illustrated how best to rescue the less fortunate members of society, and that Kirk saw no reason to elaborate upon very plain solutions to very real problems. To Kirk, to write a discourse upon how every compassionate person ought to adopt a social conscience featuring a step-by-step formula for achieving success would be to turn his own conservative belief into an ideology of the right, as surely bound for mischief and failure as any ideology of the left. He believed that the twentieth-century conservative—whatever his vocation—is concerned, first of all, for the regeneration of spirit and character.

Brightening their own corner, Russell and Annette Kirk invited refugees from communist lands, unwed mothers-to-be, and a host of others into their home for as long as it took for them to receive the help, education, and training they needed before moving out into society at large and establishing themselves within their own communities. The phrase "Brighten your corner" found its way into his writings during those years, the emphasis here being that the family and the small community take care of their own, a way of life with deep roots in American history and that strikes compelling chords in the nation's collective psyche.

Many Americans, even those from large cities, can remember a time when the comings and goings of children within the neighborhood were watched closely by the people next door and across the street. Children were held accountable for their conduct, not by an intrusive political mechanism but by concerned neighbors, fellow communicants at the local church, and members of other small corporate communities. Parents often taught their children to accord these unofficial guardians the honorific "Uncle" or "Aunt" before their first names. ("If you're ever down at the other end of the street and a stranger in a car starts following you, run to Aunt Martha's house.") To the jaded, progressive-minded individual of the late twentieth century, this may seem an idyllic fantasy; but it was, in fact, a manner of living by which Kirk was raised in Plymouth during the 1920s (and by which the author of this book was raised a generation ago in Virginia). It was not a perfect upbringing to be sure—there were always neighbors who were overzealous in watchfulness, or outspokenly judgmental about children's conduct—but it worked tolerably well, and Kirk saw much value in it. It indeed "takes a village to raise a child," but this does not mean, as many liberals intend it to mean, that the state should have a loud and intrusive say in, and responsibility for, raising children; nor does it mean that children can and should be raised by a succession of caregivers other than their parents. It means simply that parents, who are primarily responsible for the upbringing of their young, do not labor in a vacuum, but that they raise their children supported by trusted neighbors, fellow parishioners, close relatives, teachers in the local school, and other circles of immediate influence in a child's life. Where those circles of voluntary influence break down, from the parental level and on through the other levels, the likelihood increases markedly for the individual to acquire a sense of rootlessness and anxiety; a link is broken in the community of souls, and the individual is endangered by all the temptations and opportunities for antisocial mischief—all the "holes in the social safety net"—with which the postmodern world is riddled. In the concluding pages of Mark Helprin's novel *Memoir from Antproof Case*, the first-person narrator and central protagonist writes of his being fortunate enough to be raised in such a way that the contract of eternal society was unbroken: "I was graduated from the finest school, which is that of the love between parent and child. Though the world is constructed to serve glory, success, and strength, one loves one's parents and one's children despite their failings and weaknesses—sometimes even more on account of them." He adds:

> In this school you learn the measure not of power but of love; not of victory, but of grace; not of triumph, but of forgiveness. You learn as well . . . that love can overcome death, and that what is required of you in this is memory and devotion. Memory and devotion. To keep your love alive you must be willing to be obstinate, and irrational, and true, to fashion your entire life as a construct, a metaphor, a fiction, a device for the exercise of faith. Without this, you will live like a beast and have nothing but an aching heart. With it, your heart, though broken, will be full, and you will stay in the fight unto the very last.

Just so. But with the change of culture the nation has undergone noticeably since mid-century, this manner of upbringing and neighborly care has vanished throughout much of America. The vast sense of mobility that came into being with the twentieth century makes for impermanence—the latest occupational promotion, a longstanding misunderstanding with one's parents, the opportunity to acquire a bigger and better house, or even a tiff with the neighbors leads us to move on to other pastures, and the sense of rootedness in place is broken. A largely rootless society is prey to a whole raft of social ills at which Kirk took aim throughout his career. To address these ills, the nation has called for progressive legislation to "fix" them, and often the fix has been a cure that makes the sickness worse. The burden has shifted from the little platoons of society to the tender care of the liberal ideologue. And to Kirk, as Wesley McDonald has noted, the ideologue, often a self-anointed expert, is the great enemy of humanity, holding as he does to his own abstract formulas for progress with an intolerant rigidity that would astonish a medieval pope. Writing of Kirk, McDonald claims, "The chief cause of modern social and cultural decadence, in his estimation, is the impoverishment of the imagination by ideology. The ideologist erects inflexible abstract doctrines in which there is an arrogant assumption that the world can be governed and all problems solved."[6] There are ideologues of both the left and the right of the cultural and political spectrum, both to be distrusted.

In his essays of social criticism, then, Kirk offered not a point-by-point agenda of how to defeat the problems he perceived in society—widespread indifference or outright contempt for unborn human life, acceptance of pornography in the name of free expression, a lack of accountability by school administrators and faculty, a lack of accountability by the parents of disruptive students in the nation's schools, the practice of thinking in slogans instead of thinking, the mistaking of the newest ideas for the best ideas, the degeneracy of the Christian faith as practiced within both modern Catholicism and Protestantism, and other issues—but rather a set of principles grounded in tradition by which social problems ought to be viewed and the culture strengthened.

CULTURAL HEALTH—AND SICKNESS

What did Kirk mean by culture? ("Culture," after all, was a word they used in Nazi Germany, as New York Governor Mario Cuomo pointed out with bathetic ominousness.) He was in much agreement with what Eliot wrote in *Notes towards the Definition of Culture* (1949), which Kirk considered one of the most significant books of the twentieth century. Eliot identified three different senses of the term, concerning the development of the culture of the individual, of a group or class, and of a whole society; but in general he held that by culture he meant "the way of life of a particular people living together in one place. That culture is made visible in their arts, in their social system, in their habits and customs, in their religion. But these things added together do not constitute the culture, though we often speak for convenience as if they did. These things are simply the parts into which a culture can be anatomised, as a human body can. But just as a man is something more than an assemblage of the various constituent parts of his body, so a culture is more than the assemblage of its arts, customs, and religious beliefs. These things all act upon each other, and fully to understand one you have to understand all." Eliot elaborated:

Now there are of course higher cultures and lower culture, and the higher cultures in general are distinguished by differentiation of function, so that you can speak of the less cultured and the more cultured strata of society, and finally, you can speak of individuals as being exceptionally cultured. The culture of an artist or a philosopher is distinct from that of a mine worker or field labourer; the culture of a poet will be somewhat different from that of a politician; but in a healthy society these are all parts of the same culture; and the artist, the poet, the philosopher, the politician and the labourer will have a culture in common, which they do not share with other people of the same occupations in other countries.[7]

In its original sense, "culture" meant cultivation of the land. From this connotation concerning tilling the soil, the word expanded outward in meaning like the ripples from pebbles cast into a pond, to include animal husbandry, the building of houses and outbuildings, the setting of property boundaries, the development of standards of conduct and laws, the establishment of customs and conventions, and the ordering of all society—all the things necessary to maintain a sense of stewardship over the land and nature. As Eliot's words imply, the people of any particular culture, fed by religious faith, draw upon the legacy of past generations while looking to the well-being of future generations to establish an underlying sense of remembrance, order, and meaning within the natural world.

The conservative is the conservator of culture. He need not be pharisaical in this role, forever being of the mind that everything new is wrong; for if he is wise he knows, with Burke, that change is the means of our preservation. To the liberal, the only form of change that is harmful is a change toward conservatism, but to the conservative that change is harmful which is injudicious and harmful to the culture at large. To the conservative living during the second half of the twentieth century, change for the sake of efficiency and change for the sake of newness have been the theme of American culture, and much of this change has been for the worse. The symptoms of decay Kirk witnessed in the West—some already listed above but also including the growth of pornography, abortion, drug abuse, skullduggery at all levels of business and government, the vapidity of television, the decline of education, the unscrupulousness and dishonesty of the press, the elevation of utter cowardliness aligned with strong administrative skills as the primary qualification for leadership, psychological habituation to the general coarsening of the social order—pointed to an underlying sickness of the spirit in the cultures of what had once been known as Christendom. He addressed this cultural malady in numerous essays he published throughout his career and that were collected in such volumes as *A Program for Conservatives* (1954), *Beyond the Dreams of Avarice: Essays of a Social Critic* (1956), *Confessions of a Bohemian Tory* (1963), *The*

Intemperate Professor and Other Cultural Splenetics (1965), and *Redeeming the Time* (1996), which incorporates (in large part) material from a short book with a long title, *The Wise Men Know What Wicked Things Are Written on the Sky* (1987) as well as another short collection of lectures, *Reclaiming a Patrimony* (1982).

It may be worthwhile to note here that it was in Kirk's social criticism that several critics, especially during the 1950s, the decade of postwar conservatism's first steps, found material useful in their sometime attempts to dismiss Kirk as a hidebound, out-of-touch champion of a vanished, probably imagined, past. The preferred method of these critics was to snatch at isolated sentences within Kirk's essays, display them out of context, and then make sarcastic remarks about conservatism in general and Kirk in particular. "When reality becomes overbearing," chuckled one anonymous writer for *The New Republic*, "one can always turn for escape to the writings of Russell Kirk, editor of *The Conservative Review* [sic] and columnist for *The National Review*." Eager to share the wacky hilarity to come, the critic plunged ahead:

> More successfully than any current historical novelist, in our opinion, Dr. Kirk captures the spirit of English life at the time of Jane Austen and makes us wish we had lived then. Occasionally, he convinces us we *are* living then. This accomplishment appears the more remarkable when we consider that Dr. Kirk writes contemporary political tracts, not novels, and that he lives in Mecosta, Michigan, not Steventon, Hampshire. For those unacquainted with Kirkian romanticism, here is a sample: "No social institution does more to develop decent leadership and a sense of responsibility than does the inheritance of large properties."[8]

(Having smirkingly ridiculed Squire Kirk, author of such "political tracts" as *The Conservative Mind* and *Randolph of Roanoke*, the unnamed critic homed in on the contents of *The Intelligent Woman's Guide to Conservatism*, a collection of essays that might be likened to a popular version of the scholarly *Conservative Mind*. Briefly, the critic takes issue with a passage written by Kirk about Shaw regarding the voting patterns of women. He compares this with a passage from Shaw's *The Intelligent Woman's Guide to Socialism* which—apparently unbeknownst to the critic—confirms Kirk's, rather than Shaw's, interpretation of how women tend to vote immediately upon being enfranchised.)

Kirk addressed the particulars of how the conservative approaches the challenges of the future in his first (and, arguably, most important) work of social criticism, *A Program for Conservatives*, a collection of related essays that was in time revised and published as *Prospects for Conservatives*. It is an extended discussion of certain fundamental moral and political questions as seen in the light of circumstances during the second half of the twentieth century. As he wrote in his foreword to a later edition of the work, "The reader will not find in this book of mine anything resembling a partisan platform; indeed, I ignore many of the political controversies of the hour, and touch but glancingly upon others. By the word 'prospects' I signify long views—that is, a survey of the difficulties and the opportunities that conservatives probably will encounter for a good while to come."[9]

In *A Program for Conservatives*, Kirk, referring repeatedly to Burke as a guide, addressed several questions facing conservatives in the immediate and extended aftermath of World War II, which he identified as follows.

1. *The question of the mind.* Here Kirk addressed the decline of "the unbought grace of life"—the sense of honor and honorable being as the hallmark of the good individual in society and the end of a liberal education. Burke described the state of being that characterizes the honorable mind, writing:

> To be bred in a place of estimation; to see nothing low and sordid from one's infancy; to be taught to respect one's self; to be habituated to the censorial inspection of the public eye; to look early to public opinion; to stand upon such elevated ground as to be enabled to take a large view of the widespread and infinitely diversified combinations of men and affairs in a large society; to have leisure to read, to reflect, to converse; to be enabled to draw the court and attention of the wise and learned wherever they are to be found; to be habituated in the pursuit of honor and duty; to be formed to the greatest degree of vigilance, foresight, and circumspection, in a state of things in which no fault is committed with impunity, and the slightest mistakes draw on the most ruinous consequences; to be led to a guarded and regulated conduct, from a sense that you are considered as an instructor of your fellow-citizens in the highest concerns, and that you act as a reconciler between God and man....[10]

A high calling, needless to say, and one that critics of Burke have doubtless mocked as belonging to an imagination detached from the hard knocks of everyday life. "To see nothing low and sordid from one's infancy" may seem overly protective as a goal for child-rearing, what with the horrid things and events children today face from the earliest ages: widespread divorce and the mutual recriminations that surround it; grisly violence on television, in movies, and in the electronic games they play; not to mention the news that is beamed into their lives every evening on television. To sneer at the very idea of "protectiveness" is to assume that there is really nothing so bad out in the world that children need protecting; and even if there is, children should become calloused to it in order to mature properly. But there is a mean to be observed here, and Burke and

Kirk understood it well. That children should learn to stand up for themselves and not be thin-skinned about life's challenges is a worthy goal; to inundate a child in violence and filth under the idea that "the kid's gotta learn about this kinda stuff someday, so he might as well learn it now," is irresponsible and harmful. The virtuous citizen, not the mass-citizen—gullible, readily susceptible to demagoguery, thinking in clichés, living for pleasure alone—is the goal of right upbringing, the former possessing clear discernment and tending to view the present in terms of eternity.

2. *The question of the heart.* Kirk addresses here the question of human nature as it relates to differences between the conservative and the liberal cast of mind. The liberal believes, with Jean-Jacques Rousseau, that humanity is basically good, and that with a bit more social tinkering here and there—new drugs for the mentally unstable, truant officers with degrees in child psychology, the lowering of testing standards in schools to enhance self-esteem among the students, a tad more abortions so that unwanted children will not affront us by their presence, liberalized laws on assisted suicide so that the unwanted elderly and infirm will not affront us by *their* presence—the world will be made a better place, in the course of what the Irish playwright Sean O'Casey termed, in all seriousness, "the slow, the certain, the glorious ascent of man."[11] Some have as their goal a terrestrial paradise; others, less given to delusions, seek something much more within the realm of possibility: an existence of widespread fairness, equality, pleasure, and good will, a world not unlike that described in Aldous Huxley's novel *Brave New World.* On the other hand, the moral imagination of the conservative perceives man not in the ascendant, but as a flawed creature with a bent toward sin and error. Not a contemptible worm, but a being beloved by God and destined for eternity. The conservative conceives of the good society as one in which there is a tolerable social order, not constant political tinkering in an attempt to bring about perfection; he realizes that prudential wisdom governing a tolerable social order is preferable to a regime of efficiency experts, professional administrators, and would-be commissars who strive to control others in the name of a bright new tomorrow of perfection, but who end by leveling down and bringing on the pervasive grayness and boredom of sameness.

3. *The question of social boredom.* In this, the strongest essay in *A Program for Conservatives,* Kirk discourses at length upon the causes and symptoms of social boredom, which he had introduced in the previous chapter. If a people will not have a tolerable social order, they will have anarchy or (more likely) a tyranny of professional social improvers whose goal, so they say, is fairness, freedom, equality, fraternity, or any combination of

the god-words that will best persuade the masses to acquiesce to their leadership. The result, if the examples of postwar Eastern Europe and certain island nations are any indication, is bleakly multifoliate: a bland landscape of sameness and boredom, in which it is widely understood that striving, self-reliance, the gathering of small, voluntary associations, the very concept of virtue, are all a snare and a delusion. Against such as this, conservatives see their role as that of keeping humanity human. The role of the liberal is to transcend humanity—and never mind that all such past efforts have been dismal failures, some ending in mere muddlement, others in unimaginable bloodshed. The ideological failures of Gerrard Winstanley, Georges Danton, Karl Marx, Adolf Hitler, Pol Pot, and Jim Jones notwithstanding; this time we'll all plan better, be nicer to each other, try harder, reach farther, until one fine morning. . . . ("So we beat on," noted Nick Carroway in *Gatsby*, "boats against the current, borne back ceaselessly into the past.") To the liberal, the very idea that noble-minded social experiments may become tyrannies, or at the very least remove the incentive of a regime's citizens to strive to better themselves and their situation in life, is a hard-hearted factoid, probably cobbled together at a right-wing think tank for the purpose of doing nothing about society's problems. There is not a scrap of scientific research to prove such an assertion, they conclude. (For that matter, there exists no official, juried, scientific study to suggest that putting one's hand on a hot stove hurts.)

In "The Question of Social Boredom," Kirk relates the issue under discussion to the writings of David Riesman, Thorstein Veblen, and Alfred Kinsey, noting especially the ignorance and presumptuousness that permeate the latter's two volumes on human sexual behavior. The failure of certain liberal thinkers is often that they reason not from illation, but from raw reason alone: reason divorced from any sense of the historical experience of the human race or ethical sense. Kirk was not against reason by any means (for one thing, his marriage to a Thomist would have been excruciatingly difficult rather than the harmonious blend it was); but rather, he was against that form of reason described above, which he referred to as defecated rationality. He used the term *defecated* not as a ribald term of abuse, but in its old sense—in the sense Burke used it on occasion, as in his *Letter to a Noble Lord* (1796)—of connoting unmixed or unmitigated. Governed by ideologues who are themselves driven by a combination of raw lust for power and rhetorical skills that appeal to the most basic of human failings—envy—society in time becomes filled with a well-fed, sullen proletariat, bored easily, incapable of love, eager to hate. Of such was Nazi Germany fashioned, as well as Soviet Russia. For there remain civic leaders who refuse to embrace ideology, who "still retain a degree of moral and political ascendancy over the masses," and "if the men who still retain a degree of moral and political ascendancy over the masses have in them the courage to make the endeavor, it is not yet too late to preserve to posterity the unbought grace of life, and to keep at bay the squalid oligarchs who detest the world of silence and of freedom."[12]

4. *The question of social justice.* "The concept of social justice is bound up ineluctably with questions of community and of political economy," declared Kirk near the beginning of this chapter. "What should be the relationships among classes? How do we secure the cooperation of the many interests within a complex society? Does 'justice' signify equality of condition? What are the differences between community and collectivism? Do there exist religious and moral foundations upon which a tolerably just society rests? Is American society, though indubitably democratic, nevertheless unjust?" These are hard but necessary questions that cannot be answered by mere appeals to prescription, wrote Kirk in addressing this issue. In a world in which the loudly stated manner of bringing about social justice lies in appropriating a portion of the earnings of the productive in order to support a host of social programs designed to help the nonproductive, those who cannot or will not support themselves, conservatives, Kirk thought, ought to serve as a voice of common sense about the meaning of social justice.

In light of the failure of ideologues and levelers to bring about social justice, what is the conservative's proposal for seeking that justice? First, said Kirk, the prudent witness to social justice should seek to insure that there shall be a clear, rational relationship between endeavor and reward, between honest labor and fruit of labor. "The most unjust of organized societies is that in which no man retains title to anything of consequence; in which everything belongs, theoretically to everybody, and nothing in particular to anybody," Kirk claimed. For any people, the just society is that which protects the things that are by right their own. One is reminded of Whittaker Chambers's story of talking with an old dirt farmer in Maryland who had been approached by a smug, power-drunk wheat inspector, who instructed the old man that his farm was overplanted. Chambers asked the old-timer how he had responded to the veiled threat of this would-be commisar, and learned that he had run the petty bureaucrat off his land: "My neighbor set down each pail, somewhat with the air of a President laying a State of the Union message on a lectern, and eyed me for a moment of dense silence. Then he said: 'You know he's a black-hearted skunk,' adding with immense relish: 'I run 'im.' I thought I heard the fifes of '76."[13]

Also, as a signal step toward recovering a sense of social justice, the conservative must not buy into the Marxist's primary axiom: that man is first and foremost an economic creature, whose fulfillment is found in material comfort and prosperity, however humble. Political figures who boast of the nation's economic growth as a sign of government fulfilling its role, believing that making a people fat, sassy, and smug is the end of government, are misguided. Bent upon converting human existence into a gigantic whirl of getting and spending, making economic prosperity the be-all and end-all of existence while viewing virtue as an afterthought, is the path toward hedonism and selfishness during the best of times, the leveling impulse during the worst, and cultural homogenization at all times. This last-named feature, if obtained, may make fairness (of sorts) a reality, but would also entail the creation of a society marked by intolerable sameness and boredom—and perhaps worse. "Who rationally could prefer the social justice of democratic Kampuchea under Pol Pot, say, to the social justice of Switzerland under its bourgeois government?" asked Kirk rhetorically. "Yet there are plenty of irrationalists about"; and while it seems unlikely that the United States will be led by them along the path to Cambodia's killing fields, it is far more likely that the nation will be led in the direction of the brave new world envisioned with loathing by Aldous Huxley, whose Mustapha Mond demands, in the name of economic prosperity, "Self-indulgence up to the very limits imposed by hygiene and economics." It is the role of the thinking conservative, then, to enlighten and persuade the "irrationalists" to embrace a preferable vision of life and its purpose.

5. *The question of wants.* Prudence is the primary virtue of the conservative, and the prudent individual has no truck with the culture of expanding wants and expectations. In this chapter, Kirk takes to task the highly specialized, consumerist society of the mid- to late twentieth century, its citizens, many of them, tempted to view every new gadget and device they see advertised, especially on television, as a must-have item.

Kirk segues from broadsides against vacant-minded consumerism, in which the appetite for more reigns supreme, to a discussion of prospects for a humane political economy, noting that an economy based on a humane scale, as advocated by Wilhelm Röpke and put into practice in Central Europe after World War II, may offer a strong, sensible alternative to both a command economy and *laissez-faire* capitalism. Of Röpke, Kirk has high praise, writing:

Loathing "doctrinaire rationalism," Röpke is careful not to propound an arbitrary scheme of alteration and renovation. Yet his suggestions for deproletarizing are forthright. Family farms, farmers' co-operatives for marketing, the technical and administrative possibilities of industrial decentralization, the diminution of the average size of factories, the gradual substitution for "the old-style welfare policy" of an intelligent trend toward self-sufficiency—none of these projects is novel, but they are urged by an economist possessing both reputation and frank common sense. . . .

In Wilhelm Röpke's pages, the political economist recollects that the art of politics has an ethical foundation, and that the purpose of industry is private contentment, not an abstract Production. And throughout Röpke's work, man is regarded as a member of a civilized community, a true person, not merely a factor in industrial output.[14]

Only when most people embrace the need for such a civilized community, giving more attention to their duties and less to their wants, Kirk believed, will society turn from the clutch of dehumanizing ideology and enchantment by the temptations of Vanity Fair.

6. *The question of order.* By the end of the twentieth century, there still lived a small number of individuals who retained firsthand memories of the October Revolution in Russia. A common thread to their reminiscences is that there was, in the days immediately after the storming of the Winter Palace, a complete breakdown of order throughout the nation: everywhere there were bands of armed, masterless men who might at any minute smash their way into a person's house for purposes of stealing bread or, for that matter, murdering anyone in residence just for the obscene joy of it. Several years ago I spoke to a man, himself a Russian émigré who remembered those days still, who said that the main thing he could remember as he and his parents fled before the coming of the Bolsheviks was "People running, running, running, and more running." A society without order is a society in anarchy, and those who write and speak on behalf of anarchy know little of the dark forces they would unleash were their efforts successful. Order is the prerequisite for any society.

In an eloquent definition, Kirk wrote, "Order, in society, is the harmonious arrangement of classes and functions which guards justice and gives willing consent to law and ensures that we all shall be safe together." If the very concept of order in Western society should decline, how then shall its citizens "be safe together"? Kirk saw just such a decline in process in the West, and he wrote that he considered "that one of the principal causes of this disorder is the enervation of the idea of order in its traditional sense— that is, the spirit of class, duty, and honor, the sense of responsibility and common interest within long-established social groups which is closely bound up with Burke's 'unbought grace of life.'" When order within the soul and the community of souls breaks down, then order is maintained, with declining degrees of success, by external controls alone; and it is the sign of a culture in decline where the citizenry and its leaders seek greater freedom from the inner restraints afforded by "the spirit of class, duty, and honor, the sense of responsibility and common interest within long-established social groups" and instead call for a larger police force and other external restraints upon conduct to save society from itself.

Proposing and legislating into existence more external restraints in the cause of social order is the forte of the liberal activist, for he believes that circumstances, external forces, are at the heart of human misery. His appeals for greater external control finds a ready audience among the masses, for it appeals to widespread belief that any social problem can be solved if enough money is poured its way, and it appeals to human vanity: people often initially reject what the conservative knows, that the heart of human misery is often the human heart itself. To restore order and community requires the moral imagination, patient and honest persuasiveness, and intelligence, "ten times as much intelligence as we have displayed in recent years," wrote Kirk. He concluded, "Money, and most of the media of communication, are still on the side of the liberals and radicals; but the key to order is in the possession of the conservatives."

7. *The question of power.* "Power, generally defined, is such an absence of external restriction and limitation that only the inward determination of the subject causes the subject to act or to refrain from action," wrote Kirk. Power over men, he added, is the ability to do as one likes, whether others like that course of action or not. The conservative, having learned the lessons of history, seeks to erect a hedge about power with strong restrictions, and to separate authority among many groups and institutions, that concentrated power, capable of becoming a law unto itself, may reside nowhere. Thus the separation of powers within the state and federal governments in the United States, for example. Believing in the human proclivity for sin, that the voice of the masses is not the voice of seasoned thought (much less the voice of God), the conservative looks with suspicion upon the gradual breaking down of the walls separating power in government, knowing that the resulting concentration of power is a fertile field for demagoguery to flourish. The latest NBC News/ *Wall Street Journal* poll might provide an interesting commentary upon what a questionably representative cross section of the American people are thinking about one issue or the other, amid the passions of the moment; but it is not a useful tool for governance. When used as such, especially in instances wherein "the people" demand that laws be ignored or sidestepped, it is the voice of a benevolent mob, who may someday become a lynch mob, writ large. "The conservative, believing that not goodwill unaided can put a check upon power, defends that just order in society which puts laws above men and prescriptive rights above present expediency," concluded Kirk, on the question of power. "At present, this problem of power is not

merely a question of social well-being, but unmistakably a question of the survival of civilization, or even the survival of human life as a whole. The conservative, however oppressed by this responsibility, brings to it a cast of mind far better suited for the task than the disintegrating optimism of liberals and radicals."[15]

8. *The question of tradition.* Of tradition Kirk wrote and argued through-out his career, for two reasons. First, he believed that tradition, a guide to those permanent qualities in society, philosophy, and private life that need to be conserved, whether intact or adjusted somewhat to fit present expediencies, throughout the process of inevitable change, was central to maintaining a bearable and whole life. It is the preservation of continuity, a filter by which humanity separates its mistakes from its truly progressive discoveries, an instrument for the retention of unifying principle despite the acquisition of fresh knowledge. In the realm of ethics, Kirk wrote, "Most men and women are good only from habit, or out of deference to the opinions of their neighbors, the friend to tradition argues; and to de-prive them of their habits, customs, and precepts, in order to benefit them in some novel way, may leave them morally and socially adrift, more harmed by their loss to ethical sanctions than helped by the fancied new benefit."[16]

Second, he wrote and argued often about tradition because both his philosophical opponents and allies pressed him constantly for *distinguos;* after all, what did Kirk mean by tradition? Which traditions ought to be kept, and why? Is tradition its own highest value? If so, how ought we to view such "traditions" as chattel slavery, marital "wandering" by males, dueling, "redlining" in the real estate business to prevent minorities from moving into all-white neighborhoods, and so on. Which ancestors are worth attending, and how can they be discerned? As Richard M. Weaver put it:

> Traditions grow up insensibly and, as it were, vegetatively; they are adaptations and include strong emotional preferences. These facts in themselves may be good, yet they certainly create problems when traditions come into conflict and have to be reconciled. Since they are not rational creations, they are not suscep-tible to rational adjustment unless one is willing to isolate intellectually their el-ements of value and of truth. Yet this is a process disrespectful of tradition in the sense that it transcends tradition and looks for some higher guide. The only way a traditionalist can object to this is by saying that tradition expresses something not in the arguable realm, which is itself a grave commitment.[17]

The "higher guide" by which the wise person separates the wheat from the chaff in regard to traditions is that mindset that appeals to the permanent things, what C. S. Lewis called the *tao*. To sift traditions through this grid Kirk did not consider "a process disrespectful of tradition," but an act of prudential wisdom. One need not be a slave to tradition to find a usable past. In words that echo Eliot's seminal essay "Tradition and the Individual Talent," Kirk answered his questioners:

> If tradition sinks into mere unquestioning routine, it digs its own grave; for man then approximates vegetable nature, disavowing reason and conscience as correctors and restorers of tradition. It was one of the more eloquent apologists for tradition, Chateaubriand (in his *Memoires d'outre-tombe*) who lamented "the mania for adhering to the past, a mania which I never cease impugning. . . . Political stagnation is impossible; it is absolutely necessary to keep pace with human intelligence. Let us respect the majesty of time; let us reverentially contemplate past centuries, rendered sacred by the memory and the footsteps of our fathers; but let us not try to go back to them, for they no longer possess a vestige of our real nature, and if we endeavored to seize hold of them, they would fade away." This is the traditionalist of elevation, appealing to his generation to hold by living tradition, but not to be governed by a letter from which the spirit has departed.[18]

The nineteenth-century French novelist Chateaubriand lamented that sort of materialist described by Allen Tate in his "Ode for the Confederate Dead," to whom the narrator asks rhetorically, "Shall we, more hopeful, set up the grave / In the house? The ravenous grave?" To remember and emulate the better qualities and traditions of the dead while avoiding their errors is noble; to worship the dead is sacrilege. The conservative never forgets the grand question that so few in modern society seem to ask themselves: "Is life worth living? Are men and women to live as human persons, formed in God's image, with the minds and hearts and individuality of spiritual beings, or are they to become creatures less than human, herded by the masters of the total state, debauched by the indulgence of every appetite, deprived of the consolations of religion and tradition and learning and the sense of continuity, drenched in propaganda, aimless amusements, and the flood of sensual triviality which is supplanting the private reason? Are they to be themselves endowed with personality and variety and hope, or are they to be the vague faces in the Lonely Crowd, devoid of all the traditional motives to integrity?"[19]

These questions, first discussed in *A Program for Conservatives*, were revisited thematically throughout the essays of social criticism Kirk wrote for the rest of his life. Reviewing this volume, social theorist and historian James Burnham wrote, "*A Program for Conservatives* does not present an itemized political platform. Ranging over the great political, social, moral, and religious issues that confront us, it throws on and around them the light of those conservative principles that Mr. Kirk finds most fully and finely expressed in Edmund Burke."[20] Renowned journalist Dorothy Thompson wrote to Kirk to say she was reading *A Program for Conservatives* "conscientiously," and to thank him enthusiastically for the book.[21] Historian of ideas Richard M. Weaver, author of *Ideas Have Consequences* (1948), wrote that the true conservative "is defined essentially by belief in the following principles":

> There is an order higher than that devised by man which it is our duty to find out and to respect.
>   Civilization shows itself in variety and complexity and individual attachment; and standardization is the death alike of vitality and interest.
>   There is no social justice thru mechanical leveling, but rather the reverse.
>   Society thrives on distinctions so long as they are distinctions of natural ability, earned leadership, and sympathetic attachment.
>   History is a storehouse of wisdom, whereas the abstract designs of collectivist reformers are the fancies of an overheated brain.
>   Society must be receptive to change, but change is most likely to be gained when it is the work of private endeavor and sagacity.
>   Doctrinaire breaks with the past are costly failures because they take too little account of the substance of history and human nature.
>   All of these thoughts, so discerning of the nature of man in society, he develops into a program for order, community, loyalty, and tradition.[22]

It is no accident that there are throughout this list of principles echoes of the "six canons" of conservatism Kirk had outlined in *The Conservative Mind*, published the year before *A Program for Conservatives*. In its essentials, Kirk's philosophy changed not at all during his lifetime, though his understanding and interpretation of certain historical figures and their effect upon conservative thought did change somewhat, as we have seen in the chapter on Kirk's historical writings. To Kirk, society changes organically, if not one life at a time, then within small communities of voluntary association, the "little platoons we belong to in society," as Burke called them.

CUSTODIAN OF WESTERN CULTURE

The ideologue, governed by a passion not for wealth but power over the lives of others, with his contempt for all things venerable and prickly intolerance toward any questioning of his own motives and policies, was targeted by Kirk in a number of essays published during the 1950s and then brought together in the well-received collection *Beyond the Dreams of Avarice*. For the most part, these essays reflect Kirk's ruminations upon the debasement of numerous ancient, storied estate houses in Scotland (which he visited during his walking trips through Britain), the vanishing way of life among the crofters of the Hebrides, and, in a special tribute to a friend, a warm assessment of Wyndham Lewis's accomplishment as an artist and writer. The world Kirk describes is one in which, on one hand, there is a people grown languid with the ancient sin of *acedia* (sloth), indifferent to tradition and transcendent truths, concerned only with external comforts and benefits. Into this decadent world there steps the quarter-educated reformer with his endless envy-driven regulations designed to level down the "rich" and their flawless plans to build hideous new housing projects of unremitting sameness and boredom in which every inhabitant will be at long last equal. Writing from London, T. S. Eliot had much praise for Kirk's volume, citing news that even a prominent liberal social critic had found value in it: "I am glad to hear that Dwight Macdonald has approved *Beyond the Dreams of Avarice*, as he is one of the small number of left-wingers whose brains I respect and whose personality I like. I have dipped into it myself again and again, and usually find something that meets with my agreement. It pleased me to read your appreciation of Wyndham Lewis—a just and well-balanced one, I think. Much of what you say about this country supports my own gloomy views, and I think it is very true to say of any country, that a decline in private morality is certain to be followed in the long run, by a decline in public and political morality."[23] Writing in *The Commonweal*, Frederick D. Wilhelmsen found several prize essays amid Kirk's collection, as well as a point of weakness. "When commenting on American life today," he wrote, "Kirk seems at his best in 'The Age of Discussion'—an analysis of the decline of the literate journal in America—and in 'The Ethics of Censorship'—a penetrating judgment not only of official but also of the unofficial censorship exercised by publishing houses, universities, librarians and government officials. He judges this censorship to be directed more often against the friends of tradition and religion than against their enemies." However,

The author is weakest when he sweeps Bentham, Marx, Dewey, and Freud indiscriminately into his radical Inferno. This is not quite fair. Although the climate surrounding official Freudianism has been anti-Christian and depersonalizing, the weight of latter-day scholarship is against any essential link between the conclusions of psychoanalysis and the forces making for an impersonal world of broken men. Kirk is dead right when he states that the psychiatrist will never save us. But it is also true, as Karl Stern insists in *The Third Revolution*, that depth psychology has positive value. When exercised with delicacy by a man sensitive to the mystery of human nature and the tragedy of illness, it is capable of bringing to light those archaic forces lying within the depths of every man, forces paradoxically linked with what Augustine and

Aquinas called "the natural desire" of spirit and flesh for union with the common Father. Eminently concrete, fully being, those archaic forces surge forth from the veiled center of the psyche to reach beyond the artificial and abstract world modern man has built around him. They speak to the heart of Love and Death and God. I develop this issue simply because I think Kirk could string Freud to his own bow.[24]

During his career, Kirk never did seek to "string Freud to his own bow," holding to a strong suspicion of the mischievous uses psychiatrists could make of their vocation by "bringing to light"—and, as has come to light in recent years, *creating* where none before existed—"those archaic forces lying within the depths of every man." In regard to psychologists, Kirk had a sympathetic interest not in Sigmund Freud, but in Carl Jung, finding a great interest and soundness in Jung's theory of archetypes as they relate to history and literature; he also found Jung's openness to the possibility of a spiritual dimension to life fascinating. Rethinking human truth is a consequent of obedience to divine truth, wrote Flannery O'Connor in her review of *Beyond the Dreams of Avarice*, "and it is such a rethinking in the obedience to divine truth which must be the mainspring of any enlightened social thought, whether it tends to be liberal or conservative." She continued:

> Since the Enlightenment, liberalism in its extreme forms has not accepted divine truth and the conservatism which has enjoyed any popularity has shown no tendency to rethink human truth or to reexamine human society. Mr. Kirk has managed in a succession of books which have proved both scholarly and popular to do both and to make the voice of an intelligent and vigorous conservative thought respected in this country.[25]

In the lengthy *Confessions of a Bohemian Tory*, Kirk addressed cultural decadence again, in the one book of his which was criticized by even his publisher for its title and for much else besides. "Publishers are notoriously wary of such books: made up as they nearly always are of previously published pieces on various, often fleeting subjects, they usually lack coherence and are difficult to sell," wrote Henry Regnery, many years after the book's appearance. He added, "*Confessions of a Bohemian Tory* probably comes closest to what a publisher fears in such a book: it is not well titled, is somewhat uneven, many of the pieces included are rather ephemeral and several could have been omitted, but many are well worth reading and pleasant to turn back to—'The Valor of Virginia,' for example, an amusing short piece; 'The Class Struggle in Jos,' describing the effect—unexpected and violent—of the showing of the American film 'Death of a Salesman' in an outdoor movie in Nigeria; or 'A House on Mountjoy Square,' on the charm and contradiction of modern Dublin."[26] Not sur-

prisingly this book is out of print, one of Kirk's few such books, though un-
deservedly so because of the worthwhile essays among the slighter material as described by Regnery. Contemporary reviewers were somewhat
cool to *Confessions of a Bohemian Tory;* there was a "yes—but" element in
their assessments. Kirk's "emphasis on the value of tradition, of free enterprise, of personal freedom, is the kind of conservatism which merits a
hearing and analysis," wrote reviewer Joseph A. Ruef in *The Library Journal.* "Unfortunately this book is too disorganized and too weak to serve
that purpose well."[27] "One need not agree with Mr. Kirk . . . to enjoy much
of this collection, wrote John Blake in *The New York Times Book Review.* "Old
inns, churches, thoughts on social institutions, the making of Carragheen
pudding and talks with well-known persons met on the author's travels,
are among the subjects of these vignettes. The main fault of the collection
is the brevity of the essays, most of which run to less than two pages. Just
as the reader settles in, he is turned out."[28] Even in the usually sympathetic
pages of *National Review,* John Chamberlain was moved to write, tongue-
in-cheek, that Kirk "is delightful because he is precisely what he urges
other people not to be." That is, "Two rhetorical strains that run through
his advocacy of conservatism are a professed dislike of reasoned consistency in principle and a stated prejudice against cultivating individualism
as such. But his collection of columns and magazine essays, *Confessions of
a Bohemian Tory,* reveals him as a comrade-in-arms of the reasonably consistent Frank Meyer (whom he erroneously dismisses as an 'ideologue')
and as an individualist almost to the point of eccentricity in the grand old
English style."[29]

Of the "two rhetorical strains" Chamberlain mentioned, the second is a
matter of opinion alone, stemming from a (perhaps deliberate) confound-
ing of the word "individualist"; for Kirk had earlier written in *A Program
for Conservatives* words by which he strove to live: "The real conservative
is all in favor of sound individuality; he is all against doctrinaire 'individualism,' the belief that we exist solely in ourselves, and for ourselves, so
many loveless specks in infinite time and space, like the unfortunate youth
in Mark Twain's *Mysterious Stranger* to whom Satan reveals that nothing
exists except the boy and empty space, and that his very informant is no
more than a random thought of the desolate Self."[30]

I use the words "perhaps deliberate" above because there are wheels
within wheels in Chamberlain's remarks, especially in regard to the first
of the two "rhetorical strains." For Kirk and Meyer had been on uneasy
footing with each other for years, since at least 1953, when Meyer had published a luke-warm review of *The Conservative Mind* in *The American Mercury.* One of the key reasons Kirk refused to allow his name to appear in
the masthead of *National Review* was that the names of Meyer and other

ex-Marxists appeared there, and he did not want to give the impression that he and they were philosophically close. While their letters to each other were cordial and respectful (if a bit stiff), and while Meyer frequently approached Kirk with offers to review specific books for *National Review*, in the arena of ideas they were at odds for some time, involved in one of those squabbles that to many outside the world of conservatism may seem much ado about nothing.

In brief, their differences concerned the claims of order versus the claims of freedom. As a traditionalist, Kirk believed that the essence of conservatism is wisdom and virtue; Meyer, coming to conservatism out of Marxist and individualist beginnings, believed that the essence of conservatism is freedom. To Kirk, wisdom and virtue make for order, and freedom without order is hedonism and the social fragmentation that is the fruit of individualism run amok. To Meyer, virtue and wisdom are indeed important, but there can be no virtue without freedom first—how can virtuous choices be truly virtuous unless there is the freedom to choose good over evil?—and there was, he believed, far more reason to fear an oligarchy of legalistic moralists than a national descent into individualistic anarchy. At the time Chamberlain wrote his review of *Confessions of a Bohemian Tory*, Meyer's study *In Defense of Freedom*, a work published late in 1962, was still very much in the air; and in this study Meyer had singled out Kirk as no friend of freedom. For his part, Kirk had just recently published an unflattering appraisal of *In Defense of Freedom* in *The Sewanee Review*, one in which Kirk, according to historian George H. Nash, blasted Meyer "for being 'filled with detestation of all champions of authority,' for striving to turn conservatism into an ideology, for seeking 'to supplant Marx by Meyer,' for deification of liberty in the abstract, and for arrogant zealotry."[31] Chamberlain, I suspect, was attempting in his review to make light of the two men's philosophical differences in the hope of easing tensions between Kirk and Meyer, which were at their highest at the time *In Defense of Freedom* appeared. (In the years that followed, their differences largely dissipated, though the two were never close. Meyer had long sought to bring about within the conservative movement a "fusion" of libertarian freedom and traditionalist concern with "the permanent things," and this became a widespread reality among movement conservatives by the mid-1960s, even in Kirk, who had long considered a healthy individualist mindset, but not eccentric individualism, as a largely unspoken element of cultural conservatism. In fact, a careful reading of the writings of both Kirk and Meyer indicates that for all their skirmishing, the two men shared much in common philosophically; like T. S. Eliot and C. S. Lewis, who quarreled throughout much of their careers until near the end, Kirk and Meyer had far more bridges than walls between them.)

In *The Intemperate Professor and Other Cultural Splenetics,* Kirk brought together a collection of "studies in the afflictions of modern culture" that were "meant as diagnoses of certain present intellectual and social discontents," he wrote, adding, "The failure of our great wealth to produce greatness of mind and art; the decay of religious sentiments into mere sociability; the conversion of universities into amusement-parks, and of schoolmen into ideologues; the false premises and disastrous techniques of much schooling; the decay of apprehension of political theory; and the decline of public interest in town and country—these are some of my subjects." Despite the book's subtitle, there is nothing really splenetic about the essays in *The Intemperate Professor;* Kirk works through his essays with the coolness of a seasoned heart surgeon; there is no sense of raging, name-calling, or any of the other characteristics of spleen-venting in this volume. Comparing this volume favorably to *Confessions of a Bohemian Tory,* Regnery found much to commend, saying, "*The Intemperate Professor* has a tighter, more unifying theme—Kirk describes the essays collected in it as 'studies in the afflictions of modern culture [which] are meant as diagnoses of certain present intellectual and social discontents.' A particularly perceptive essay on the American private college proposes a drastic, radical reform, that the college turn its back on 'relevance' and revert to its original purpose, in Kirk's words to 'produce a body of high-principled and literate men' and 'then send them into the world with a cast of character and mind fitted for ethical and intellectual leadership.' "[32] Reviewer Charles F. Donovan, writing in the Jesuit journal *America,* found that the essays collected in *The Intemperate Professor* read "like a minority report on the 20th century." He found—rightly, I believe—the essay "The Rarity of the God-Fearing Man," Kirk's "most telling and forceful essay," describing it as "a sober and profound lay sermon" concerning the degradation of the Christian faith into a soppy, sentimental exercise far removed from the rigors commanded by its founder.[33] In *National Review,* Thomas Molnar wrote, "The cumulative effect is a quiet but persistent critique of the prevailing ideology. Not so much a radical critique in the sense of exposing the roots, as one proceeding by description of the Liberal environment in its poverty of imagination, it oversimplifications—and its victims." On the issue of cultural decadence, Molnar found Kirk accurate in his diagnosis: "If there is decadence, Kirk implies, we need not look for hidden sociological poisons, but for conscious individuals who make the wrong decisions or for institutions that fail in their tasks."[34]

The first line of defense against cultural decadence, as Burke wrote, lies in the realization that the individual is foolish but the species is wise; but even he, in his cautionary wisdom, knew that the species can degenerate into foolishness during periods of cultural decadence. One of the hall-marks of such eras is the elevation of popularly beloved scoundrels, dem-agogues of ideology, to positions of authority. In *Lanterns on the Levee* (1941), William Alexander Percy described one such charismatic individ-ual, an expert in character assassination attached to the Mississippi state senatorial campaign of James K. Vardaman. The individual in question be-came a character type transferable to any decadent age, and was described by Percy as "a pert little monster, glib and shameless, with that sort of cun-ning common to criminals which passes for intelligence." Percy adds dryly, "The people loved him. They loved him not because they were de-ceived in him, but because they understood him thoroughly; they said of him proudly, 'He's a slick little bastard.' He was one of them and he had risen from obscurity to the fame of glittering infamy—it was as if they themselves had crashed the headlines." To guard against the deceptions of slick demagogues, the virtuous citizen must turn and turn again to the pre-scriptive wisdom of the past, to "redeem the time," as Eliot phrased it.

In the posthumous collection *Redeeming the Time*, Kirk supplied his final words of cultural criticism. Originally lectures, most of them delivered at the Heritage Foundation in Washington, these essays revisited themes fa-miliar to Kirk's longtime readers, the themes being readily discernible in their titles, which include: "Can Virtue Be Taught?," "The Perversity of Re-cent Fiction: Reflections on the Moral Imagination," "Humane Learning in the Age of the Computer," "The Injustice of Equality," and one of his most widely reprinted essays, "Criminal Character and Mercy," which concerns the question of capital punishment and recounts the story of the time Kirk's grandfather, president of the bank in the north end of Plymouth long ago, was robbed and kidnapped at the point of a tommy-gun. Kirk suggests through various "incidents and images that capital punishment possesses certain merciful aspects. It may be merciful, first, in that it may relieve a depraved criminal of the horror of being what he is. It may be merciful, second, in that it can help to protect the less guilty from the more guilty. And in a third way . . . capital punishment may mercifully protect the guiltless from the more extreme forms of violence."[35]

But Kirk's true "final word" of social criticism could arguably be the es-say with which he concluded an earlier collection, *The Politics of Prudence*. Published a year before his death, *The Politics of Prudence* has about it an autumnal tone, the sense of a man who knows that his life is drawing rapidly to a close. This is borne out in the wording of Kirk's dedication of the work ("To my four daughters—Monica, Cecilia, Felicia, and Andrea—now embarking hopefully upon the turbulent sea of modern discontents. May they steer clear of Scylla and Charybdis! Emulating Yeats, I set strong ghosts to watch over them.") and in the final essay, "An Exhortatory Epilogue: May the Rising Generation Redeem the Time?" In that concluding essay, which originally served as an address to a college graduating class, he issued a challenge and a warning:

> Many among the rising generation have not known a tranquil and confident America. They scarcely can imagine a time, not many decades past, when it was the diversion of families or couples to strolling of an evening in New York's Central Park or Detroit's Belle Isle Park or Los Angeles' MacArthur Park. Families and couples do not venture to stroll there now. Most of the rising generation have experienced little of continuity and stability; the expectation of distressing change has been greater far. Yet many of them sense that much remains to conserve, and that much ought to be restored.
>
> In the later 'Sixties, some of the rising generation fancied it amusing to pull down what earlier generations patiently had built up. In the early 'Nineties, I trust, many of the rising generation will find it satisfying to restore and redeem their patrimony—so to save the world from suicide.[36]

What is needed, Kirk believed, is not (on the one hand) government-mandated, government-directed "service"; nor (on the other hand) shallow, public exercises in self-congratulation and conspicuous moral one-upmanship: rather, prudent action arising from intelligent thought. Citing words originally spoken by Orestes Brownson at Dartmouth College in 1843, words that were echoed in one of the best-known speeches written by Theodore Sorensen for President John F. Kennedy, Kirk defined the essence of the American scholar's mission, the mission of the rising generation: "Ask not what your age wants, but what it needs; not what it will reward, but what, without which, it cannot be saved; and that go and do; and find your reward in the consciousness of having done your duty, and above all in the reflection that you have been accounted to suffer somewhat for mankind."[37] Kirk's social philosophy, wrote Donald Atwell Zoll, "is ultimately a defense of simplicity, an ability to see the moral import in common experience, the final dignity, the joys of the elemental experiences that loom behind the 'winds of doctrine.' The strength, finally, of Kirk's humanism lies in its ability to connect in ethical, aesthetic and spiritual terms the glories of racial attainment with the prosaic obligations and satisfactions that are the universal lot of men. The defense of standards is thus blended with the indispensable elements of compassion, of mutuality, of sensitivity to the tragic predicament."[38]

MORDANT LAST WORDS

"If civilization is to be spared from further descent into the abyss of decadence," warned Wesley McDonald, "then conservatives must recognize the prior need for 'a politics of imagination,' concerned with far more than

merely conserving 'our goods and chattels.' The battleground for the future of the West, Kirk believes, will be won in neither the boardrooms of
the great corporations nor out in the political hustings, but in the realm of
the imagination."[39] Failure on this battleground, a failure of imagination
and action, will lead to a continuation of the spiritual Waste Land described eloquently by Kirk's friend Malcolm Muggeridge, in his essay
"The Great Liberal Death Wish": "As the astronauts soar into the vast eter-
nities of space, on earth the garbage piles higher; as the groves of academe
extend their domain, their alumni's arms reach lower; as the phallic cult
spreads, so does impotence. In great wealth, great poverty; in health, sickness; in numbers, deception. Gorging, left hungry; sedated, left restless;
telling all, hiding all; in flesh united, forever separate. So we press on
through the valley of abundance that leads to the wasteland of satiety,
passing through the gardens of fantasy; seeking happiness ever more ar-
dently, and finding despair ever more surely."[40]

On the day of Kirk's funeral, May 3, 1994, *The Detroit News* reprinted a
speech Kirk had delivered at the Heritage Foundation a year and a half earlier. Its text is a shortened version of his final essay in *Prospects for Conservatives*, "Enlivening the Conservative Mind." In the speech, Kirk spoke in
cautionary but guardedly hostile phrases on the state of late twentieth-century Western culture, working in an anecdote concerning a boyhood game
he had played years before near the Pere Marquette railroad yards in Plymouth:

> Near the end of the 20th century, the human condition fast becomes a global
> game of prisoners' base, kidnappers and hostages, ideology justifying every
> atrocity. Ignorant armies, supplied with the weapons of annihilation, clash by
> night on our darkling plain. By Anno Domini 2000, what will remain?
>
> This, as I write, is the prospect which conservatives confront. Their obliga-
> tion is the recovery of moral order and political order, a task to stagger Her-
> cules. Their adversaries are the Four Horsemen of the Apocalypse—in partic-
> ular that Fourth Horseman, who is called Revolution.
>
> Yet my young comrades and I, pursued and pursuing through the ponds
> and scrub of the Pere Marquette railway years in the dark, rescued prisoners
> from the enemies' base: We found it possible to win against odds. If we defy
> the Four Horsemen, it may come to pass that the Permanent Things will not
> fall trophy to Chaos and old Night.[41]

Finding himself by vocation a part-time Cassandra throughout his life,
warning against the dire forces of ideology, Kirk was nevertheless cheerful as he faced life, and it shone through in his essays of social criticism.
(It is not true, as some have stated, that Kirk's brand of conservatism dif-
fered from Ronald Reagan's in that Kirk tended toward doom and gloom
while Reagan was all sunny optimism. Both men were cheerful at

prospects for the future, but where one tended to have a cautionary bent and emphasized the dire possibilities of "chaos and old Night," the other focused primarily upon the joy of triumph over those dark forces.) In one of his most often reprinted essays, "Cultural Debris: A Mordant Last Word," Kirk succinctly summarized both the cautionary and the hopeful aspects of his cultural criticism, warning that if conservative men and women, who know what makes life worth living, choose to be silent, if they cannot make common cause, then "the garment of our civilization will slide to the rag bin, and the cultural debris of the twentieth century will drift down the rubbish heaps of the future. Not many years of indulgence, I fancy, remain to us. But—as Henry Adams was fond of saying— the fun is in the process."[42]

NOTES

1. Chesterton, *Autobiography*, pp. 223–24.
2. *The Portable Conservative Reader*, pp. xvii–xviii.
3. Eliot, *The Rock* (New York, 1934), p. 42.
4. Cargas, review of *Enemies of the Permanent Things*, in *America* 20, May 17, 1969, 596.
5. Marx to Kirk, February 25, 1964.
6. McDonald, "Russell Kirk: Conservatism's Seasoned Sage," *The Wall Street Journal*, November 19, 1984, 32.
7. Eliot, in *Christianity and Culture: The Idea of a Christian Society* and *Notes towards the Definition of Culture*, p. 198.
8. "Kirk on Shaw," *The New Republic* 136, May 6, 1957, 7.
9. *Prospects for Conservatives*, p. ix. As the 1989 edition of *Prospects* represents Kirk's most mature statement of the principles and discourses upon those principles originally stated in *A Program for Conservatives*, I have chosen to quote from this edition throughout.
10. Burke, quoted in Kirk, *Prospects for Conservatives*, pp. 45–46.
11. O'Casey, *The Green Crow*, p. 204.
12. *Prospects for Conservatives*, p. 127.
13. Chambers, in Teachout, ed., *Ghosts on the Roof: Selected Journalism of Whittaker Chambers, 1931–1959*, p. 320.
14. *Prospects for Conservatives*, pp. 183–84.
15. *Prospects for Conservatives*, p. 226.
16. *Prospects for Conservatives*, p. 235.
17. Weaver, "Which Ancestors?" *National Review* 2, July 25, 1956, 21.
18. *Prospects for Conservatives*, p. 236.
19. *Prospects for Conservatives*, p. 253.
20. Burnham, review of *A Program for Conservatives*, in *The Annals of the American Academy of Political and Social Sciences* 298, March, 1955, 216.
21. Thompson to Kirk, May 29, 1956. This letter is on file at the Russell Kirk Center for Cultural Renewal, Mecosta, Michigan.

22. Weaver, "Battle for the Mind," *Chicago Sunday Tribune Magazine of Books*, October 24, 1954, Part 4, 3.

23. Eliot to Kirk, October 31, 1956.

24. Wilhelmsen, "Contemporary Criticism in the Georgian Manner," *The Commonweal*, 64, July 13, 1956, 375–76.

25. O'Connor, review of *Beyond the Dreams of Avarice*, in Leo J. Zuber and Carter W. Martin, eds., *The Presence of Grace and Other Book Reviews by Flannery O'Connor*, p. 23. O'Connor's short review originally appeared in the June 23, 1956 issue of her diocesan paper, *The Bulletin of the Catholic Laymen's Association of Georgia*.

26. Regnery, "Russell Kirk: An Appraisal," in Person, ed., *The Unbought Grace of Life: Essays in Honor of Russell Kirk*, p. 24.

27. Reuf, review of *Confessions of a Bohemian Tory*, in *The Library Journal* 88, December 15, 1963, 4761.

28. Blake, review of *Confessions of a Bohemian Tory*, in *The New York Times Book Review*, December 8, 1963, 26.

29. Chamberlain, "A Conservatism of Reflection," *National Review* 16, March 10, 1964, 198.

30. *Prospects for Conservatives*, p. 34.

31. Nash, *The Conservative Intellectual Movement in America since 1945*, 2d ed., pp. 161–62. Kirk's review of *In Defense of Freedom* appeared in *The Sewanee Review* 72, Spring, 1964, 349–50.

32. Regenery, "Russell Kirk: An Appraisal," p. 24.

33. Donovan, review of *The Intemperate Professor and Other Cultural Splenetics*, *America* 114, January 22, 1966, 145.

34. Molnar, " 'The Fault, Dear Brutus . . .'," *National Review* 18, March 22, 1966, 277.

35. Nelson, ed., *Redeeming the Time*, p. 245.

36. *The Politics of Prudence*, pp. 292–93.

37. *Politics of Prudence*, p. 292.

38. Zoll, "The Social Thought of Russell Kirk," *The Political Science Reviewer* 2, Fall, 1972, 136.

39. McDonald, "Russell Kirk on Decadence in an Age of Ideology," *The Hillsdale Review* 7, Winter-Spring, 1985, 58–59.

40. Muggeridge, in Kirk, ed., *The Portable Conservative Reader*, p. 624.

41. "Reason, Imagination Enliven the Conservative Mind," *The Detroit News*, May 3, 1994, 9A.

42. *The Portable Conservative Reader*, p. 709.

10

Two Cheers for the
Market Economy:
Kirk on "the Dismal Science"

If you will first make men prosperous, they will become happy and enabled to become spiritually minded, if they so choose. Thus opined Andrew Undershaft in Bernard Shaw's Fabian play *Major Barbara*. In this, Shaw reflected not only socialist thought on humanity's relationship to capital, but the attitude of many dyed-in-the-wool adherents of democratic capitalism. Likely as not, by common perception, well-off people are good people. On the other hand, poor people tend toward crime and anti-social behavior.

Not necessarily, believed Russell Kirk, who knew many honest poor firsthand and saw man as something other than an economic creature only. (His own origins were humble, and his wife's family, though by no means poor, was far from wealthy; the Courtemanches were nevertheless refined, generous, and honest to a fault.) Having leaned toward socialism during his teens, he embraced the concept and practice of the market economy ever afterward; yet while he saw much good in that system, he did not see it as a panacea for the ills of the United States, much less the world.

"It's mistaken to use the word capitalism, which is a Marxist word," said Kirk in an interview with *Detroit News* editor Thomas J. Bray. "It tries to make us all part of a system, an ideology. That cannot long endure, any more than communism could long endure, because life is so much more complex. Most people in the long run are not content with getting and spending. And that's the sort of prospect presented by neoconservatives like Irving Kristol and his *National Interest* crowd—the whole world will be one vast copy of the United States. Life isn't like that."[1]

"Life isn't like that." Considering Kirk's vision of humanity, shaped by the moral imagination, this view is not surprising. Man is indeed something more than the sum of his appetites, and any ideology ("the science of idiocy," in old John Adams's scathing words) drew his scorn, no matter how dear to the heart it might be to neoconservatives and libertarians.

Given his disdainful attitude toward democratic capitalism, the question remains as to what political economy (or economies) Kirk did embrace, and how it differs from laissez-faire capitalism or even the government-regulated (some would same government-*dominated*) "democratic capitalism" that has been touted by various neoconservatives during the 1990s. (Kirk once wrote, "One might as well speak of 'egalitarian quantum mechanics' or 'autocratic horticulture' as to speak of 'democratic capitalism,'" noting that the political terms *democratic* and *democracy* imply decision making by the mass of people, and the concept of equality; while the economic term *capitalism* describes a system that "does not count noses, is conducted for the most part by an elite of managers, does not exercise judicial or police functions, and emphatically does not dole out its rewards on any principle of equality.")[2] Although he often referred to economics by Thomas Carlyle's term as "the dismal science" and considered the discipline overstressed in American society, Kirk had much to say about economics, going so far as to write a textbook, *Economics: Work and Prosperity*. Little has been written on this aspect of Kirk's interest and writings, but the few articles that have appeared are rich in content. The starting point for anyone seeking to understand Kirk's view of economics, aside from Kirk's writings themselves, are the essays of John Attarian, a conservative social critic and economist of considerable insight.

Attarian has summarized Kirk's outlook succinctly, noting that Kirk's embrace of the permanent things was central to his worldview, from which his political economy would descend. Kirk saw man not as a cosmic accident, the result of random combinations of colliding molecules, but as a creation of God, made for eternity, and though flawed with sin, beloved of his creator. Man is a complex creature of choices and opportunities, made in such a way that he can endure anything but boredom. From this position, Attarian has written, "Kirk believed that economics has been overstressed. 'The true contest in our time is not between economies merely, but between opposing concepts of human nature.' Are we embodied souls created by a transcendent God, whose purpose is to struggle upward toward Heaven? Or are we creatures of matter, rational animals, pleasure-seeking and pain-shunning, with utility maximization as our life's goal?" Attarian added, "Kirk affirmed the former, economic utopians of Left and Right, the latter."[3]

Historian Bruce Frohnen, one of the most astute scholars to engage with Kirk's ideas, has written, "Those who find in free markets the key to happiness have fallen under the same spell of ideology that controls Marxists and other worshippers of the state. They seek a ready, universal mechanism—be it market or state—that will solve all life's problems. But there is no mechanism that can produce utopia. And the attempt to build one produces only misery. Any decent life requires that we seek to protect and enrich our culture—the historically given institutions, beliefs, and practices that make up our way of life."[4]

With this insight in mind, it can be seen that Kirk's ideas on economics ran along lines remarkably similar to those of a German economist he greatly admired, Wilhelm Röpke, advocate of a "middle way" between laissez-faire capitalism, with its devil-take-the-hindmost ethic, and the tightly regulated command economies beloved by statists that stifle economic initiative, punish the creative and prudent, reward the dull, the lazy, and a host of petty administrative toadies, and in general oversee a society that fosters a sense of dependency rather than individual and community initiative to make one's way in life. Röpke, the principal architect of West Germany's economic recovery after World War II, advocated what he termed a "humane economy," that being "an economic system suited to human nature and to a humane scale in society, as opposed to systems bent upon mass production regardless of counterproductive personal and social consequences."[5] The two men were on friendly terms, with Kirk advising Röpke through letters on matters related to getting his *Economics of the Free Society* published in the United States. Like Kirk, Röpke was a formidable opponent of socialist and other command economies—and no friend of the libertarians' version of laissez-faire capitalism. Both Kirk and Röpke rebelled at the notion of the individual's, the community's, or the state's economic health descending from the decision making of commissars possessing wisdom of dubious quality, much less a handful of tinkerers and experts, or even the chairman of the Federal Reserve.

The essence of a humane economy, Kirk and Röpke believed, lies in creating and sustaining economic independence for a wide array of artisans, farmers, small-and medium-size businesspeople, members of the free professions, and trusty community leaders. Among such "traditional human nature still has its healthiest roots, and throughout most of the world they are being ground between 'capitalistic' specialization and 'socialistic consolidation.'"[6] Kirk notes that at one time local and national leadership in the United States and other republics arose from the ranks of this array of people, rather than from the fairly narrow band of mostly attorneys and career politicians who today wield power.

Disdaining utilitarianism, neither Kirk nor Röpke advocated an arbitrary scheme of economic alteration and renovation. Kirk described Röpke's suggestions for "deproletarianizing" a political economy in terms indicating his assent to them, given his preference for variety and ordered liberty, writing:

> Family farms, farmers' cooperatives for marketing, encouragement of artisans and small traders, the technical and administrative possibilities of industrial decentralization, the diminution of the average size of factories, the gradual substitution for the "old-style welfare policy" of an intelligent trend toward self-sufficiency—none of these projects is novel, but they are commended by an economist possessing both grand reputation and sound common sense. To cushion society against the fluctuations of the business cycle, for instance, the better remedy is not increased centralization, a most dubious palliative, but instead the stimulating of men to get a part of their sustenance from outside the immediate realm of financial disturbance. Specialization often works mischief, he [Röpke] says:
>
> "The most extreme examples of this tendency are perhaps some American farmers who had become so specialized and so dependent on their current money incomes when the crisis came they were as near starvation as the industrial worker. At the other, more fortunate end we see the industrial worker in Switzerland who, if necessary, can find his lunch in the garden, his supper in the lake, and can earn his potato supply in the fall by helping his brother clear his land."[7]

If this sounds somewhat similar to Distributism, an economic system promoting self-sufficiency by small landholders advocated by G. K. Chesterton, it is no wonder, for Distributism is but a variation on Röpke's theme. Humanizing the economic structure was at the core of Chesterton's and Röpke's proposals. For them, as for Kirk, political economy had an ethical foundation upon which to support the linking of generations in virtuous continuity and the sustenance of a tolerable social order. Chesterton's once described William Cobbett's worldview in terms that, with some little adjustment, could describe the views of Kirk or Röpke:

> What he saw was the perishing of the whole English power of self-support, the growth of cities that drain and dry up the countryside, the growth of dense dependent populations incapable of finding their own food, the toppling triumph of machines over men, the sprawling omnipotence of financiers over patriots, the herding of humanity in nomadic masses whose very homes are homeless . . . the wealth that may mean famine and the culture that may mean despair; the bread of Midas and the sword of Damocles. In a word, he saw

what we see, but he saw it when it was not there. And some cannot see it—even when it is there.[8]

If the sky should fall we would all catch larks, runs an old English saying. If men were virtuous, the humane economy would be a working possibility. But, instead, pragmatism and self-serving crowd out virtue in the economic contest. Given this, it might be argued, is it not best that the free-market economy be regulated by experts to "level the playing field" (in the overworked phrase) and thus seek to ensure fairness and at least a middling prosperity for all?

Nay, not so, Kirk would say; for humanity's fallen nature afflicts the experts who would regulate as it does the population at large. There will doubtless be instances of unfairness among even the most enlightened and virtuous leaders and administrators. The humane economy makes no Rousseauesque assumptions about human nature; humanity is flawed and thus needs some regulation—Kirk, it might be noted, considered trust-busting Theodore Roosevelt among his "ten conservative heroes" in *The Politics of Prudence*—but not overregulation. Both Kirk and Röpke were far from supposing that the free market is perfect or immune to corruption; and unlike many of their conservative colleagues, both believed that government must be strong within its given limits. However, the function they assign government lies not in regulating wages, prices, and production, but rather in placing a check upon monopoly. In *Economics of the Free Society*, Röpke wrote:

> The State can effectively fight monopoly by energetically opposing restrictions of competition and by carefully avoiding economic policies which favor the formation of monopolies. For this, however, it is necessary to have a strong state—impartial and powerful—standing above the melee of economic interests. . . . The state must not only be strong; unmoved by ideologies of whatever brand, it must clearly recognize its task: to defend "capitalism" against the "capitalists" when they are tempted to take comfortable short cuts to profits.[9]

Theodore Roosevelt could not have put this more bluntly. This said, though, Röpke and Kirk would agree, it is the strong, virtuous family, neighborhood, community, church, and other "little platoons" of society that make the free economy work as it should. Kirk held that a competitive, free economy is the best economic system for encouraging loyalty to the permanent things. In his vastly underrated short book *The American Cause,* he wrote, "Men and women are industrious, thrifty, honest, and ingenious, in economic life, only when they expect to gain certain rewards for being industrious, thrifty, honest, and ingenious. Some few human beings, in any age, work simply out of altruism, desire to benefit their fellows; but the vast majority work principally out of self-interest, to benefit themselves and their families."

He adds that there is nothing wrong with this, as it is merely a condition of ordinary human nature, one which can be bent to wrongful purposes but is in essence normal. In support, Kirk cites the writings of the eighteenth-century professor of moral philosophy Adam Smith, whom he hailed in one of his better-known essays as one of Western civilization's "three pillars of order." Smith is best known for observing that the wealth of nations is contingent upon a competitive economy in which there are sufficient rewards for thrift, industriousness, and "the ordinary motives to ordinary integrity." "Such a society, such an economy," wrote Kirk, "is guided by an 'invisible hand': the natural law of economic existence which rules that every man, though laboring for his own benefit, actually increases the common good through his private labors."[10] Kirk recognized that a society that does not reward private industry and private saving will stagnate, if not degenerate into one that produces a citizenry given to alternate grasping and wastefulness.

Kirk believed that the free market provides a fine economic framework insofar as it is employed prudently by a people conscious of their relation to a transcendent order and to their fellow pilgrims in this world. In this sense, he saw capitalism as something of a tool: used properly, it can accomplish much good; used as a weapon, it can cause great harm. (Kirk had little but scorn for those corporate executives and upper-echelon labor representatives who seem to go through life striving mightily, it would seem, to live down to stereotype as self-absorbed, high-living demigods.) In an essay on Donald Davidson written toward the end of his life, Kirk wrote grimly, "While we talk windily still of free enterprise, the industrial and commercial conglomerates move toward oligopoly on a tremendous scale. Religious belief and observance have been first reduced to the ethos of sociability, and then to ignorant discourses on revolution. Leviathan, the monstrous society, has swallowed his myriads."[11]

To some, Kirk's loathing of the leviathan state and insistence upon the centrality of morality to political economy may seem very much of the ivory tower. However, he was also very much of the workaday world; he had a strong understanding of economic reality and was no fancier of high-sounding theory based outside the experience of custom, continuity, and convention. Kirk recognized that "some people would like to separate economics from morals, but they are unable to do so. For unless most men and women recognize some sort of moral principles, an economy cannot function except in a small and precarious way. Moral beliefs, sometimes called moral values, make possible production, trading, saving, and the whole economic apparatus."[12]

Importantly, as Attarian has written, a key element in Kirk's understanding of culture in general and economics in particular was a strong belief in the right to hold property. If the right to hold property is transgressed, all rights are then vulnerable and likely to be overridden in time by political expediency, a tyranny, no matter how smiling its aspect. Kirk went so far as to say that property is a prerequisite of civilization and culture. "Unless property is secure," Attarian quotes Kirk, from *The Intelligent Woman's Guide to Conservatism*, "there can be no civilized life; for without the right to keep what is one's own, and to add to that if possible, there can be no leisure, no material improvement, no culture worthy of the name."[13] In short, without the security of property, there can be no order except that which is administered by a large, intrusive military or police presence. And order is at the foundation of any culture worthy of the name.

Without order and normative conduct, people cannot live together in true community. Lacking a moral order, wrote Edmund Burke in his *Reflections on the Revolution in France*, "the law is broken; nature is disobeyed, and the rebellious are outlawed, cast forth, and exiled, from this world of reason, and order, and peace, and virtue, and fruitful penitence, into the antagonist world of madness, discord, vice, confusion, and unavailing sorrow." In such a world, the meek, the humble, and the virtuous are caught up in a relentless, no-quarter-asked-or-given competition for life and livelihood; such activities as storytelling, walking for pleasure, or other acts of leisure time, cannot be practiced, and the contract of eternal society is broken. Kirk had heard of such societies from his readings in Burke and Aleksandr Solzhenitsyn; he knew whereof he spoke.

This concern about holding the sphere of government in check is understandable, given Kirk's view of human nature as flawed by sin, not the least of sin's manifestations being the ravening will to power masked as a force for fairness and human betterment. One modern manifestation of this is called *ideology*. "Of all tyrannies a tyranny sincerely exercised for good of its victims may be the most oppressive," wrote C. S. Lewis of ideologies. "It may be better to live under robber barons than under omnipotent moral busybodies. The robber baron's cruelty may sometimes sleep, his cupidity may at some point be satiated; but those who torment us for our own good will torment us without end, for they do so with the approval of their own conscience."[14]

What about the greed, selfishness, and pauperization of the working masses that competitive, free-market capitalism allegedly produces? A good question, which Kirk addressed, writing that it is not competition that is ruthless; rather, it is the lack of competition that makes a society ruthless, for in a competitive economy people work voluntarily for decent rewards, while in a noncompetitive economy, whether it be socialist or one of capitalism tightly managed by a central government, a few experts or commissars "employ the stick to get the world's work done."[15] Further, competition does not rule out love and pity, for a competitive society in which sound moral principles are observed is not on the whole selfish or ruthless. The inflammatory phrase "Social Darwinism" need not come into play, for "Enlightened competition does not mean 'dog eat dog,'" wrote Kirk. He added significantly, "Successful competition makes possible successful charity; for the increased productivity of a competitive free economy gives society a surplus of goods and services with which to relieve the poor, the infirm, the handicapped, the old, and the young"—those who are unable to provide for themselves in "the economic contest." In words to which Röpke would nod assent, Kirk wrote:

> A free economy is one in which men and women can make their own choices. They can choose the kind of work they want to do, and where they want to do it. They can buy what they choose, and abstain from what they choose. They can work when they like, within limits, and rest when they like. They can change occupations and employers and their material circumstances much as they like. These are great benefits; they help to satisfy the fundamental human longing for self-reliance. They make men and women free.[16]

So while Kirk saw the free economy of the United States as a good thing in itself, he did not see economic well-being as the whole of life. "No economy," he wrote, "however productive materially, could be a good thing if it were founded upon injustice, disorder, slavery, and dishonor." He added:

> The slave-labor camps of the Communist Chinese are economically efficient, after a fashion—but only because they take no reckoning of human lives or moral principles. Thus our American economy, though good in itself, is important not merely for its own sake—its real importance is the contribution it makes to our justice and order and freedom, our ability to live in dignity as truly human persons.[17]

To live in dignity means to live in right relation to God and our fellow man, Kirk believed. There is a time to devote oneself to politics, to raising children, to traveling, to courtship and love, to devotion to the arts, to telling stories at home among friends, and a hundred other pursuits. There is also a time to devote one's attention to concerns related to the nation's political economy. And one of the most normal and innocent ways of doing so is the act of working for a living. "A man is seldom more innocently occupied than when he is engaged making money," said Samuel Johnson in an aphorism Kirk often quoted. This said, Kirk believed that for the most part, impediments to this innocent occupation should be minimal, and that the American government ought to stay within its constitutional limits, if only to help ensure domestic tranquillity. "So, like Mr. Irving Kristol, I send up two cheers for capitalism," he once said, in a debate with socialist Michael Harrington.[18] Kirk took a dim view of confiscatory taxation (which, in effect, punishes the productive and the thrifty), excessive regulation, unfair trade policies, needlessly high federal expenditures in the form of entitlements and transfer payments, and infringements upon the right to own and hold property. (It ought to be reaffirmed at this point that Kirk was no enemy of government, believing that there is a proper and minimal sphere and role for government in regard to maintaining ordered liberty and providing for the national defense. However, he was conscious that the tendency of the federal government, especially from the 1930s to the present day, is to grow, with myriad departments and agencies justifying their continued existence by discovering ever-more dire "needs" and "crises" that need addressing, and thus expanding their influence incrementally into the private sector.)

In a press release prepared for Patrick J. Buchanan's run for the Republican nomination for president in 1992, Kirk applauded Buchanan's proposed economic policies, notably his stated intent to reduce federal expenditures drastically, revive the economy by restoring sound fiscal policies, and reduce income taxes as had President Ronald Reagan. Kirk also supported Buchanan's position as a "trade hawk," who would encourage American productivity and commerce by insisting that if other countries desire free trade with the United States, they must first demolish their trade barriers against American goods.[19] In the end, of course, Buchanan lost the Republican nomination to George Bush, who in turn lost the presidential election to Bill Clinton, primarily because of a shaky economy and because he had lost the faith of his followers after breaking his keystone "no new taxes" pledge of 1988.

"A citizen can hardly distinguish between a tax and fine, except that the fine is generally much lighter," wrote Chesterton in 1931.[20] Indeed so, Kirk would agree, for in a speech given at the Heritage Foundation in 1991, he quoted C. Northcote Parkinson as having written, "Taxation, taken to the limit and beyond, has always been a sign of decadence and a prelude to disaster. For government expenditure is the chief cause of inflation and is also the means of government interference in commercial, industrial, and social life"[21]—this because the burden of neighborly responsibility that inheres in small voluntary associations is removed and replaced by a program, a department, a handout from on high, weakening society's cohesiveness and creating dependency. It is for this reason primarily, and because he believed that the working individual has far more warrant to keep a substantial portion of his earnings than his government has to

confiscate it, that Kirk opposed excessive taxation—not because of stereo-
typical conservative "greed and selfishness."

As Attarian has noted, in further regard to the issue of taxation, Kirk was
a scathing critic of Social Security. "Centralized, compulsory, wielding
ever-expanding arbitrary power, it 'bears nearly all the marks of a re-
morseless collectivism.'"[22] Drawing upon Kirk's *A Program for Conservatives* for supporting quotations, Attarian tackles the issue of Social Security
and Kirk's position on it boldly, writing:

> While acknowledging that some people wouldn't save on their own, he main-
> tained that it would be better "morally and economically" to let them make
> their own mistakes and to provide voluntary charity, than to embrace forced
> saving. He argued that Social Security's stated motive, provision for the poor
> elderly, is disingenuous; the real reason for Social Security's expansion is that
> it gives the government access to "a vast reserve of money and credit," and is
> "disguised taxation," evading opposition to new taxes. [The "poor elderly"
> have Supplemental Security Income to sustain them in lieu of Social Security.
> —JP] Kirk's robust moral denunciation of Social Security, as tyrannical and
> mendacious, towers over today's conservatives' ingratiating endorsement
> and proposals to "save" it.[23]

As conservative politicians discovered during the second Clinton administration, Social Security is an effective "wedge" issue in the hands of
the more skillful among their opponents; for while many citizens would
agree with Kirk's dire assessment of Social Security, they still want and expect that check every month—this among many who describe themselves
as able-bodied and (in a fashion) conservative, not "the poor elderly" only.
With Edmund Burke, Kirk knew that the ablest statesman is one who combines a disposition to preserve with an ability to reform, and that a changing of the national consciousness in regard to Social Security can only come
about through the efforts of patient, intelligent, ethical, and imaginative
leaders who can effectively answer the demagoguery of statists—who
loudly assure all who will listen that the efforts of would-be reformers are
really part of a plan to throw the elderly into the street to fend for themselves—while promoting the moral and economic sense of private saving.

The concept of the family and the community taking care of its own has
a special place in the American psyche. To some, it invokes images of an
earlier, republican America, the days in which people would say, "The
United States are . . ." rather than "The United States is. . . ." To others, it
brings to mind a cruel sink-or-swim way of life disguised in benevolent
words, with no fine-woven economic safety net to catch those who cannot
or will not compete in the economic contest. To Kirk, product of a small
town in which the "little platoons" of family, church, and small group
were a living reality, the concept was good and right. On occasion he called

himself a "Northern Agrarian," aligning himself with Donald Davidson, Andrew Lytle, Allen Tate, and the other Southerners who contributed to *I'll Take My Stand,* a now-classic statement for a simpler, more community-grounded, agrarian, and small-town way of life.

Agrarianism was near to his heart, and while Kirk was no advocate of "three acres and a cow" for each family in America, he was nonetheless a concerned champion of the American farmer and a harsh critic of American agricultural policy. He mistrusted the proposed North American Free Trade Agreement during his lifetime, primarily because he believed its passage and implementation would cause economic harm to the small farmer, even as it would prove a boon to the agricultural giants. (After Kirk's death and the passage of the NAFTA, his concerns were vindicated.) In words written in 1957, which still hold hauntingly true today, Kirk said:

When we take up our farm problems . . . we phrase it in terms which imply that the farmer is simply a servant of Mammon; that his function is simply to feed the cities. If the farmer is found "inefficient," or in any respect less prosperous than his city cousins, then, in our present-day view, either he ought to be shipped off to the city and fitted into the process of automation, or else subsidized as if he were a disagreeable mendicant whose vote, regrettably, does count.

Almost no one asks just what is going to happen to a country in which the rural population, already scarcely a seventh of the total, sinks toward extinction; or whether the rural life is not worth conserving at some cost to total efficiency; or whether the farmer really ought to be expected to live a life, in creature comfort and aims, precisely like that of his city cousin. If we think of aiding the farmer at all, it is merely with a view toward converting him into an agricultural capitalist, I suggest that we are suffering from a decline of social imagination, extending to—and sometimes caused by—economic theory.[24]

To remedy this, though without putting forward any specific blueprint for the future (as would befit an ideologue), Kirk urged the "middle way" or "third way" advocated by Röpke, that the American people would learn to

humanize mass-production, and to restore craftsmanship and personal accomplishment to work, and to teach ourselves how to make our leisure something better than boredom. We need to infuse into modern industrial life a sense of community and purpose and hope and deep-rooted security. We need more genuinely educated businessmen and more genuinely responsible labor-union leaders. We need decentralization of industry and more penetrating regard for the claims of rural life.[25]

In Kirk, despite his sometimes gloomy words, "cheerfulness keeps breaking in," as he liked to say. He believed that periods of dullness and even decadence in a nation's existence are often followed by periods of imagination and hope. Kirk had high hopes for the future of the market economy, writing that while many strange economic doctrines are preached today, "there is reason to believe that the productive market economy will be functioning well a century from now. The errors of command economies and the blunders of utopian welfare states have become obvious to a great many people, while Adam Smith continues to make economic sense." He warns, though:

> So long as many people work intelligently, with good moral habits, for their own advantage and for the prosperity of our nation, an economy will remain healthy. But hard work and sound habits may be undone by foolish public policies or by the violent envy of totalist states. There is a strong need for watchfulness on behalf of the economy.[26]

Kirk probed deeply and systematically into economics, articulating a vision that was, in Attarian's words, "a major advance in conservative thought toward a systematic and explicitly articulated political economy grounded in awareness of a transcendent reality."

NOTES

1. Bray, "The Long View from Piety Hill," *The Detroit News*, November 4, 1990, 2B.
2. "Capitalism and the Moral Basis of Social Order," *Modern Age* 35, Winter, 1992, 100.
3. Attarian, "Russell Kirk's Political Economy," *Modern Age* 40, Winter, 1998, 87–97.
4. Frohnen, "Russell Kirk on Cultivating the Good Life," *The Intercollegiate Review* 30, Fall, 1994, 63–64.
5. "The Humane Economy of Wilhelm Roepke," in *The Politics of Prudence*, Wilmington, 1993, p. 115.
6. "Humane Economy of Roepke," pp. 119–20.
7. "Humane Economy of Roepke," p. 120.
8. Chesterton, in *William Cobbett*, p. 14.
9. Quoted in Hart, *The American Dissent: A Decade of Modern Conservatism*, p. 230. For a fuller understanding of Röpke's economic ideas, his *A Humane Economy: The Social Framework of the Free Market*, originally published in 1960 by Henry Regnery, is a good starting point. This work, with a helpful introduction by Dermot Quinn, is now available in a new edition (1998) published by the Intercollegiate Studies Institute.
10. *The American Cause*, p. 90.
11. *The Politics of Prudence*, pp. 111–12.
12. *Economics: Work and Prosperity*, p. 365.
13. Attarian, "Russell Kirk's Economics of the Permanent Things," *The Freeman* 46, April, 1996, 233.
14. Lewis, in Walter Hooper, ed., *God in the Dock: Essays on Theology and Ethics*, p. 292.

15. *The American Cause,* p. 94.

16. *American Cause,* p. 95.

17. *American Cause,* p. 86.

18. "Is Capitalism Still Viable?" *The Hillsdale Review* 3, Winter, 1981, 5.

19. "Why We Support Mr. Patrick Buchanan's Presidential Candidacy," a press release written by Kirk, 1992.

20. Chesterton, "Our Note Book," *The Illustrated London News* 178, May 23, 1931, 860.

21. "Political Errors at the End of the Twentieth Century, Part I: Republican Errors," *The Heritage Foundation, Lecture #321,* February 27, 1991.

22. Attarian, "Russell Kirk's Economics of the Permanent Things," 234.

23. Attarian, "Russell Kirk's Economics of the Permanent Things," pp. 234–35.

24. "Ideology and Political Economy," *America* 96, January 5, 1957, 390.

25. Attarian, "Russell Kirk's Political Economy," 94.

26. *Economics: Work and Prosperity,* pp. 368–69.

11

Kirk's Significance
and Influence

Although I have lived twenty years with General Lee and have
lived for ten years with General Washington, I am prepared
humbly to submit to you that I do not know what either of them
ever was thinking at a given moment unless he happened to have
written it down himself. We cannot be too sure. Of all the frauds
that ever have been perpetrated on our generation, this "psy-
chography" is, in my opinion, the worst. How dare a man say
what another man is thinking when he may not know what he
himself is thinking! That is the fate of a good many of us.
—Douglas Southall Freeman, Pulitzer Prize-winning
biographer, author of *R. E. Lee* and *George Washington*

"No intellectual phenomenon has been more surprising in recent years
than the revival in the United States of conservatism as a respectable social
philosophy," wrote historian Arthur Schlesinger Jr. in 1955, adding true
words that proved prescient when applied to the 1960s and '70s, "For
decades liberalism seemed to have everything its way." But in a short time,
"it has all seemed to change. Fashionable intellectual circles now dismiss
liberalism as naive, ritualistic, sentimental, shallow. With a whoop and a
roar, a number of conservative prophets have materialized out of the
wilderness, exhuming conservatism, revisiting it, revitalizing it, preaching
it. . . ."[1]

Kirk did not tend to whoop or roar, but the impact of his writings was seismic. As journalist Patricia Cohen wrote in 1998, "Since postwar leftist radicalism peaked in 1968, conservatives have affixed Ronald Reagan's name to a revolution, the South has deserted the Democrats for the Republican, the Christian right has pushed its way onto the national stage, and liberal confidence in government action has become about as commonplace as the rotary phone."[2]

With Kirk's death in 1994, one of the giants of twentieth-century thought left our midst. Seventy-five years old at his death, he had accomplished much during his life, not the least being his work as an articulate and influential conservator of the true and enduring in Western culture. As a defender of what his friend T. S. Eliot called "the permanent things," Kirk may have taken his famous friend's phrase "Redeem the time, redeem the dream" as his own watchword.

Despite his many accomplishments as a conservative writer and public figure, Kirk was not nearly as well known to the general public as many other conservative figures, such as William F. Buckley or George F. Will. Truth be known, this lack of fame probably pleased him. For despite his fondness for walking tours across the European continent and Scotland, he enjoyed being "happy at home," in the phrase of one of his heroes, Samuel Johnson, spending much time at his ancestral home in Mecosta. Writing from that setting, a forested land that is itself a throwback to the Midwestern villages and "dark fields of the Republic" spoken of by Nick Carraway in *The Great Gatsby*, Kirk was one of the few quietly influential voices that reminded and reassured many persons that the permanent things are to be remembered, cultivated, and passed on to one's children and to society.

Kirk held by the permanent things: those enduring norms of honor, courage, character, virtue, constancy, humility, godly wisdom, order, and prudence—as well as faith, hope and charity. His was a voice of reassurance that spoke eloquently through both the well-turned essay and the well-told tale in an adept melding of the intellect and the imagination.

In the previous pages, I have attempted to illuminate the life and works of this man. This slim book has neither presumed to plumb Kirk's innermost being nor venture a greatly ambitious interpretation of his works, but to offer instead a clear, insightful reading of his life and works through revisiting his own writings and those of his critics. I have demonstrated that Kirk articulated an intelligent conservatism, consistent in all its parts, a manner of viewing the world that is in essence much more intelligent and humane than that described by Schlesinger in his early appraisal; in 1955 the great Harvard historian described conservatism as something designed to remonstrate with "New Dealers, trade-union leaders, reformers, and evidently, all those who can read without moving their lips," in works wherein the reader "can find very little . . . calculated to upset a slum landlord." (The very concept of the moral imagination places Kirk and the slum landlord on opposite sides of a great divide.)[3] Anything more ambitious I leave to other, better scholars than myself.

In writing this study I have incidentally demonstrated something stated in the opening chapter: Kirk was a remarkable man, though difficult to pigeonhole. As conservatives go, he was certainly not an "aginner" merely, one of those cranks who despise everything modern and grumble their way through life until in the end they become little more than a grumble. I cannot improve upon the assessment of Wilfred McClay, who has written that Kirk "may have fancied himself a Bohemian Tory, but he was never that most tiresome of bores, 'the alienated American intellectual,' a restless species that grazes in herds of independent minds." Kirk knew and never forgot that he was fortunate to live in a country in which he was left alone to pursue a career as a writer, unattached to any university and thus not beholden to bureaucrats, petty "admin" types, and envious colleagues. At the same time, as McClay notes, Kirk was never an uncritical idolizer of American culture; and though he loved his country, "he held it accountable to a transcendent standard, against which he often found it seriously wanting." Kirk, then, spent his life attempting to do something characteristic of traditionalist conservatives: "charge both ways!" as a famous American cavalry leader is reputed to have said, and fight on two fronts at once. Kirk defended American culture against those who would radically alter or replace it—while at the same time challenging many elements of that culture by comparing it to its classical and Judeo-Christian antecedents.

On this point, Kirk had little use for what he perceived as the deification of progress, the mass appeals to envy masking as a concern for absolute social equality, the encroachments of an intrusive, omnicompetent government, the cult of the autonomous self, the decay of belief in the wisdom of the species, and the various abstractions that transformed American culture for the worse during his lifetime. He fought with every weapon at his disposal against ideology on both the American left and right wings, ideology tending to sacrifice timeless wisdom upon the altar of expediency and utility. As McClay has written of Kirk, "He comforted the afflicted and afflicted the comfortable—and sometimes they were the same people."[4]

With a nod to Henry Regnery's assessment of Kirk's significance in *Memoirs of a Dissident Publisher,* it is plain that one of the most remarkable aspects of Kirk's career was its uninterrupted consistency in terms of conveying much wisdom in an accessible manner. In a disorderly age he tirelessly and eloquently made clear the necessity and sources of order.

Against those voices who proclaimed that all values are relative and drive from will and appetite, he showed the immutability of enduring norms. And to those who believe that man is capable of all things, he taught humility, and that the beginning of wisdom is respect for creation and the order of being.

Kirk was well aware that for conservative philosophy to be anything other than what Schlesinger called "the politics of nostalgia," a mindset driven by emotions that are "honorable, generous—and irrelevent," it is necessary for intelligent conservative men and women to live and work faithfully within the circles of influence in which they live, to work faithfully in their chosen vocations, to actively engage with the life of their local communities, and, in matters political, to take their stand and hold by the permanent things. Kirk's works have been read, admired, and taken to heart by thousands of readers, including numerous political figures across the political spectrum, some of whom claim to have been influenced by him, perhaps most notable among these being his longtime friend John Engler, governor of Michigan. Engler visited Piety Hill many times during Kirk's life, holds to distinctly Kirkian ideas on the goals of education, the limitation of government, and curbs upon taxation, and even mentioned "the permanent things" in his 1999 State of the State address. Other political figures who have read and spoken highly of Kirk include Senator Fred Thompson of Tennessee, Senator Paul Simon of Illinois, Senators Joanne Emmons and Spencer Abraham of Michigan, Senator Eugene McCarthy of Minnesota, President Ronald Reagan, and Congressman Henry Hyde of Illinois. Even those political and scholarly figures who disagree with Kirk's philosophy deeply respected the man himself.

Of Kirk's enduring importance in political thought, Lee Edwards gave him pride of place in assessing his importance to the success of the conservative Heritage Foundation, writing, "Because the Heritage Foundation rests securely on the ideas of Kirk, Hayek, Weaver, and a hundred other conservative thinkers, it has become the most influential think tank in the most important city in the most powerful nation in the world."[5]

Kirk's enduring significance extends well beyond the political realm. His name appears on virtually every list of those figures who proved seminal in the revitalization of conservatism as a way of looking at life in the twentieth century. In an article published in 1988, Edwards identified the three progenitors of modern conservatism as Kirk, Buckley, and Goldwater.[6] Years later, in his study *The Conservative Revolution* (1999), he explained that these men and several others represent a logical progression: First came the men of ideas, the intellectuals, among them Kirk; next came the men of interpretation, popularizers, among them Buckley; last came the policy makers and politicians, such as Goldwater and Reagan. Edwin Feulner, on the other hand, cited conservatism's three prime movers as Kirk, Friedrich A. von Hayek, and Milton Friedman.[7] William A. Rusher considers Hayek's *The Road to Serfdom*, Whittaker Chambers's *Witness*, and *The Conservative Mind* the three most powerful philosophical contributions to the conservative movement that awakened in the 1950s.[8] *American Spectator* editor R. Emmett Tyrrell Jr. has named Buckley, Friedman, and Kirk as "superb role models" for the conservative movement as he encountered it during the 1960s.[9] Whichever group of influential conservatives is named, then, it seems Russell Kirk is the constant. Indeed, as Buckley has written, "It is . . . inconceivable to imagine an important, let alone hope for a dominant, conservative movement in America, without his labor."[10]

What, finally, was the sum of Kirk's life and accomplishment? What Kirk wrote of Eliot applies entirely to himself, as well: "What the man believed in, he became. The gentle dignity of his life won over some who had denigrated . . . his prose; others, hostile at first to his writings, gradually found themselves persuaded by his honesty and his depth of feeling. And the seed of the spirit that he sowed, though falling among tares, may yet germinate in fields that have lain barren."

Lifelong, he contended against the spirit of his age, as he deemed it a spirit of deception and cultural decadence. Kirk, the son of a locomotive engineer, joined with his friend William Buckley in seeing that the conservative's role is not always one of standing athwart history yelling "Stop" (for history will not stop), but of climbing aboard history, actively remaining true to one's vocation in life while counseling those in positions of influence to "Slow Down," to ensure that the signs are read aright, that signals and switches are correctly set, and that there are no bloody derailments or collisions. By the choices made by individuals living by the permanent things within their small communities of influence, history is changed. In the teeth of winds of doctrine, Kirk, like Eliot, attested those same permanent things, and thereby triumphed; knowing the community of souls and his place within it, he freed others from captivity to time and the lonely ego. In 1992 David L. Schindler wrote, "All of us concerned with the humane traditions of Western culture are indebted to Russell Kirk, whose sweeping erudition has been carried with gentleness, humility, dignity, and charm."[11] In the years to come, some of those who rise up against a domination of boredom and materialism may find in Kirk a mind and a conscience that endure.

NOTES

1. Schlesinger, "The New Conservatism: Politics of Nostalgia," *The Reporter* 12, June 16, 1955, 9. This essay was reprinted in Schlesinger's *The Politics of Hope*.

2. Cohen, "Leftist Scholars Look Right at Last, and Find a History," *The New York Times,* April 18, 1998, B7.

3. Schlesinger, *"The New Conservatism,"* 11. In debate and in their firsthand relations, Schlesinger and Kirk were on respectful and friendly terms, despite the tenor of this appraisal, which is a fascinating mixture of insightful discourse and genteel, off-the-mark sarcasm.

4. McClay, "The Mystic Chords of Memory," *Heritage Lecture.* no. 550, 1995.

5. Edwards, *The Power of Ideas: The Heritage Foundation at 25 Years,* p. 225.

6. Edwards, "The Other Sixties: A Flag-Waver's Memoir," *Policy Review,* no. 46, 1988, 59.

7. Feulner, in an interview in *Policy Review,* no. 58, 1991, 13.

8. Rusher, *The Rise of the Right,* p. 28.

9. Tyrrell, *The Conservative Crack-up,* p. 59.

10. Buckley, "Notes & Asides," *National Review* 41, October 30, 1981, 1255.

11. Schindler, in Person, ed., *The Unbought Grace of Life: Essays in Honor of Russell Kirk,* p. 222.

Selected Bibliography

PRIMARY SOURCES

A. Books

Randolph of Roanoke: A Study in Conservative Thought, University of Chicago Press, 1951; enlarged and published as *John Randolph of Roanoke: A Study in American Politics*, Henry Regnery, 1964; third ed., Liberty Fund, 1997.

The Conservative Mind: From Burke to Santayana, Regnery, 1953; third rev. ed. published as *The Conservative Mind: From Burke to Eliot*, 1960; seventh rev. ed., 1986.

St. Andrews, Batsford, 1954.

A Program for Conservatives, Regnery, 1954; abridged and published as *Prospects for Conservatives*, 1956; rev. ed., 1989.

Academic Freedom: An Essay in Definition, Regnery, 1955.

Beyond the Dreams of Avarice: Essays of a Social Critic, Regnery, 1956.

The Intelligent Woman's Guide to Conservatism, Devin-Adair, 1957; revised and published as *The Intelligent American's Guide to Conservatism*, Spence Publishing, 1999.

The American Cause, Regnery, 1957; second ed., with an introduction by John Dos Passos, 1966.

Old House of Fear, Fleet Press, 1961; second ed., 1963.

The Surly Sullen Bell: Ten Stories and Sketches, Uncanny or Uncomfortable, with a Note on the Ghostly Tale, Fleet Press, 1962.

Confessions of a Bohemian Tory: Episodes and Reflections of a Vagrant Career, Fleet Press, 1963.

The Intemperate Professor and Other Cultural Splenetics, Louisiana State University Press, 1965; rev. ed., Sherwood Sugden, 1988.

A Creature of the Twilight: His Memorials. Being Some Account of Episodes in the Career of His Excellency Manfred Arcane, Minister without Portfolio to the Hereditary

221

President of the Commonwealth of Hamnegri, and de facto Field Commander of the Armies of That August Prince, Fleet Press, 1966.
Edmund Burke: A Genius Reconsidered, Arlington House, 1967; rev. ed., Sugden, 1985; second rev. ed., 1988; reprinted with foreword by Roger Scruton, 1997.
(With James McClellan) *The Political Principles of Robert A. Taft*, Fleet Press, 1967.
Enemies of the Permanent Things: Observations of Abnormity in Literature and Politics, Arlington House, 1969; rev. ed., Sugden, 1984.
The Roots of American Order, Open Court, 1974; second ed., Pepperdine University Press, 1980; reprinted with epilogue by Frank Shakespeare, Regnery, 1991.
Decadence and Renewal in the High Learning, Regnery, 1978.
Lord of the Hollow Dark, St. Martin's Press, 1979; reprinted, prefaced with the short story "Balgrummo's Hell," Christendom College Press, 1989.
The Princess of All Lands, Arkham House, 1979.
Reclaiming a Patrimony: A Collection of Lectures, Heritage Foundation, 1982.
Watchers at the Strait Gate, Arkham House, 1984.
The Wise Men Know What Wicked Things Are Written on the Sky, Regnery, 1987.
Economics: Work and Prosperity, Beka, 1989.
The Conservative Constitution, Regnery, 1990; rev. ed. published as *Rights and Duties: Reflections on Our Conservative Constitution*, edited by Mitchell S. Muncy, introduction by Russell Hittinger, Spence Publishing, 1997.
The Politics of Prudence, Intercollegiate Studies Institute, 1993.
America's British Culture, Transaction, 1993.
The Sword of Imagination: Memoirs of a Half-Century of Literary Conflict, Eerdmans, 1995.
Redeeming the Time, edited by Jeffrey O. Nelson, Intercollegiate Studies Institute, 1996.

B. Books Edited

The Portable Conservative Reader, Viking, 1982.
The Assault on Religion: Commentaries on the Decline of Religious Liberty, University Press of America/Center for Judicial Studies, 1986.
The Library of Conservative Thought, by Transaction Publishers, including:
   Collected Letters of John Randolph of Roanoke to Dr. John Brockenbrough, 1812–1833 (edited by Kenneth P. Shorey; foreword by Kirk).
   Burke Street, by George Scott-Moncrieff (introduction by Kirk).
   Orestes Brownson: Selected Political Essays, by Orestes Brownson (introduction by Kirk).
   Regionalism and Nationalism in the United States: The Attack on Leviathan, by Donald Davidson (introduction by Kirk).
   Edmund Burke: The Enlightenment and Revolution, by Peter J. Stanlis (introduction by Kirk).
   The Social Crisis of Our Time, by Wilhelm Röpke (foreword by Kirk).
   We the People: The Economic Origins of the Constitution, by Forrest McDonald (foreword by Kirk).
   A Historian and His World: A Life of Christopher Dawson, by Christina Scott (introduction by Kirk).

C. Selected Periodical Publications and Uncollected Essays

"Mementos." *Scholastic: The American High School Weekly* 28, no. 12 (12 April 1936): 5, 12.
"Two Plays of Resignation." *The Month* 10 (October 1953): 223–29.
"The Measure of Abraham Lincoln." *The Month* 12 (April 1954): 197–206.
"The Poet as Conservative." *The Critic* 18, no. 4 (February-March 1960): 19–20, 84–86.
"The Popularity of Robert Frost." *Los Angeles Times* (20 January 1963): G7.
"The Wisdom of Evelyn Waugh." *The Times-Picayune*, New Orleans (25 April 1966): (I)15.
"The Moral Imagination of Children." *The Times-Picayune*, New Orleans (5 October 1966): (I)13.
"Tolkien and Truth through Fantasy." *The Times-Picayune*, New Orleans (29 June 1968): (I)11.
"In Defense of the South." *The Times-Picayune*, New Orleans (12 May 1969): (I)13.
"Chesterton, Madmen, and Madhouses." *Modern Age* 15 (Winter 1971): 6–16.
"Twenty Years of Conservative-Mindedness." *The Detroit News* (24 April 1973): B9.
"The School of the Open Road." *National Review* 30 (3 March 1978): 282.
"Imagination against Ideology." *National Review* 32 (31 December 1980): 1576–83.
"Right Reason Does Not Pay." *Modern Age* 26, nos. 3–4 (Summer-Fall 1982): 228–34.
Introduction to *The Portable Conservative Reader*, edited by Russell Kirk, pp. xi-xl, Penguin, 1982.
"Religion in the Civil Social Order." *Modern Age* 28, no. 3 (Fall 1984): 306–9.
"Babbitt and the Ethical Purpose of Literary Studies." Introduction to *Literature and the American College: Essays in Defense of the Humanities*, by Irving Babbitt, pp. 1–68, National Humanities Institute, 1986.
"Capitalism and the Moral Basis of Social Order." *Modern Age* 35 (Winter 1992): 99–105.
"Reason, Imagination Enliven the Conservative Mind." *The Detroit News* (3 May 1994): 9A.
"The Salutary Myth of the Otherworld Journey." *The World & I* (October 1994): 425–37.

D. Letters

Kirk's correspondence is on file at the Clarke Historical Library, Central Michigan University, in Mount Pleasant, Michigan, and at the Russell Kirk Center for Cultural Renewal in Mecosta, Michigan.

SECONDARY SOURCES

Attarian, John. "Russell Kirk's Economics of the Permanent Things." *The Freeman* 46, no. 4 (April 1996): 232–36. Insightful discussion of Kirk's theory of economics and their Christian-humanist underpinnings.
———. "Russell Kirk's Political Economy." *Modern Age* 40, no. 1 (Winter 1998): 87–97. Enlarges upon many points and illustrations included in the critic's earlier *Freeman* essay. Here, Atttarian again stresses the moral dimension of Kirk's

economics, compares Kirk's understanding of economics with that of Ludwig von Mises and Wilhelm Röpke, and defends Kirk's statements on the American political economy from several neoconservative detractors.

Bliese, John R. E. "Richard M. Weaver, Russell Kirk, and the Environment." *Modern Age* 38, no. 2 (Winter 1996): 148–58. Argues that conservatives, far more than liberals and centrists, should be in the forefront of the conservation movement in America. Bliese cites key examples from the writings of Kirk, Weaver, Peter Viereck, and George Nash in building his case.

Brown, Charles, ed. *Russell Kirk: A Bibliography*. Mount Pleasant, Mich.: Clarke Historical Library, 1980. Detailed primary and secondary bibliography concerning Kirk's writings through 1980. A complete and up-to-date bibliography, really an extension of this book, has been compiled by Brown and is available in electronic form at the Russell Kirk Center for Cultural Renewal.

Chalmers, Gordon Keith. "Goodwill Is Not Enough." *The New York Times Book Review* (17 May 1953): 7, 28. Major review of *The Conservative Mind*, though one that leans toward assessing that work in primarily political terms. With a deft use of the telling quotation, Chalmers, president of Kenyon College, hails *The Conservative Mind* as a "vigorous book" that describes a "rededication to human freedom by independent lovers of liberty throughout the past century of expanding democratic collectivism."

Cheney, Brainard. "The Conservative Course by Celestial Navigation." *The Sewanee Review* 62, no. 1 (Winter 1954): 151–59. Lengthy, favorable review of *The Conservative Mind* written, in part, to answer the criticisms of John Crowe Ransom, which had earlier appeared in an issue of *The Kenyon Review*.

East, John. "Russell Kirk as a Political Theorist." *Modern Age* 27, no. 2 (Winter 1984): 33–44. An eloquent, informative treatise on the centrality of virtue and the moral imagination, as opposed to decadence and ideology, in Kirk's thought, and how these elements inform his political beliefs.

Filler, Louis. "'The Wizard of Mecosta': Russell Kirk of Michigan." *Michigan History* 63, no. 5 (September-October 1979): 12–18. Lively, accurate biographical essay on Kirk and his accomplishments. Illustrated.

Frohnen, Bruce. *Virtue and the Promise of Conservatism: The Legacy of Burke and Tocqueville*. University Press of Kansas, 1993. Indispensable study of the key role of virtue in the thought of Burke, Tocqueville, and Kirk. This work also sharply contrasts the views of the above-mentioned individuals with those of Leo Strauss and Eric Voegelin.

———. "Has Conservatism Lost Its Mind? The Half-Remembered Legacy of Russell Kirk." *Policy Review*, no. 67 (Winter 1994): 62–66. Examines several beliefs common to conservatives of the mid-1990s, finding them overly simplified first cousins of beliefs held by Kirk, whose Burkean view focused (unlike these others) upon virtue maintained through the individual's voluntary associations and relations to his God.

Frum, David. "The Legacy of Russell Kirk." *The New Criterion* 13, no. 4 (December 1994): 10–16. Reprinted in Frum's *What's Right: The New Conservative Majority and the Remaking of America*, pp. 159–69. Warm assessment of Kirk's significance, particularly as effected through the influence of *The Conservative Mind*. Frum takes the position that this tome is less a history than it is a work of romantic imagination; the essayist claims, "it ought to be esteemed as something in some ways more important [than history]: a profound critique of contemporary mass society, and a vivid and poetic image—not a program, an image—of how that society might better itself."

Genovese, Eugene D. "Captain Kirk." *The New Republic* 213, no. 24 (11 December 1995): 35–38. Favorable, insightful review of *The Sword of Imagination*, inaccurate in a few particulars but for the most part a well-read introduction to Kirk's memoir.

Hart, Jeffrey. "The Varieties of Conservative Thought." In *The American Dissent: A Decade of Modern Conservatism*, pp. 187–238. Garden City, N.Y.: Doubleday, 1966. Contains material on Kirk (pp. 190–201) and Wilhelm Röpke (pp. 227–31). Hart outlines the rationale behind Burke's centrality to Kirk's thought, and then engages with a question posed of Kirk's position by numerous liberal and libertarian critics, including Frank S. Meyer, who on one occasion wrote, "The question is, What do you want to conserve?" To the cultural conservative, is tradition its own highest value? Hart then endeavors to answer this question, finding Kirk no conservative historicist—though he does respectfully question Kirk for not replying to his critics on this matter in "any systematic and serious way."

Herron, Don. "The Crepuscular Romantic: An Appreciation of the Fiction of Russell Kirk." *The Romantist*, no. 3 (1979): 1–12. Enthusiastic overview of Kirk's imaginative literature, with special emphasis upon the horror fiction.

Hittinger, Russell. Introduction to *Rights and Duties: Reflections on Our Conservative Constitution*, by Russell Kirk, pp. xiii-xxxi. Dallas: Spence Publishing, 1997. Essential reading, in which Hittinger examines the question of how it is possible for the written Constitution to change not at all while the "unwritten Constitution," modern interpretation of original intent, changes dramatically, and how this issue relates to Kirk's understanding of the subject.

The Intercollegiate Review 30, no. 1 (Fall 1994). A special tribute issue to Kirk, containing top-drawer essays on his accomplishments by George A. Panichas, Roger Scuton, George H. Nash, Russell Hittinger, Peter J. Stanlis, Francis Canavan, Bruce Frohnen, Gerhart Niemeyer, and several other scholars and essayists.

Kirk, Annette. "The Conservative Heart: Life with Russell Kirk." *Heritage Lecture*, no. 547. Washington, D.C.: Heritage Foundation, 1995, n.p. Examines the bond that drew together Russell and Annette Kirk, two individuals very unalike in temperament, and concludes that the couple's shared "first principles" and illative sense for apprehending "the permanent things" provided the sinews of that bond.

McClay, Wilfred M. "The Mystic Chords of Memory: Reclaiming American History." *Heritage Lecture*, no. 550. Washington, D.C.: Heritage Foundation, 1995, n.p. Explores Kirk's historical consciousness as it relates to the need for America's need to embrace a genuine historical consciousness to unite the culture at large and build toward the linking of generations while strengthening what is best in the American heritage.

Meyer, Frank S. "Collectivism Rebaptized." In his *In Defense of Freedom, and Related Essays*, pp. 3–13. Indianapolis: Liberty Fund, 1996. Ruminates upon the implications of Kirk's thought, finding *The Conservative Mind* a well-meant but insufficient answer to the advance of liberal collectivism. Categorizing Kirk as one of the "New Conservatives" of the 1950s, Meyer states that Kirk "lacks the standards to effectuate politically and socially his undoubtedly genuine concern for the integrity of the individual person as a philosophical and spiritual truth," thus inadvertantly blurring the line between the traditionalist's concern for community and the twentieth-century liberal's tendency to view the nation as a "community" in need of centralized guidance. Meyer's essay originally appeared in *The Freeman* in 1955, and an early edition of *In Defense of Freedom* was published in 1962 by Regnery.

Nash, George H. *The Conservative Intellectual Movement in America since 1945*. Wilmington, Del.: Intercollegiate Studies Institute, 1997. Invaluable historical survey that defines and explains Kirk's place among the traditionalist conservatives who, with anticommunists and libertarians, formed the three-stranded helix of postwar conservatism.

Person, James E. Jr. *The Unbought Grace of Life: Essays in Honor of Russell Kirk*. Peru, Ill.: Sherwood Sugden, 1994. Contains especially insightful essays on Kirk's accomplishments by Peter J. Stanlis, Forrest McDonald, John Lukacs, M. E. Bradford, and Andrew Lytle, among others.

Ransom, John Crowe. "Empirics in Politics." In his *Poems and Essays*, pp. 135–45. New York: Vintage Books, 1955. Review of *The Conservative Mind* originally published in *The Kenyon Review*, Autumn, 1953. Ransom offers a lengthy, ruminative, faintly condescending assessment of Kirk's best-known work. The review is especially interesting as a reflection of Ransom's thinking, coming as it does from a man who, by the mid-1950s, had changed his own political and cultural viewpoint to align more fully with progressive statism, after years of being associated with the traditionalist Nashville Agrarians.

Regnery, Henry. "Russell Kirk: Conservatism Becomes a Movement." In his *Memoirs of a Dissident Publisher*, pp. 146–66. New York: Harcourt, Brace, Jovanovich, 1979. Warmly assesses Kirk's importance in the founding of postwar conservatism and appraises each of the first six (of seven) books written by Kirk and published by the Henry Regnery Company. Regnery gives much space to the genesis of *The Conservative Mind* (his single greatest publishing success), Kirk's intent in writing this work, and its critical reception.

Russello, Gerald J. "The Jurisprudence of Russell Kirk." *Modern Age* 38, no. 4 (Fall 1996): 354–63. Examines Kirk's writings insofar as they deal with the bases of law. The essayist demonstrates that Kirk's writings on legal theory and legal issues reveal a deep concern with returning law, in its Roman sense of being "at base a knowledge of the ethical norms for the human being," to a form of public discourse, and with reminding lawyers that there is more to their calling than mere technique. Along with Russell Hittinger's essay, noted above, Russello's is crucial to understanding Kirk's view of jurisprudence.

Whitney, Gleaves. "Seven Things You Should Know about Russell Kirk: The Origins of the Modern Conservative Movement in the U.S." *Vital Speeches of the Day* 63, no. 16 (June 1997): 507–11. Text of an address to the Russell Kirk Society at Michigan State University. Whitney focuses upon the relevance of Kirk's accomplishments to readers of the present day, identifying the following achievements as key to understanding Kirk's significance: a founder of modern conservative thought, a leading voice in conservatism for four decades, a political observer and advisor, a conductor of path-breaking scholarship, an advocate of the classical liberal arts education, a man of letters, and a cultural critic.

Wolfe, Gregory. "The Catholic as Conservative: Russell Kirk's Christian Humanism." *Crisis: A Journal of Lay Catholic Opinion* 11, no. 9 (October 1993): 25, 27–32. Engages the criticisms that have been leveled against Kirk and determines their degree of accuracy. In this assessment, Wolfe, a former assistant at Piety Hill, finds his former teacher in danger of being honored but not read, cited but not understood, and appropriated by rightward-leaning individuals who actually have little use for Kirk's cultural conservatism.

Zoll, Donald Atwell. "The Social Thought of Russell Kirk." *The Political Science Reviewer* 2 (Fall 1972): 112–36. Ruminative, even-handed essay that examines the significance of, and praiseworthy social possibilities presented by, the cultural conservatism articulated by Kirk.

Sources Consulted

In addition to the sources listed in the primary and secondary bibliography, the author also consulted the following items.

"The American Right." *The Times Literary Supplement*, no. 3443 (22 February 1968): 176.

Babbitt, Irving. *Literature and the American College*. Boston: Houghton Mifflin, 1908.

Barfield, Owen. *Worlds Apart*. Middletown, Conn.: Wesleyan University Press, 1963.

[Barnes, John A.] "Russell A. Kirk: Man of Letters." *The Virginian-Pilot/The Ledger-Star*, Norfolk (7 May 1994): A12.

BeVier, Thomas. "The Nonconformist." *Detroit* (Sunday magazine supplement of the *Detroit Free Press*) (11 January 1987): 10–15, 20.

Blake, John. Review of *Confessions of a Bohemian Tory*. *The New York Times Book Review* (8 December 1963): 26.

Bradford, M. E. "The Wizard of Mecosta." *National Review* 32, no. 25 (12 December 1980): 1513–14.

———. *A Better Guide than Reason: Federalists & Anti-Federalists*. New Brunswick, N.J.: Transaction Publishers, 1994.

Bray, Thomas J. "The Long View from Piety Hill." *The Detroit News* (4 November 1990): 2B.

Brookhiser, Richard. "Hail to the Chief." *National Review* 33, no. 21 (30 October 1981): 1263.

Buckley, William F. Jr. *God and Man at Yale: The Superstitions of Academic Freedom*. Chicago: Henry Regnery, 1951.

———. "Essay in Confusion." *The Freeman* 5 (July 1955): 576.

———. "Notes and Asides." *National Review* 33, no. 21 (30 October 1981): 1254–55.

———. "Russell Kirk, RIP." *National Review* 46, no. 10 (30 May 1994): 19–20.

Bundy, McGeorge. "The Attack on Yale." *The Atlantic Monthly* 188, no. 5 (November 1951): 50–52.

Burnham, James. Review of *A Program for Conservatives*. *The Annals of the American Academy of Political and Social Science* 298 (March 1955): 216.

Cargas, Harry. Review of *Enemies of the Permanent Things*. *America* 120, no. 20 (17 May 1969): 596.

Chamberlain, John. "A Conservatism of Reflection." *National Review* 16 (10 March 1964): 198–99.

———. Review of *Eliot and His Age*. *The Freeman* 22, no. 11 (November 1972): 700–703.

Chamberlin, William. "A Study of Conservative Thought and Its Progress in the Past Two Hundred Years." *The Wall Street Journal* (10 June 1953): 6.

Chambers, Whittaker. *Ghosts on the Roof: Selected Journalism of Whittaker Chambers, 1931–1959*. Edited by Terry Teachout. Washington: Regnery Gateway, 1989.

Chesterton, G. K. "Our Note Book." *The Illustrated London News* 127, no. 3474 (18 November 1905): 714.

———. Introduction to *George MacDonald and His Wife*. London: George Allen & Unwin, 1924.

———. *William Cobbett*. New York: Dodd, Mead & Co., 1926.

———. "Is Humanism a Religion?" *The Bookman* 69, no. 3 (May 1929): 236–41.

———. "Our Note Book," *The Illustrated London News* 178, no. 4805 (23 May 1931): 860.

———. *Autobiography*. London: Hutchinson, 1936.

———. *The Everlasting Man*. Garden City, N.Y.: Image Books, 1955.

———. *Orthodoxy*. Garden City, N.Y.: Image Books, 1959.

Cohen, Patricia. "Leftist Scholars Look Right at Last, and Find History." *The New York Times* (18 April 1998): B7, B9.

Colson, Charles. *Against the Night: Living in the New Dark Ages*. Ann Arbor, Mich.: Servant Publications, 1989.

Como, James. *Branches to Heaven: The Geniuses of C. S. Lewis*. Dallas: Spence Publishing, 1998.

Cook, Fred J. "Freedom Medalist." *The Nation* 238 (10 March 1984): 277.

Dakin, Arthur Hazard. *Paul Elmer More*. Princeton: Princeton University Press, 1960.

Dante. *Hell (L'Inferno)*. Translated by Dorothy L. Sayers. London: Penguin, 1949.

Dante. *Heaven (Paradiso)*. Translated by Dorothy L. Sayers. London: Penguin, 1962.

Donoghue, Denis. "Eliot and His Age." *Commonweal* 96 (12 May 1972): 242–44.

Donovan, Charles F. Review of *The Intemperate Professor and Other Cultural Splenetics*. *America* 114, no. 4 (22 January 1966): 144–45.

Edwards, Lee. "The Other Sixties: A Flag-Waver's Memoir." *Policy Review*, no. 46 (Fall 1988): 58–65.

———. *The Power of Ideas: The Heritage Foundation at 25 Years*. Ottawa, Ill.: Jameson Books, 1997.

———. *The Conservative Revolution: The Movement That Remade America*. New York: Free Press, 1999.

Eliot, T. S. *Four Quartets*. New York: Harcourt Brace Jovanovich, 1971.

———. *Christianity and Culture: The Idea of a Christian Society and Notes towards the Definition of Culture*. New York: Harcourt Brace Jovanovich, 1988.

———. *To Criticize the Critic, and Other Writings*. Lincoln: University of Nebraska Press, 1991.

————. *The Sacred Wood and Major Early Essays.* Mineola, N.Y.: Dover Publications, 1998.

Ericson, Edward E. Jr. Review of *The Sword of Imagination. Books & Culture* 1, no. 1 (November-December 1995): 30–31.

Evans, M. Stanton. "The Triumph of Taft." *National Review* 20, no. 14 (9 April 1968): 351–54.

Feulner, Edwin J. Jr. *The March of Freedom: Modern Classics in Conservative Thought.* Dallas: Spence Publishing, 1998.

Flynn, James J. Review of *The American Cause. Annals of the American Academy of Political and Social Science* 316 (March 1958): 143.

Fuller, Edmund. *Man in Modern Fiction: Some Minority Opinions on Contemporary American Writing.* New York: Random House, 1958.

Genovese, Eugene D. "Captain Kirk." *The New Republic* 213, no. 24 (11 December 1995): 35–38.

Guroian, Vigen. *Tending the Heart of Virtue: How Classic Stories Awaken a Child's Moral Imagination.* New York: Oxford University Press, 1998.

Harrigan, Anthony. "Great Conservative." *The Freeman* 2, no. 16 (5 May 1952): 511–12.

Harris, Bernice Kelly, ed. *Strange Things Happen.* Murfreesboro, N.C.: Johnson Publishing, 1971.

Hart, Jeffrey. "The Relevance of Burke." *National Review* 19, no. 37 (19 September 1967): 1022–23.

————. "Christopher Dawson and the History We Are Not Told." *Modern Age* 39, no. 3 (Summer 1997): 211–24.

Hatch, Robert. "Enforcing Truth." *The New Republic* 125, no. 23 (3 December 1951): 19.

Heckscher, August. "Toward a True, Creative Conservatism." *New York Herald Tribune Book Review* (2 August 1953): 4.

Hicks, Granville. "On the Conservative Side." *The New York Times Book Review* (30 September 1956): 38.

Hook, Sidney. "The Faiths of Whittaker Chambers." *The New York Times Book Review* (25 May 1952): 1, 34–35.

Howard, Thomas. *The Achievement of C. S. Lewis: A Reading of His Fiction.* Wheaton, Ill.: Harold Shaw, 1980.

Jaffa, Harry V. "On the Education of the Guardians of Freedom." *Modern Age* 30, no. 2 (Spring, 1986): 131–40.

James, M.R. *More Ghost Stories of an Antiquary.* London: Edward Arnold, 1911.

Jamieson, T. John. Review of *Watchers at the Strait Gate. The American Spectator* 18, no. 2 (February 1985): 43–44.

Judis, John B. "Three Wise Men." *The New Republic* 210, no. 22 (30 May 1994): 20–21, 24.

Kermode, Frank. "There Was Time for Visions and Revisions." *The New York Times Book Review* (26 March 1972): 6–7, 20, 22.

Kilpatrick, William. *Why Johnny Can't Tell Right from Wrong.* New York: Simon and Schuster, 1992.

Kirk, Russell. "Who's Theatening Academic Freedom?" *Chicago Sunday Tribune Magazine of Books* (20 November 1955): 2.

————. "The Mood of Conservatism," *The Commonweal* 78, no. 11 (7 June 1963): 297–300.

————. "An Ideologue of Liberty." *The Sewanee Review* 72, no. 2 (Spring 1964): 349–50.

————. "Professor? What Professor?" *National Review* 20 (21 May 1968): 503.

————. "Conservation Activism Is a Healthy Sign." *The Sun*, Baltimore (4 May 1970): A17.

————. "Imagination against Ideology." *National Review* 32, no. 26 (31 December 1980): 1576–83.

————. "The End of Learning: A Place to Stand." *Discipleship Journal*, no. 23 (1984): 26–28.

————. *Eliot and His Age: T.S. Eliot's Moral Imagination in the Twentieth Century*. Rev. ed. LaSalle, Ill.: Sherwood Sugden & Co., 1988.

————. "Men of Letters as Statists: Locke, Montesquieu, Hume, Burke." In *Literature Criticism from 1400 to 1800*, vol. 7, edited by James E. Person Jr., pp. xiii-xix. Detroit: Gale Research, 1988.

————. Unpublished message delivered at First United Methodist Church of Plymouth, Michigan, October 16, 1988.

————. "Natural Law and the Constitution." *Notre Dame Law Review* 69, no. 5 (1994): 1035–48.

Lewis, C. S. *Rehabilitations, and Other Essays*. London: Oxford University Press, 1939.

————. *God in the Dock: Essays on Theology and Ethics*, edited by Walter Hooper. Grand Rapids, Mich.: William B. Eerdmans Publishing, 1970.

————. *The Screwtape Letters*. New York: Collins, 1976.

————. *On Stories, and Other Essays on Literature*, edited by Walter Hooper. New York: Harcourt Brace Jovanovich, 1982.

Lytle, Andrew. *A Wake for the Living*. Nashville: J.S. Sanders & Co., 1992.

Macdonald, Dwight. "God and Buckley at Yale." *The Reporter* 6, no. 11 (27 May 1952): 35–38.

MacDonald, George. *A Dish of Orts: Chiefly Papers on the Imagination and on Shakespeare*. 1893. Reprint. Norwood, Pa.: Norwood Editions, 1977.

Mapp, Alf J. Jr. *The Virginia Experiment: The Old Dominion's Role in the Making of America, 1607–1781*. 2d ed. La Salle, Ill.: Open Court, 1974.

————. *Frock Coats and Epaulets: Psychological Portraits of Confederate Military and Political Leaders*. Lanham, Md.: Hamilton Press, 1982.

————. *Thomas Jefferson: A Strange Case of Mistaken Identity*. Lanham, Md.: Madison Books, 1987.

————. *Three Golden Ages: Discovering the Creative Secrets of Renaissance Florence, Elizabethan England, and America's Founding*. Lanham, Md.: Madison Books, 1999.

Margolis, John D. Review of *Eliot and His Age. The Western Humanities Review* 26, no. 3 (Summer 1972): 279–82.

McDonald, Forrest. "Russell Kirk: The American Cicero." *National Review* 37, no. 25 (31 December 1985): 92–94.

McDonald, W. Wesley. "Russell Kirk: Conservatism's Seasoned Sage." *The Wall Street Journal* (19 November 1984): 32.

————. "Russell Kirk on Decadence in an Age of Ideology." *The Hillsdale Review* 7 (Winter-Spring 1985): 53–59.

Meixner, John A. "Morrison, Kirk, Malamud." *The Sewanee Review* 72, no. 3 (Summer 1964): 540–42.

Metzger, Walter P. Review of *Academic Freedom*. *Political Science Quarterly* 70, no. 4 (December 1955): 598–600.

Meyer, Frank. "Conservatism and Individualism." *The American Mercury* 67, no. 3 (July 1953): 140–42.

Molnar, Thomas. "'The Fault, Dear Brutus . . .'." *National Review* 18, no. 12 (22 March 1966): 275, 277–78.

Montgomery, John Warwick. *The Shaping of America*. Minneapolis: Bethany House Publishers, 1981.

More, Paul Elmer. *Shelburne Essays*, seventh series. Boston: Houghton Mifflin, 1910.

Moss, Chuck. "Kirk: Godfather of Modern Conservatism." *The Detroit News* (1 March 1989): 15A.

Muggeridge, Malcolm. Review of *The Roots of American Order*. *Esquire* 82, no. 2 (February 1975): 20.

Newman, R. Andrew. "Pilgrimages and Easter Destinations in the Ghostly Tales of Russell Kirk." *Modern Age* 40, no. 3 (Summer 1998): 314–18.

"Kirk on Shaw." *The New Republic* 136, no. 18 (6 May 1957): 7.

Review of *Old House of Fear* in *The New Yorker* 37, no. 26 (12 August 1961): 92.

Niemeyer, Gerhart. "In Praise of Tradition." *Modern Age* 36, no. 3 (Spring 1994): 233–36.

Nisbet, R. A. Review of *Academic Freedom*. *The Western Political Quarterly* 9, no. 1 (March 1956): 216–17.

Oakeshott, Michael. "Conservative Political Thought." *The Spectator* 193 (15 October 1954): 472, 474.

O'Brien, Conor Cruise. *The Great Melody: A Thematic Biography and Commented Anthology of Edmund Burke*. London: Sinclair-Stevenson, 1992.

O'Casey, Sean. *The Green Crow*. London: George Braziller, 1956.

O'Connor, Flannery. *The Presence of Grace, and Other Book Reviews*, edited by Leo J. Zuber and Carter W. Martin. Athens: University of Georgia Press, 1983.

Orwell, George. *The Collected Essays, Journalism and Letters of George Orwell*, vol. IV, *In Front of Your Nose, 1945–1950*. New York: Harcourt, Brace and World, 1968.

Panichas, George A. "*Academic Freedom* Views Modern Educational Trends." *The Springfield Republican* (10 July 1955): 5C.

———. *Modern Age: The First Twenty-Five Years, a Selection*. Indianapolis: Liberty-Press, 1988.

———. "The Inspired Wisdom of Burke." *Modern Age* 40, no. 2 (Spring 1998): 214–18.

Percy, William Alexander. *Lanterns on the Levee: Recollections of a Planter's Son*. New York: Alfred A. Knopf, 1941.

Person, James E. Jr. "Russell Kirk: A Giant of 20th Century Thought." *The Observer*, Plymouth, Mich. (30 May 1994): 10A.

———. "The Sharpening of the Conservative Mind." *Modern Age* 36, no. 4 (Summer 1994): 373–76.

Regnery, Henry. "Russell Kirk: A Life Worth Living." *Modern Age* 38, no. 3 (Summer 1996): 211–17.

Robson, W. W. "The Unread Eliot." *Partisan Review* 40, no. 1 (Winter 1973): 136–40.

Rodman, Selden, and Frank D. Ashburn. "'Isms' & the University." *The Saturday Review of Literature* 34, no. 50 (15 December 1951): 18–19, 44–45.

Röpke, Wilhelm. *A Humane Economy: The Social Framework of the Free Market*. Wilmington, Del.: Intercollegiate Studies Institute, 1998.

Rozell, Mark J., and James F. Pontuso, eds. *American Conservative Opinion Leaders*. Boulder, Colo.: Westview Press, 1990.

Ruef, Joseph A. Review of *Confessions of a Bohemian Tory*." *The Library Journal* 88, no. 22 (15 December 1963): 4761.

Rusello, Gerald J. "The Jurisprudence of Russell Kirk." *Modern Age* 38 (Fall 1996): 354–63.

Rusher, William A. *The Rise of the Right*. New York: William Morrow, 1984.

Schlesinger, Arthur Jr. "The New Conservatism: Politics of Nostalgia." *The Reporter* 12, no. 12 (16 June 1955): 9–12.

Schock, David B. "Mecosta New Home for Refugees," *Chippewa Hills Courier*, Big Rapids, Mich. (24 September 1975): 1.

Schoyer, George. Review of *The Political Principles of Robert A. Taft*. *The Library Journal* 92, no. 18 (15 October 1967): 3648.

Scott-Moncrieff, George. "Eliot Remembered." *The Sewanee Review* 80, no. 4 (Autumn 1972): 632–38.

Scruton, Roger. Foreword to *Edmund Burke: A Genius Reconsidered*, by Russell Kirk, pp. vii-ix. Wilmington, Del.: Intercollegiate Studies Institute, 1997.

Shackelford, George Green. Review of *Randolph of Roanoke*. *The Virginia Magazine of History and Biography* 60, no.1 (January 1952): 188–89.

Solzhenitsyn, Aleksandr. *A World Split Apart*. New York: Harper and Row, 1978.

Spitz, David. "Confusion of Principles." *The Nation* 186, no. 15 (12 April 1958): 326, 328.

Stanlis, Peter J. "The Conservative Mind of Russell Kirk." *The Newman Review* 5, nos. 3–4 (1954): 20–27.

Stegner, Wallace. *Where the Bluebird Sings to the Lemonade Springs: Living and Writing in the West*. New York: Penguin Books, 1992.

Stokes, Harold Phelps. "Whittaker Chambers' Story." *The Yale Review* 42, no. 1 (Autumn 1951): 123–27.

Sullivan, Jack. "Zombies and Other Spooks." *The New York Times Book Review* (1 November 1979): 15, 35.

Tate, Allen. *Reactionary Essays on Poetry and Ideas*. New York: Charles Scribner's Sons, 1936.

Theroux, Paul. "The Way to East Coker." *Book World—The Washington Post* (12 March 1972): 5.

Tonsor, Stephen. "Russell Kirk: 1918–1994." *Modern Age* 37, no. 2 (Winter 1995): 98–101.

Trilling, Lionel. *The Liberal Imagination: Essays on Literature and Society*. New York: Harcourt, 1978.

Twelve Southerners. *I'll Take My Stand: Essays by Twelve Southerners*. Baton Rouge: Lousiana State University Press, 1977.

Tyrrell, R. Emmett. *The Conservative Crack-up*. New York: Simon and Schuster, 1992.

Vanauken, Sheldon. "Old Western Man: C. S. Lewis and the Old South (and Other Dinosaurs)." *Crisis: A Journal of Lay Catholic Opinion* 11, no. 11 (December 1993): 26–30.

Weaver, Richard M. "Which Ancestors?" *National Review* 2 (25 July 1956): 20–21.

————.*Visions of Order: The Cultural Crisis of Our Time*. Baton Rouge: Louisiana State University Press, 1964.

Wheeler, Harvey. "Russell Kirk and the New Conservatism." *Shenandoah* 7, no. 2 (Spring 1956): 20–34.

Whitney, Gleaves. "The Roots of American Disorder." *Vital Speeches of the Day* 63, no. 1 (15 October 1996): 15–18.

Wilhelmsen, Frederick D. "Contemporary Criticism in the Georgian Manner." *The Commonweal* 64, no. 15 (13 July 1956): 375–76.

Wood, Ralph C. "Russell Kirk: Knight of Cheerful Conservatism." *The Christian Century* 113, no. 30 (23 October 1996): 1015–21.

Wriston, Henry M. "A Conservative View of Academic Freedom." *The Yale Review* n.s. 44, no. 4 (June 1955): 608–10.

Yancey, Philip. "Nietzsche Was Right," *Books & Culture* 4, no. 1 (January-February 1998): 14–17.

Index

About the Author

James E. Person Jr. is a senior editor at The Gale Group, where he has worked on such major reference resources as *Major Twentieth-Century Writers, Literature Criticism from 1400 to 1800,* and *Twentieth-Century Literary Criticism.* His essays and book reviews have been published in *Modern Age, National Review, The University Bookman,* and *The Sewanee Review.* He is the editor of *The Unbought Grace of Life: Essays in Honor of Russell Kirk.* He and his family live in Northville, Michigan.